Revelation

The Easy Study Bible Commentary

Trennis E. Killian

D1736062

Trennis E. Killian

Christ Centered Ministries
Black Canyon City, Arizona

ISBN: 978-1-6930-3123-6

The eBook edition of this book may be obtained through
http://www.trenniskillian.com

The Easy Study Bible Commentary Series

Ephesians

Philippians

Titus and Philemon

James

Jude

Revelation

Table of Contents

Commentary on Revelation

End Matters (Index)

Introduction

I want to make it clear right away that this commentary series is not for Bible scholars, pastors, or anyone else who is well versed in the Greek New Testament.

Instead, this commentary series is for everyone else who does not fit into that group of scholars. I wrote this commentary series for those of you who would like to study the New Testament with the knowledge of what the significant Greek words mean and how they fit into the context of each verse, chapter, and book that you may be studying.

As a pastor, I have watched many Christians (not just new Christians either) struggle to better understand what God is saying to them through His Word.

I started doing this process more than twenty years ago when I was teaching a new member class at my church. As it turned out, I started with eight adults who were all either totally new to studying the Bible or they were not the strongest readers. Therefore, both groups were having a difficult time understanding the Bible.

So, I began by placing the verses of each lesson in a diagram form. When that proved to be helpful, I then began to take the Greek words and define them so they could understand the different meanings that each Greek word could have when translated into English.

The result was that the class soon became the largest class in the church and we all (especially me) learned a great deal about God's Word in the process.

Therefore, this is the approach I have taken with this new Bible commentary series. I will show you how this is done with the example provided below,

* * *

The Easy Study Bible Commentary takes *The Easy Study Bible Diagramed* and examines, describes and expounds upon each New Testament book, chapter by chapter, paragraph by paragraph, verse by verse, phrase by phrase and finally word by word.

In my many years of Bible study and teaching, I have found this arrangement to be the easiest to follow and understand.

I have done my best to write this commentary with the idea in mind of making it easier for you to understand and therefore apply the great teachings that God gave to each of us through the various books of the New Testament.

There is one thing I need to make note of right here. There are two different Greek texts of the New Testament that most translations are based on from 1611 forward.

The Textus Receptus text which the King James Version and some other older translations are based on.

The Nestle Aland text on which most of the modern translations are based.

The Nestle Aland is an older text and therefore, is considered by most

Bible experts as being the more reliable text.

Whenever there is a difference in the two texts, I will bring your attention to it by including the following phrase: "This is another one of those differences between the Textus Receptus (KJV) and the Nestle Aland (modern translations)."

Then I will go on to explain the differences.

I will go on record right now as saying that I have personally examined dozens of New Testament passages where the two texts are not the same and I have never found a major difference that could possibly affect our interpretation of God's word.

Now, on to how this commentary is laid out.

Following is an example of how I bring in the Greek definition of all significant words. I don't put in the Greek word or the transliteration of the Greek word. I simply put the word as it is translated into English, then I give the definition of the Greek word as it is in the context of the verse being studied.

This example is taken from the book of Revelation, Chapter 1, Verses 1-2:

* * *

Verses 1-2
Prologue
[1] The Revelation of Jesus Christ, that God gave Him to show to His slaves, what must soon take place. He sent and signified it by His angel to His slave John, [2] who testified to the word of God and to the testimony of Jesus Christ, to all that he saw.

[1] The Revelation of Jesus Christ,
    that God gave Him
      to show
        to His slaves,
        what must soon take place.
    He sent and signified it
      by His angel
      to His slave John,
        [2] who testified
          to the word of God
          and
          to the testimony
            of Jesus Christ,
            to all that he saw.

Verse: 1
¹ The Revelation of Jesus Christ, that God gave Him to show to His slaves, what must soon take place. He sent and signified it by His angel to His slave John,

Revelation – a disclosure of truth, instruction; concerning things before unknown; manifestation, appearance
give – give, give out, hand over, entrust, give back, give up; to give; to bestow a gift; to grant, give to one asking, let have; to supply, furnish, necessary things; to grant or permit one; to commission
show – to show, expose to the eyes; to give evidence or proof of a thing; to show by words or teach
take place – to become, to come into existence, begin to be, receive being; to come to pass, happen; to arise, appear in history, come upon the stage; to be made, finished
signified – to give a sign, to signify, indicate; to make known

Sometimes this book is called the Apocalypse (an event involving destruction or damage on an awesome or catastrophic scale).

Jesus was telling John what the future would be like and there are a lot of frightening things depicted. But those who are saved don't have to worry about any of those events. We do need to worry about our relatives and friends who are not saved though.

Verse: 2
² who testified to the word of God and to the testimony of Jesus Christ, to all that he saw.

testified – to be a witness, to bear witness, i.e. to affirm that one has seen or heard or experienced something, or that he knows it because taught by divine revelation or inspiration
saw – to see with the eyes; to see with the mind, to perceive, know; to take heed, beware; to care for, pay heed to

John is simply saying that what he is writing is exactly what Christ told him to do and also all the things he, John, saw in the visions that Christ gave him.

(Note that sometimes a Greek definition will have a ';' in it. The semi-colon is used to separate two different meanings of subtle differences in how the word can be translated. In cases like these, we must rely on the context of the verse it is used in.)

* * *

At the end of each verse or group of verses that we study, I will give you what I call my Greek Paraphrase. What I do is I take all the expanded Greek definitions and put them together to help us better understand the passage.

The following example is also from Revelation Chapter 1, Verses 1-2:

(First is the Easy Study Bible Translation and then my Greek Paraphrase.)
¹ The Revelation of Jesus Christ, that God gave Him to show to His slaves, what must soon take place. He sent and signified it by His angel to His slave John, ² who testified to the word of God and to the testimony of Jesus Christ, to all that he saw.

Greek Paraphrase of Verses: 1-2
***This is* the disclosure of the truth of Jesus Christ, the unveiling of the divine mysteries, which God the Father gave to Him to show to those who believe in Him, the things which must soon take place in their entirety. He sent and made it known by His divine messenger to His bond-servant John, who witnessed *and* gave supporting evidence to the word of God and to the testimony of Jesus Christ, *even* to everything that he saw in his visions.**

* * *

I use this method whenever I study any part of the Bible, whether I'm just studying for my own enrichment or to teach it to others. It helps me to understand each passage well enough to apply it to my life as well as to help others do the same. This makes the whole experience so much more enjoyable for both my students and for me as well.

I sincerely hope this commentary will make the Bible more understandable for you too. Please let me know how it works for you.

You can reach me through the 'Contact Us' tab on the menu of my web page.
http://www.trenniskillian.com

The Book of Revelation

Introduction

The true, original title of this book is "The Revelation of Jesus Christ." This happens to be the first three Greek words: "Revelation Jesus Christ." That beginning leaves no doubt as to what will follow.

Normally, whenever someone takes on the monumental job of writing a commentary on a book of the New Testament it is expected that he or she should make every effort to explain every single sentence, word and expression of the book.

My goal was to do just that. But ... Isn't there always a but? I personally think there have been way too many commentaries on the book of Revelation that are guilty of over explaining to the point of making wild speculations (guesses).

So, here goes!

Revelation is not only the last book of the Bible, but it is not like any other book of the Bible. The only possible exception would be the Old Testament book of Daniel which mentions alludes to some of the things in Revelation. This is especially true of Daniel Chapter Seven.

The four gospels record the life of Christ at His first coming, but the book of Revelation records His second coming and all the events leading up to it and even afterward for a while.

Without oversimplifying things, I can safely say that the entire book of Revelation was written to make sure that all people then and since know that Jesus Christ is coming again and that we should every one of us be ready by accepting Him as our Lord and Master by bringing Him into our hearts.

Author
The apostle John

Date Written
Approximately A.D. 95 from the island of Patmos

Purpose
To reveal the full identity of Christ and to give warning to all and hope to believers

Original Audience
The seven churches in Asia: Ephesus, Smyrna, Pergamos, Thyatira, Sardis, Philadelphia, Laodicea, and all believers everywhere.

Setting
Most scholars believe that the seven churches of Asia to whom John writes were experiencing the persecution that took place under Emperor Domitian (A.D. 90-95).

It seems that the Roman authorities had exiled John to the island of Patmos. Patmos is a rocky, treeless, ten-mile-long island about sixty miles southwest of Ephesus. John may have been sentenced to hard labor in the quarries. But it's doubtful that a ninety plus year old man would be forced to do much.

John, who had been an eyewitness of the incarnate Christ, had a vision of the glorified Christ. God also revealed to John what would take place in the future—judgment and the ultimate triumph of God over evil.

Themes

God's Sovereignty

Explanation:
God is sovereign. He is greater than any power in the universe. God is not to be compared with any leader, government, or religion. He controls history for the purpose of uniting true believers in loving fellowship with him.

Importance:
Though Satan's power may temporarily increase, we are not to be led astray. God is all-powerful. He is in control. He will bring his true family safely into eternal life. Because he cares for us, we can trust him with our very life.

Christ's Return

Explanation:

Christ came to earth as a "Lamb," the symbol of his perfect sacrifice for our sin. He will return as the triumphant "Lion," the rightful ruler and conqueror. He will defeat Satan, settle accounts with all those who reject him, and bring his faithful people into eternity.

Importance:

Assurance of Christ's return gives suffering Christians the strength to endure. We can look forward to his return as king and judge. Since no one knows the time when he will appear, we must be ready at all times by keeping our faith strong.

God's Faithful People

Explanation:

John wrote to encourage the church to resist the demands to worship the Roman emperor. He warns all God's faithful people to be devoted only to Christ. Revelation identifies who the faithful people are and what they should be doing until Christ returns.

Importance:

You can take your place in the ranks of God's faithful people by believing in Christ. Victory is sure for those who resist temptation and make loyalty to Christ their top priority.

Judgment

Explanation:

One day God's anger toward sin will be fully and completely unleashed. Satan will be defeated with all of his agents. False religion will be destroyed. God will reward the faithful with eternal life, but all who refuse to believe in him will face eternal punishment.

Importance:

Evil and injustice will not prevail forever. God's final judgment will put an end to these. We need to be certain of our commitment to Jesus if we want to escape this great final judgment. No one who rejects Christ will escape God's punishment.

Hope

Explanation:

One day God will create a new heaven and a new earth. All believers will live with him forever in perfect peace and security. Those who have already died will be raised to life. These promises for the future bring us hope.

Importance:

Our great hope is that what Christ promises will come true. When we have confidence in our final destination, we can follow Christ with unwavering dedication no matter what we must face. We can be encouraged by hoping in Christ's return.

1. The Apocalypse contains a prophetical description of the destruction of Jerusalem, of the Jewish war, and the civil wars of the Romans.

2. It contains predictions of the persecutions of the Christians under the heathen emperors of Rome, and of the happy days of the Church under the Christian emperors, from Constantine downwards.

3. It contains prophecies concerning the tyrannical and oppressive conduct of the Roman pontiffs, the true antichrist; and foretells the final destruction of popery.

4. It is a prophetic declaration of the schism and heresies of Martin Luther, those called Reformers, and their successors; and the final destruction of the Protestant religion.

Keys

KEY VERSE:
"God blesses the one who reads the words of this prophecy to the church, and he blesses all who listen to its message and obey what it says, for the time is near" (1:3).
KEY PEOPLE:
John, Jesus
KEY PLACES:
Patmos, the seven churches, the new Jerusalem
SPECIAL FEATURES:
Revelation is written in "apocalyptic" form— a type of Jewish literature

Subject Outline

Part I, The Letters to the Churches (1:1 – 3:22)
The vision John received opens with instructions for him to write to seven churches. He both commends them for their strengths and warns them about their flaws. Each letter was directed to a church then in existence but also speaks to conditions in the church throughout history. Both in the church and in our individual lives, we must constantly fight against the temptation to become loveless, immoral, lenient, compromising, lifeless, or casual about our faith. The letters make it clear how our Lord feels about these qualities.

Part II, The Message for the Church (4:1 – 22:21)

1. Worshiping God in heaven
2. Opening the seven seals
3. Sounding the seven trumpets
4. Observing the great conflict

5.Pouring out the seven plagues
6.Seizing the final victory
7.Making all things new

This revelation is both a warning to Christians who have grown apathetic and an encouragement to those who are faithfully enduring the struggles in this world. It reassures us that good will triumph over evil, gives us hope as we face difficult times, and gives guidance when we are wavering in our faith. Christ's message to the church is a message of hope for all believers in every generation.

Aids to Understanding Revelation

What it says about Christ:

He is referred to as:

      The One: thirty-three times
    The Lamb: twenty-eight times.
      Jesus: ten times
      Jesus Christ: three times
      Son of Man: three times
      Lord Jesus: one time

For a total of seventy-eight times.

Outline of Revelation

I. The Things That You Have Seen – 1:1-20
    A. Prologue: The Communication of Christ 1:1-8
    B. The Vision of the Glorified Christ 1:9-20

II. The Things That Are – 2:1-3:22
    A. The Seven Churches
        1. Ephesus 2:1-7
        2. Smyrna 2:8-11
        3. Pergamos 2:12-17
        4. Thyatira 2:18-29
        5. Sardis 3:1-6
        6. Philadelphia 3:7-13
        7. Laodicea 3:14-22

III. The Things That Will Be Hereafter 4:1-22:21
    A. The Throne Set in Heaven 4:1-5:14
        1. The Heavenly Door 4:1
        2. The Heavenly Throne 4:2-5
        3. The Twenty-four Elders 4:4, 10-11
        4. The Four Living Creatures 4:6-11
        5. The Seven-Sealed Scroll 5:1-14

    B. The Seven Seals 6:1-8:1
        1. One - White Horse 6:1-2
        2. Two - Red Horse 6:3-4
        3. Three - Black Horse 6:5-6
        4. Four - Pale Horse 6:7-8
        5. Five - Souls of Martyrs 6:9-11
        6. Six - Worldwide Chaos 6:12-17

        First Interval 7:1-17
        1. Sealing of the 144,000
        2. Saved Gentile Multitude 7:9-17

        7. Seal Seven - Silence in Heaven 8:1

    C. The Seven Trumpets 8:6-11:19
        1. One - Hail, Fire, and Blood 8:7
        2. Two - Mountain Burning with Fire 8:8-9
        3. Three - Star Called Wormwood 8:10-11
        4. Four - Sun, Moon, and Stars Darkened 8:12-13
        5. Five (First Woe) - Locust Plague 9:1-12)
        6. Six (Second Woe) - Armies Loosed 9:13-21

Second Interval 10:1-11:13
1. The Mighty Angel and Seven Thunders 10:1-7
2. John and the Little Book 10:8-11
3. The Two Witnesses 11:1-13

7. Seven (Third Woe) - Kingdom Anticipated
   11:14-19

D. The Seven Personages 12:1-13:18
1. The Sun-Clothed Woman 12:1-2
2. The Great Red Dragon 12:3-4
3 The Man-Child 12:5-6
4. Michael the Archangel 12:7-12
5. The Jewish Remnant 12:13-17
6. The Beast Out of the Sea 13:1-10
7. The Beast Out of the Earth 13:11-18

Third Interval 14:1-20
1. The Lamb and the 144,000 14:1-5
2. Announcement of the Three Angels 14:6-11
3. Blessed Dead Who Die in the Lord 14:12-13
4. The Harvest 14:14-16
5. The Vintage 14:17-20

E. The Seven Vials 15:1-16:21
1. Preparation for the Seven Vials 15:1-8
1. One - Malignant Sores 16:1-2
2. Two - Sea Turned to Blood 16:3
3. Three - Rivers Turned to Blood 16:4-7
4. Four - Scorching Heat 16:8-9
5. Five - Darkness 16:10-11
6. Six - River Euphrates Dried Up 16:12

Fourth Interval 16:13-16
   Unclean Spirits Like Frogs 16:3-16

7. Seven - Great Earthquake and Hail 16:17-21

F. Judgment of Babylon 17:1-18:24
1. Ecclesiastical Babylon 17:1-18
2. Commercial Babylon 18:1-24

G. The Return of the Lord Jesus Christ 19:1-21
1. Rejoicing in Heaven 19:1-6
2. The Marriage of the Lamb 19:7-10
3. The Second Advent 19:11-16
4. The Battle of Armageddon 19:17-21

H. The Millennial Kingdom and Great White Throne
   20:1-15
   1. Satan Bound 20:1-3
   2. The First Resurrection 20:4-6
   3. Satan Loosed 20:7-10
   4. Great White Throne Judgment 20:11-15

I. The Eternal State 21:1-22:5
   1. The New Heaven and New Earth 21:1-8
   2. The Descent of the Holy Jerusalem 21:9-10
   3. A Description of Outside the City 21:9-10
   4. A Description of Inside the City 21:22-22:5

J. Epilogue 22:6-21

Revelation Commentary

Chapter One

This chapter gives us a general introduction to the whole book of Revelation. It has three parts to it.

First is an announcement that the reason for the book is to record a revelation which Jesus made to John. This revelation is about many important events which are to happen in the future.

Part of that announcement is a blessing on anyone who should read and understand the book.

It is stressed that the reader needs to pay special attention to this book because the predicted events are soon to happen.

The second part is basically a greeting to the seven churches of Asia. They seem to be who the book was written to/for.

Finally, in the third part, John tells us he is the one recording the revelation and where he was at the time.

And remember that the true title of this book is, "The Revelation of Jesus Christ."

Verses 1-2
Prologue

¹ The Revelation of Jesus Christ, that God gave Him to show to His slaves, what must soon take place. He sent and signified it by His angel to His slave John, ² who testified to the word of God and to the testimony of Jesus Christ, to all that he saw.

¹ The Revelation of Jesus Christ,
   that God gave Him
      to show
         to His slaves,
         what must soon take place.
   He sent and signified it
      by His angel
      to His slave John,
         ² who testified
            to the word of God
            and
            to the testimony
               of Jesus Christ,
               to all that he saw.

Verse: 1
¹ The Revelation of Jesus Christ, that God gave Him to show to His slaves, what must soon take place. He sent and signified it by His angel to His slave John,

Revelation – apokalupsis – a disclosure of truth, instruction; concerning things before unknown; manifestation, appearance
give – give, give out, hand over, entrust, give back, give up; to give; to bestow a gift; to grant, give to one asking, let have; to supply, furnish, necessary things; to grant or permit one; to commission
show – to show, expose to the eyes; to give evidence or proof of a thing; to show by words or teach
take place – to become, to come into existence, begin to be, receive being; to come to pass, happen; to arise, appear in history, come upon the stage; to be made, finished
signified – to give a sign, to signify, indicate; to make known

Sometimes this book is called the Apocalypse (an event involving destruction or damage on an awesome or catastrophic scale).

Jesus was telling John what the future would be like and there are a lot of frightening things depicted. But those who are saved don't have to worry about any of those events. We do need to worry about our relatives and friends who are not saved though.

Verse: 2
² who testified to the word of God and to the testimony of Jesus Christ, to all that he saw.

testified – to be a witness, to bear witness, i.e. to affirm that one has seen or heard or experienced something, or that he knows it because taught by divine revelation or inspiration
saw – to see with the eyes; to see with the mind, to perceive, know; to take heed, beware; to care for, pay heed to

John is simply saying that what he is writing is exactly what Christ told him to do and also all the things he, John, saw in the visions that Christ gave him.

Greek Paraphrase of Verses: 1-2
***This is** the disclosure of the truth of Jesus Christ, the unveiling of the divine mysteries, which God the Father gave to Him to show to those who believe in Him, the things which must soon take place in their entirety. He sent and made it known by His divine messenger to His bond-servant John, who witnessed **and** gave supporting evidence to the word of God and to the testimony of Jesus Christ, **even** to everything that he saw in his visions.*

Verse 3

³ Blessed is the one who reads and those who hear the words of the prophecy, and keep what is written in it, for the time is near.

³ Blessed is the one
 who reads
 and
 those who hear the words
  of the prophecy,
   and keep what is written in it,
   for the time is near.

reads – to distinguish between, to recognize, to know accurately, to acknowledge; to read
hear – to be endowed with the faculty of hearing, not deaf; to hear; to attend to, consider what is or has been said; to comprehend, to understand
prophecy – Prophecy; a discourse emanating from divine inspiration and declaring the purposes of God, whether by reproving and admonishing the wicked, or comforting the afflicted, or revealing things hidden; especially by foretelling future events
keep – to attend to carefully, take care of; to guard; to keep, one in the state in which he is; to observe; to reserve: to undergo something

Most people think John is saying that only those who read these words will be blessed. No! That was not all he said. He said we need to read this prophesy and do what is written in it.

Also, when John says that "the time is near," he is stressing to his readers to be ready at all times for the final judgment and the establishment of God's Kingdom. We don't know when they will happen, and they will happen so quickly we won't be able to prepare then.

Greek Paraphrase of Verse: 3

Happy, prosperous and to be admired is he who acknowledges and those who understand the words of the prophecy, and who heed the things which are written in it and take them to heart, for the time of fulfillment is near.

Verses 4-6

⁴ John to the seven churches in Asia: Grace and peace to you, from the One who is, who was, and who is coming, and from the seven Spirits who are before His throne, ⁵ and from Jesus Christ, the faithful witness, the firstborn from the dead, and the ruler of the kings of the earth. To Him who loves us and freed us from our sins by His blood, ⁶ and made us a kingdom, priests to His God and Father—to Him be the glory and the dominion forever and ever. Amen.

⁴ John
to the seven churches in Asia:
Grace and peace to you,
from the One
who is,
who was,
and who is coming,
and
from the seven Spirits
who are before His throne,
⁵ and
from Jesus Christ,
the faithful witness,
the firstborn from the dead,
and
the ruler of the kings of the earth.
To Him
who loves us
and
freed us
from our sins
by His blood,
⁶ and made us a kingdom,
priests to His God and Father
to Him be the glory and the dominion forever and ever.
Amen.

Verse: 4

⁴ John to the seven churches in Asia: Grace and peace to you, from the One who is, who was, and who is coming, and from the seven Spirits who are before His throne,

Asia – basically present-day Turkey
grace – grace; that which affords joy, pleasure, delight, sweetness, charm, loveliness: grace of speech; good will, loving-kindness, favor; benefit, bounty

John not only sent his greetings to the seven churches, but he sent the entire book of Revelation to each one of them.

This book was dedicated to the seven churches partly because they were basically under John's care. Also, because they were suffering from the same persecution that he was. They needed the consolations that come from the prediction of the final triumph of the Church of Christ.

Verse: 5

[5] *and from Jesus Christ, the faithful witness, the firstborn from the dead, and the ruler of the kings of the earth. To Him who loves us and freed us from our sins by His blood,*

Jesus is identified in three ways in this verse.

First, He is the faithful witness, the One who revealed the Father and the Holy Spirit.

Second, He is the firstborn from the dead.

Acts 26:23, that the Christ would suffer, and as the first to rise from the dead, He would be the first to proclaim light both to the people and to the Gentiles.

Third, He is the ruler of the kings of the earth.

Daniel 7:13-14, I continued watching in the night visions, and I saw One like a son of man coming with the clouds of heaven. He approached the Ancient of Days and was escorted before Him. He was given authority to rule, and glory, and a kingdom; so that those of every people, nation, and language should serve Him. His dominion is an everlasting dominion that will not pass away, and His kingdom is one that will not be destroyed.

Verse: 6

[6] *and made us a kingdom, priests to His God and Father—to Him be the glory and the dominion forever and ever. Amen.*

glory – splendor, brightness; of the moon, sun, stars; magnificence, excellence, preeminence, dignity, grace; majesty; a thing belonging to God
dominion - force, strength; power, might: mighty with great power; a mighty deed, a work of power; dominion, authority

Jesus not only cleanses us when we accept Him, but he also makes us what God has always wanted us to be, kings and priests to God the Father.

Greek Paraphrase of Verses: 4-6
John, to the seven churches that are in the province of Asia: Grace and inner calm and spiritual well-being be granted to you, from Him Who exists forever and Who continually existed in the past and Who is to come, and from the seven Spirits who are before His throne, and from Jesus Christ, the faithful *and* trustworthy Witness, the Firstborn from the dead, and the Ruler of the kings of the earth. To Him who always loves us and who has once for all freed us and washed us from our sins by His own blood through His sacrificial death, and formed us into a kingdom as His subjects, priests to His God and Father – to Him be the glory, power, majesty and the dominion forever and ever. Amen.

Verse 7

⁷ Behold, He is coming with the clouds, and every eye will see Him, including those who pierced Him, and all the families of the earth will mourn over Him. Truly. Amen.

⁷ Behold,
   He is coming
      with the clouds,
      and every eye will see Him,
         including those who pierced Him,
      and all the families
         of the earth
         will mourn over Him.
   Truly.
   Amen.

families – a tribe; in the NT all the persons descending from one of the twelve sons of the patriarch, Jacob; a nation, people
mourn – to cut, strike, smite; to cut from, cut off; to beat one's breast for grief

John is announcing the return of Jesus to the earth.

1Thessalonians 4:16, For the Lord Himself will descend from heaven with a shout, with the voice of the archangel and with the trumpet of God, and the dead in Christ will rise first.

All will mourn over Him, even the ones who pierced Him.

Greek Paraphrase of Verse: 7
Behold, He is coming with the clouds, and every eye will see Him, even those who pierced Him; and all the nations of the earth will mourn over Him realizing their sin and worried about the coming wrath. So, it is to be. Amen.

Verse 8

⁸ "I am the Alpha and the Omega," says the Lord God, "the One who is, who was, and who is to come, the Almighty."

⁸ "I am the Alpha and the Omega,"
   says the Lord God,
   "the One
      who is,
      who was,
      and who is to come,
         the Almighty."

Alpha and Omega – these are the first and last letters of the Greek alphabet. By this, He means that he is the first and the last, the beginning and the end.
to come – (different word) – come or appear – Jesus is using this word in present tense, but He is referring to the future.
Almighty - he who holds sway over all things; the ruler of all; almighty: God

This verse concludes the salutation of the book.

He is the beginning and the end. He exists now, always has existed and always will exist.

Greek Paraphrase of Verse: 8
"I am the Alpha and the Omega, the Beginning and the End," says the Lord God, "The One Who exists forever and Who continually existed in the past and Who is still to come in the future, the Almighty, Omnipotent Ruler of all."

Verse 9
John's Vision of Jesus
⁹ *I, John, your brother and companion in the tribulation, kingdom, and perseverance in Jesus, was on the island called Patmos because of the word of God and the testimony of Jesus.*

⁹ *I,*
> *John,*
> *your brother*
> *and*
> *companion*
>> *in the tribulation,*
>> *kingdom,*
>> *and perseverance*
>>> *in Jesus,*
>> *was on the island called Patmos*
>>> *because of the word of God*
>>>> *and the testimony of Jesus.*

brother – a brother, whether born of the same two parents or only of the same father or mother; having the same national ancestor, belonging to the same people, or countryman; any fellow or man; a fellow believer, united to another by the bond of affection
companion - participant with others in anything, a joint partner
tribulation – a pressing, pressing together, pressure; oppression, affliction, tribulation, distress, straits
perseverance – steadfastness, constancy, endurance; in the NT the characteristic of a man who is not swerved from his deliberate purpose and his loyalty to faith and piety by even the greatest trials and sufferings;

patiently, and steadfastly; a patient, steadfast waiting for; a patient enduring, sustaining, perseverance

Patmos – my killing – a rugged and bare island in the Aegean Sea

John wants us to know that he is writing this letter while a prisoner in exile on the island of Patmos. He wants his readers to know this because of the way he has to put things more or less in code throughout the letter.

Greek Paraphrase of Verse: 9
I, John, your brother and companion in the tribulation, kingdom and patient endurance in Jesus, was exiled on the island of Patmos, because I preached the word of God regarding eternal salvation and the testimony of Jesus *Christ*.

Verses 10-11
[10] I was in the Spirit on the Lord's day, and I heard behind me a loud voice like the sound of a trumpet, [11] saying, "Write in a scroll what you see, and send it to the seven churches: to Ephesus, Smyrna, Pergamum, Thyatira, Sardis, Philadelphia, and Laodicea."

[10] I was in the Spirit
    on the Lord's day,
    and I heard
      behind me
      a loud voice
        like the sound of a trumpet,
        [11] saying,
          "Write in a scroll
          what you see,
          and send it to the seven churches:
            to Ephesus,
            Smyrna,
            Pergamum,
            Thyatira,
            Sardis,
            Philadelphia,
            and Laodicea."

Verse: 10
[10] I was in the Spirit on the Lord's day, and I heard behind me a loud voice like the sound of a trumpet,

sound – a sound, a tone of inanimate things, as musical instruments; a voice, of the sound of uttered words, speech; of a language, tongue

In the Spirit probably means that John was projected into the future to a Day of the Lord that is yet to come. Then the voice came to him.

Verse: 11

11 saying, "Write in a scroll what you see, and send it to the seven churches: to Ephesus, Smyrna, Pergamum, Thyatira, Sardis, Philadelphia, and Laodicea."

scroll – a small book, a scroll, a written document; a sheet on which something has been written; a bill of divorcement

Ephesus – permitted – a maritime city of Asia Minor, capital of Ionia and under the Romans, of proconsular Asia, situated on the Icarian Sea between Smyrna and Miletus

Smyrna – myrrh – an Ionian city of Asia Minor, on the Aegean Sea, 40 miles north of Ephesus

Pergamum – height or elevation – a city in Asia Minor, the seat of the dynasties of Attalus and Eumenes, famous for its temple of Aesculapius and the invention and manufacture of parchment. The river Selinus flowed through it and the Cetius ran past it. It was the birthplace of the physician Galen and had a great royal library. It had a Christian church.

Thyatira – odor of affliction – a colony of Macedonia Greeks, situated between Sardis and Pergamos on the river Lycus; its inhabitants gained their living by traffic and the art of dyeing in purple.

Sardis – red ones – a luxurious city in Asia Minor, the capital of Lydia

Philadelphia – brotherly love – a city of Lydia in Asia Minor, situated near the eastern base of Mount Tmolus, founded and named by the Pergamene king, Attalus II Philadelphus. After the death of Attalus III Philometor, 133 BC, it together with his entire kingdom came by his will under the jurisdiction of the Romans.

Laodicea – justice of the people – a city of Phrygia, situated on the river Lycus not far from Colosse. It was destroyed by an earthquake in 66 A.D. and rebuilt by Marcus Aurelius. It was the seat of the Christian church.

Of course, the loud voice John heard was Jesus telling John to write everything down and send it to the seven churches.

Greek Paraphrase of Verses: 10-11

On the Lord's Day, I was in in special communication with the Holy Spirit and empowered to receive and record the revelation from Jesus Christ, and I heard behind me a loud voice like the *sound* of a trumpet, saying, "Write in a little book what you see in this revelation, and send it to the seven churches in Ephesus, Smyrna, Pergamum, Thyatira, Sardis, Philadelphia and Laodicea."

Verses 12-13

12 I turned to see the voice that was speaking with me. And having turned, I saw seven golden lampstands, 13 and among the lampstands was One like the

Son of Man, dressed in a robe reaching to the feet, and girded across His chest with a golden sash.

¹² I turned to see the voice
    that was speaking with me.
    And having turned,
        I saw seven golden lampstands,
            ¹³ and among the lampstands
            was One
                like the Son of Man,
                dressed in a robe reaching to the feet,
                and
                girded across His chest
                    with a golden sash.

Verse: 12
¹² I turned to see the voice that was speaking with me. And having turned, I saw seven golden lampstands,

lampstands – a candlestick, lamp stand, candelabrum

These were seven separate lampstands, not the seven-branched lampstand made by Moses (Exodus 25:31-37) presently called the Menorah

Of course, these seven lampstands represent the seven churches already mentioned.

Verse: 13
¹³ and among the lampstands was One like the Son of Man, dressed in a robe reaching to the feet, and girded across His chest with a golden sash.

robe – a garment reaching to the ankles, coming down to the feet
girded – to fasten garments with a girdle or belt; to gird one's self metaphorically with truth as a girdle; to equip one's self with knowledge of the truth
sash – a girdle, belt, serving not only to gird on flowing garments but also, since it was hollow, to carry money in

Don't miss the significance of Christ being in the midst of the seven lampstands. He is showing that he is still in and with the seven churches no matter what they may think.

His clothing indicated both His priestly position and His royal office.

Greek Paraphrase of Verses: 12-13
Then I turned to see the voice that was speaking with me. After turning I saw seven golden lampstands, and in the middle of the lampstands, I

saw One like the Son of Man, dressed in a robe reaching to His feet, and with a golden sash wrapped around His chest.

Verse 14

14 His head and hair were white like wool, as snow, and His eyes were like a fiery flame.

*14 **His head and hair were white like wool,***
*   **as snow,***
*   **and His eyes were like a fiery flame.***

The description of Christ in this verse and verse fifteen also apply to God Himself, especially as the powerful Judge and Ruler of the universe.

This description matches the one in:

Daniel 7:9, As I kept watching, thrones were set in place, and the Ancient of Days took His seat. His clothing was white like snow, and the hair of His head like whitest wool. His throne was flaming fire; its wheels were blazing fire.

Greek Paraphrase of Verse: 14
His head and hair were white like white wool, glistening white as snow, and His eyes were all-seeing and flashing like a fiery flame piercing into my very being.

Verse 15

15 His feet were like fine bronze fired in a furnace, and His voice was like the sound of rushing waters.

*15 **His feet were like fine bronze***
*   **fired in a furnace,***
*   **and His voice was like the sound of rushing waters.***

fine bronze – some metal like gold if not more precious
to burn with fire, to set on fire, kindle; to be incensed, indignant; full of fire, fiery, ignited
fired – to burn with fire, to set on fire, kindle; to be incensed, indignant; full of fire, fiery, ignited
furnace – furnace or oven for baking bread or burning earthenware

The voice John heard was also the voice of God coming at him the way you can hear water rushing toward you.

Greek Paraphrase of Verse: 15
His feet were like white-hot polished bronze, refined in a furnace, and His voice was like the sound of many powerful waters.

Verse 16

16 In His right hand, He held seven stars, and out of His mouth came a sharp two-edged sword; and His face was like the sun shining in its strength.

16 In His right hand,
   He held seven stars,
   and
   out of His mouth came a sharp two-edged sword;
   and His face was like the sun
      shining in its strength.

strength – strength, power, ability (the word we get dynamite from)

Again, the seven stars refer to the seven churches. It's significant that He held the seven stars in his right hand. The right hand was considered to be the hand of power (sorry lefthanders).

The sword in Jesus' mouth represents the power and force of his message. His words of judgment are as sharp as swords.

Greek Paraphrase of Verse: 16
In His right hand He held seven stars, and out of His mouth came a sharp two-edged sword of judgment; and His face reflected His majesty and glory was like the sun shining in all its power at its highest.

Verses 17-18

17 When I saw Him, I fell at His feet like a dead man. He placed His right hand on me, saying, "Do not be afraid. I am the first and the last, 18 and the living One. I was dead, and behold, I am alive forever, and I have the keys of death and Hades.

17 When I saw Him,
   I fell at His feet
      like a dead man.
   He placed His right hand on me,
      saying,
         "Do not be afraid.
         I am the first and the last,
            18 and the living One.
   I was dead,
      and behold,
   I am alive forever,
      and I have the keys
         of death
         and Hades.

Verse: 17

[17] When I saw Him, I fell at His feet like a dead man. He placed His right hand on me, saying, "Do not be afraid. I am the first and the last,

John had already seen Christ very much like this on the Mount of Transfiguration.

Matthew 17:2, He was transformed in front of them, and His face shone like the sun. Even His clothes became as white as the light.

Jesus touched John. Why? Maybe to revive him. After all he'd just fallen down at Jesus' feet like a dead man.

The custom of the time was when one person was giving a command to another, he would place his right hand on the other person's shoulder as if sealing his words. This is what I think Jesus was doing.

Verse: 18

[18] and the living One. I was dead, and behold, I am alive forever, and I have the keys of death and Hades.

Hades – name Hades or Pluto, the god of the lower regions; Orcus, the nether world, the realm of the dead; later use of this word: the grave, death, hell

Notice that instead of saying He is, was and is coming, Jesus simply said "the living One."

He also mentions for the first time that He has the keys to set free all who have died.

Greek Paraphrase of Verses: 17-18

When I saw Him, I fell at His feet like a dead man. He placed His right hand on me and said, "Do not be afraid; I am the First and the Last, and the One who lives in and beyond all time and space. I died, but look, I am alive forevermore, and I have absolute control and victory over death and of Hades, the realm of the dead.

Verse 19

[19] Therefore, write what you have seen, what is, and what will take place after these things.

*[19] **Therefore,***
 write what you have seen,
  what is,
  and what will take place
   after these things.

Jesus repeats his command to John to write all of this down. But this time, He includes not only what John sees but everything that will happen afterward too.

Greek Paraphrase of Verse: 19
Therefore, write the things which you have seen in this vision, the things which are now happening, and the things which will take place after these things.

Verse 20
20 The mystery of the seven stars you saw in My right hand, and the seven golden lampstands is this: the seven stars are the angels of the seven churches, and the seven lampstands are the seven churches.

20 The mystery
     of the seven stars
     you saw
          in My right hand,
     and
     the seven golden lampstands
          is this:
               the seven stars are the angels of the seven churches,
               and
               the seven lampstands are the seven churches.

mystery – a hidden purpose or counsel; secret will of men; in Rabbinic writings, it denotes the mystic or hidden sense of an Old Testament saying or of an image or form seen in a vision or of a dream

Finally, Jesus explains that the seven stars are the angels of the church. Each church has a special angel or messenger looking out for it.
And of course, the seven lampstands are definitely the seven churches.

Greek Paraphrase of Verse: 20
The mystery of the seven stars which you saw in My right hand, and the seven golden lampstands is this: the seven stars are the divine messengers of the seven churches, and the seven lampstands are the seven churches.

Chapter Two

In Chapters Two and Three consist of letters addressed to the seven churches. Chapter two has the first four: Ephesus, Smyrna, Pergamos, and Thyatira. The other four are included in Chapter Three.

Each church will be dealt with individually as John writes about them, but they all share five characteristics.

1. They all begin with a reference to some of the attributes of Christ.

2. Each of the introductions is followed by the formula, "I know your works."

3. Next comes advise, reprimands or promises that each one needed.

4. A serious warning to hear what the Spirit has to say to each of the churches.

5. Either at the beginning or the end of what is said to each church, there is some sort of promise or guarantee meant to encourage that church.

Verses 1-2
Letter to Ephesus
[1] *"To the angel of the church in Ephesus write: The One who holds the seven stars in His right hand, and walks among the seven golden lampstands, says this:* [2] *'I know your works, your labor and endurance, and that you cannot tolerate evil. You have tested those who call themselves apostles and you found them to be liars.*

[1] "To the angel
   of the church
   in Ephesus
   write:
     The One
       who holds the seven stars
         in His right hand,
       and walks among the seven golden lampstands,
       says this:
        [2] 'I know your works,
          your labor and endurance,
          and that you cannot tolerate evil,
       You have tested
         Those who call themselves apostles
         and you found them to be liars.

Verse: 1
[1] *"To the angel of the church in Ephesus write: The One who holds the seven stars in His right hand, and walks among the seven golden lampstands, says this:*

angel of the church – this is not referring to a spiritual angel. It is referring to the leader of the church to take this message to the church.

Ephesus – permitted – a maritime city of Asia Minor, capital of Ionia and under the Romans, of proconsular Asia, situated on the Icarian Sea between Smyrna and Miletus

The word 'angel' here is referring to the human leader of the church, not a spiritual being. The definition is more of messenger. He is to take this message to the rest of the church.

Of course, it is Christ who holds the stars (angels) of the seven churches and He walks among the seven churches.

Verse: 2

[2] *'I know your works, your labor and endurance, and that you cannot tolerate evil. You have tested those who call themselves apostles and you found them to be liars.*

works – business, employment, that which any one is occupied; that which one undertakes to do, enterprise, undertaking; any product whatever,
labor - a beating of the breast with grief, sorrow; labor; trouble; to cause one trouble, make work for him; intense labor united with trouble and toil
endurance – steadfastness, constancy, endurance; in the NT the characteristic of a man who is not swerved from his deliberate purpose and his loyalty to faith and piety by even the greatest trials and sufferings; patiently, and steadfastly; a patient, steadfast waiting for; a patient enduring, sustaining, perseverance
tolerate – to take up with the hands; to take up in order to carry or bear, to put upon one's self; to bear what is burdensome; to sustain, i.e. uphold, support

Now, Jesus is telling the leader of the church in Ephesus that He knows all that he's been doing, how he's been doing it and how long he's been doing it.

Then Jesus says the leader can't tolerate evil and he exposed the false apostles as liars.

Greek Paraphrase of Verses: 1-2
"To the divine messenger of the church in Ephesus write: "The One who firmly holds in His right hand the seven stars which are the messengers of the seven churches, and walks among the seven golden lampstands, the seven churches, says this: 'I know your works, your trouble and your patient endurance, and that you cannot tolerate those who are evil, and you have tested those who call themselves special messengers, and have found them to be liars and impostors.

Verse 3
[3] *You have endurance and have endured for My name's sake and have not grown weary.*

Trennis E. Killian

³ You have endurance
   and
   have endured
     for My name's sake,
     and have not grown weary.

endurance – steadfastness, constancy, endurance; in the NT the characteristic of a man who is not swerved from his deliberate purpose and his loyalty to faith and piety by even the greatest trials and sufferings; patiently, and steadfastly; a patient, steadfast waiting for; a patient enduring, sustaining, perseverance
endured – to take up with the hands; to take up in order to carry or bear, to put upon one's self; to bear what is burdensome; to sustain, i.e. uphold, support
sake – because of
grown weary – to grow weary, tired, exhausted (with toil or burdens or grief); to labor with wearisome effort, to toil; of bodily labor

Jesus is still talking to the leader of the church, but He said the same thing only in reverse order. I think this was for emphasis.

Greek Paraphrase of Verse: 3
I know that you who believe are enduring patiently and are bearing up for My name's sake, and that you have not grown weary of being faithful to the truth.

Verse 4
⁴ 'But I have this against you, that you have abandoned your first love.

⁴ 'But
   I have this against you,
     that you have abandoned your first love.

abandoned – to send away; of a husband divorcing his wife; to let go, let alone, let be; to disregard; to let go, give up a debt, forgive, to remit; to permit, allow, not to hinder, to give up a thing to a person; to leave, go way from one in order to go to another place; to desert wrongfully; to go away leaving something behind; to leave on dying, leave behind one; abandon, leave destitute

Now, it seems that Jesus has switched and is telling the leader that he hasn't done so well after all. The word translated 'abandoned' was usually used to refer to willful abandonment, a deliberate giving up. It can also mean long neglect.
Also, the love they abandoned is the agape love that Jesus demonstrated.

Greek Paraphrase of Verse: 4
But I have this against you, that you have abandoned the deep love that you first had for Me.
Verse 5
⁵ Therefore, remember how far you have fallen, and repent and do the works you did at first. If not, I am coming to you and will remove your lampstand from its place—unless you repent.

⁵ Therefore,
    remember how far you have fallen,
        and repent
        and do the works you did at first.
            If not,
                I am coming
                    to you
                    and will remove your lampstand
                        from its place
                        unless you repent.

remember – to be mindful of, to remember, to call to mind; to think of and feel for a person or thing; to hold in memory, keep in mind; to make mention of
repent – to change one's mind for better, heartily to amend with abhorrence of one's past sins
do – in this context: to act right, to do well

These three words are highly significant here. They are to remember where they were in relationship to where they are now. They are to stop what they're doing and change for the better. They are also to do the right things again.

For Jesus to remove their lampstand would mean that the church would stop being an effective church. That's bad.

Greek Paraphrase of Verse: 5
Therefore, remember *how far* you have fallen, repent, seek God's will and do the works you did when you first knew Me. If not then, I will come to you and remove the church and its impact from its place—unless you turn around and come back to Me.

Verse 6
⁶ Yet you do have this, that you hate the works of the Nicolaitans, which I also hate.

[6] Yet
> you do have this,
>> that you hate the works
>>> of the Nicolaitans,
>>> which I also hate.

Nicolaitans – Nicolaitans = "destruction of people" a sect who were charged with holding the error of Balaam, casting a stumbling block before the church of God by upholding the liberty of eating things sacrificed to idols as well as committing fornication

The Nicolaitans were believers who compromised their faith in order to participate in the sinful practices of the Ephesian society.

At least they weren't doing all that and even hated the Nicolaitans' works.

Greek Paraphrase of Verse: 6
Yet this is to your credit, that you hate the works and corrupt teachings of the Nicolaitans that deceive and trick the people, which I also hate.

Verse 7
[7] The one who has an ear, let him hear what the Spirit says to the churches. To the one who overcomes, I will give the right to eat from the tree of life, which is in the paradise of God.'

[7] The one who has an ear,
> let him hear what the Spirit says
>> to the churches.
> To the one who overcomes,
>> I will give the right to eat
>>> from the tree of life,
>>>> which is in the paradise of God.'

overcomes - to conquer; to carry off the victory, come off victorious; when one is arraigned or goes to law, to win the case, maintain one's cause
tree of life – One of the two trees in the Garden of Eden. Eating from the tree of life will bring eternal life with God.
paradise – among the Persians a grand enclosure or preserve, hunting ground, park, shady and well-watered, in which wild animals, were kept for the hunt; it was enclosed by walls and furnished with towers for the hunters; a garden, pleasure ground; grove, park; the part of Hades which was thought by the later Jews to be the abode of the souls of pious until the resurrection: but some understand this to be a heavenly paradise; the upper regions of the heavens. According to the early church Fathers, the paradise in which our first parents dwelt before the fall still exists, neither on the earth or in the heavens, but above and beyond the world; heaven

"The one who has an ear, let him hear" is at the end of each of the letters addressed to the seven churches. It was a custom of the time used to get the hearer or reader's attention and to emphasize to them the importance of what was coming next.

It is extremely important because it deals with eternal life. But I think the opposite is implied. If they don't conquer or overcome, they won't get to eat from the tree of life.

Greek Paraphrase of Verse: 7
He who has an ear, let him understand and heed what the Spirit says to the churches. To the one who overcomes the world through believing that Jesus is the Son of God, I will grant the privilege to eat the fruit from the tree of life, which is in the Paradise of God.'

Verses 8-9
Letter to Smyrna
⁸ And to the angel of the church in Smyrna write: The First and the Last, who was dead, and came to life, says: ⁹ 'I know your tribulation and poverty, but you are rich, and the slander of those who say they are Jews and are not, but are a synagogue of Satan.

⁸ And
  to the angel
    of the church
    in Smyrna
    write:
      The First and the Last,
        who was dead,
          and came to life,
        says:
          ⁹ 'I know your tribulation and poverty,
            but you are rich,
            and the slander of those
              who say they are Jews
                and are not,
                but are a synagogue of Satan.

Verse: 8
⁸ And to the angel of the church in Smyrna write: The First and the Last, who was dead, and came to life, says:

angel of the church – this is not referring to a spiritual angel. It is referring to the leader of the church to take this message to the church.
Smyrna – myrrh – an Ionian city of Asia Minor, on the Aegean Sea, 40 miles north of Ephesus

Christ begins the letter to the church in Smyrna by reminding them of His eternity and His death and resurrection.

Verse: 9

⁹ 'I know your tribulation and poverty, but you are rich, and the slander of those who say they are Jews and are not but are a synagogue of Satan.

tribulation – a pressing, pressing together, pressure; oppression, affliction, tribulation, distress, straits
poverty – beggary; in the New Testament poverty
rich – wealthy, abounding in material resources; metaphorically abounding, abundantly supplied; abounding (rich) in Christian virtues and eternal possessions
slander – slander, detraction, speech injurious, to another's good name; immoral and reproachful speech injurious to divine majesty
synagogue – a bringing together, gathering (as of fruits), a contracting; in the New Testament, an assembling together of men, an assembly of men; a synagogue

The city of Smyrna had gone through several hundred years of being conquered by different groups. It started out as Greek then finally came back shortly before this time. That is what the reference to "tribulation and poverty" is all about.

At that time, they were being persecuted by those who claimed to be Jews who rejected Christ. But in fact, they weren't even Jews but under the control of Satan.

Greek Paraphrase of Verses: 8-9

"And to the divine messenger of the church in Smyrna write: These are the words of the First and the Last, the Son of God who died and came to life again: 'I know your oppressive suffering and your poverty but you are rich, and how your name was attacked by those who say they are Jews and are not, but they are Jews only by blood, and do not believe and truly honor the God whom they claim to worship.

Verse 10

¹⁰ Do not fear what you are about to suffer. Behold, the devil is about to throw some of you into prison, to test you, and you will have tribulation for ten days. Be faithful until death, and I will give you the crown of life.

¹⁰ Do not fear
    what you are about to suffer.
    Behold,
    the devil is about to throw some of you
      into prison,
        to test you,
        and you will have tribulation for ten days.

Be faithful until death,
    and I will give you the crown of life.

suffer – to be affected or have been affected, to feel, have a sensible experience, to undergo; in a good sense, to be well off, in good case; in a bad sense, to suffer sadly, be in a bad plight

tribulation – a pressing, pressing together, pressure; oppression, affliction, tribulation, distress, straits

After all they'd suffered before, they were apparently very much afraid of more suffering to come. Jesus is telling them that there is more suffering coming. But the good thing is that if they remain faithful through their suffering, they will receive the crown of life. Great!

But the stickler here is that they must be faithful "until death." That sounds like a prediction to me.

Greek Paraphrase of Verse: 10
Do not fear anything you are about to suffer. Be aware that the devil is about to throw some of you into prison, to test your faith, and you will have tribulation for ten days. Be faithful if you must die for your faith, and I will give you the crown consisting of life.

Verse 11
11 The one who has an ear, let him hear what the Spirit says to the churches. The one who overcomes will not be hurt by the second death.'

11 The one
    who has an ear,
    let him hear
      what the Spirit says to the churches.
  The one who overcomes
    will not be hurt
      by the second death.'

overcomes – to conquer; to carry off the victory, come off victorious; when one is arraigned or goes to law, to win the case, maintain one's cause

hurt – to act unjustly or wickedly, to sin; to be a criminal, to have violated the laws in some way; to do wrong; to do hurt; to do some wrong or sin in some respect; to wrong someone, act wickedly towards him; to hurt, damage, harm

second death – eternal death

As a conclusion to the letter to the church in Smyrna, Jesus reminds all the churches that there is something worse than physical death. In fact, He is telling them they won't be hurt spiritually by their physical deaths.

Greek Paraphrase of Verse: 11
He who has an ear, let him understand what the Spirit says to the churches. He who overcomes the world through believing that Jesus is the Son of God will not be hurt by the lake of fire.'

Verses 12-13
Letter to Pergamum
[12] And to the angel of the church in Pergamum write: The One who has the sharp two-edged sword says: [13] 'I know where you live—where Satan's throne is. And you held on to My name, and did not deny your faith in Me, even in the days of Antipas, My faithful witness, who was killed among you, where Satan lives.

[12] And
    to the angel
        of the church
        in Pergamum
        write:
            The One
                who has the sharp two-edged sword
                says:
                    [13] 'I know where you live
                        where Satan's throne is.
And
    you held on to My name,
        and did not deny your faith
            in Me,
            even in the days of Antipas,
                My faithful witness,
                who was killed among you,
                    where Satan lives.

Verse: 12
[12] And to the angel of the church in Pergamum write: The One who has the sharp two-edged sword says:

angel of the church – this is not referring to a spiritual angel. It is referring to the leader of the church to take this message to the church.
Pergamum – Pergamos = "height or elevation" capital of the Roman province of Asia. It was also the seat of the dynasties of Attalus and Eumenes, famous for its temple of Aesculapius and the invention and manufacture of parchment. The river Selinus flowed through it and the Cetius ran past it. It was the birthplace of the physician Galen and had a great royal library. It had a Christian church.
sharp two-edged sword – Christ's ability and power to win victories over all His enemies and He is able to use the sword in the other direction to deal with those in the church who don't continue to be faithful.

Now, Jesus is addressing the leader of the church in Pergamum. He describes Himself as having "the sharp two-edged sword." He is telling them that He will come after them with the sword too if they don't remain faithful.

Verse: 13
¹³ 'I know where you live—where Satan's throne is. And you held on to My name, and did not deny your faith in Me, even in the days of Antipas, My faithful witness, who was killed among you, where Satan lives.

Antipas – like the father – a Christian of Pergamos who suffered martyrdom

Pergamum was a bad place where idolatry was heavily entrenched and a place where Christians were severely persecuted. Christ is commending them because they did not deny their faith even though Antipas was killed there.

Greek Paraphrase of Verses: 12-13
"And to the divine messenger of the church in Pergamum write: "These are the words of the One who has *and* wields the sharp two-edged sword in judgment: 'I know where you live, a place where Satan sits on his throne. Yet you are holding on to My name, and you did not deny your faith in Me even in the days of Antipas, My witness, My faithful one, who was martyred among you, where Satan lives.

Verse 14
¹⁴But I have a few things against you, because you have some there who hold the teaching of Balaam, who kept teaching Balak to put a stumbling block before the sons of Israel, to eat things sacrificed to idols and to commit acts of immorality.

¹⁴But
    I have a few things against you,
      because you have some there
        who hold the teaching of Balaam,
          who kept teaching Balak
            to put a stumbling block
              before the sons of Israel,
            to eat things sacrificed to idols
            and
            to commit acts of immorality.

Balaam – A native of Pethor a city in Mesopotamia, endued by Jehovah with prophetic power. He was hired by Balak to curse the Israelites; and influenced by the love of reward, he wished to gratify Balak; but he was compelled by Jehovah's power to bless them. Hence later the Jews saw him as a most abandoned deceiver.

Balak – Balak = "a devastator or spoiler" – a king of Moab
stumbling block – the movable stick or trigger of a trap, a trap stick; a trap, snare; any person or thing by which one is (entrapped) drawn into error or sin
immorality – to prostitute one's body to the lust of another; to commit fornication; metaphorically to be given to idolatry, to worship idols; to permit one's self to be drawn away by another into idolatry

But everything isn't good there even though the church as a whole is faithful. They have some who follow the deceptive teachings of Balaam. They are accused of eating things sacrificed to idols and of committing acts of sexual immorality.

Greek Paraphrase of Verse: 14
But I have a few things against you, because you have some among you there who are holding to the corrupt teaching of Balaam, who kept teaching Balak to put a stumbling block before the sons of Israel, enticing them to eat things that had been sacrificed to idols and to commit acts of sexual immorality.

Verse 15
15 So you also have some who hold the teaching of the Nicolaitans.

15 So
  you
    also
    have some
      who hold the teaching of the Nicolaitans.

Nicolaitans – Nicolaitans = "destruction of people" a sect who were charged with holding the error of Balaam, casting a stumbling block before the church of God by upholding the liberty of eating things sacrificed to idols as well as committing fornication

Some think that Balaam was also a reference to the Nicolaitans, but I don't think that's true. Those following the teachings of Balaam were also into idol worship. Even though the Nicolaitans taught unrestrained indulgence, they didn't seem to worship idols.

Greek Paraphrase of Verse: 15
You also have some there with you who are holding to the teaching of the Nicolaitans.
Verse 16
16 Therefore, repent. Otherwise, I am coming to you quickly, and will make war against them with the sword of My mouth.

¹⁶ Therefore,
  repent.
    Otherwise,
    I am coming
      to you
      quickly,
      and will make war against them
        with the sword of My mouth.

repent – to change one's mind for better, heartily to amend with abhorrence of one's past sins
make war – to war, carry on war; to fight
sword – a large sword; properly a long Thracian javelin, also a kind of long sword worn on the right shoulder

    This is the sword of God's judgment. Jesus is telling them that unless they keep the faith, He will fight against them with the sword of His mouth.

Greek Paraphrase of Verse: 16
Therefore, change your inner self from your old way of thinking, your sinful behavior and seek God's will. If not, I am coming to you quickly, and I will make war and fight against them in judgment with the sword of My mouth.

Verse 17
¹⁷ The one who has an ear, let him hear what the Spirit says to the churches. To the one who overcomes, to him I will give some of the hidden manna, and I will give him a white stone, and a new name written on the stone that no one knows but the one who receives it.'

¹⁷ The one
    who has an ear,
    let him hear what the Spirit says
      to the churches.
  To the one
    who overcomes,
    to him I will give some of the hidden manna,
    and
    I will give him a white stone,
      and a new name written on the stone
        that no one knows but the one who receives it.'
manna = "what is it" – the food that nourished the Israelites for forty years in the wilderness; symbolically, that which is kept in the heavenly temple for the food of angels and the blessed
white stone – possibly the stone of forgiveness and acquittal

If they overcome, they will receive the hidden manna. This may refer to the food of life given to the Israelites in the wilderness or it could be a totally new type of reward for faithfulness.

(Just a note here: the Hebrew word for Manna means "what is it?")

The white stone has a new name written on it. The new name means they will have a new nature and a full inheritance.

Greek Paraphrase of Verse: 17

He who has an ear, let him understand *and* do what the Spirit says to the churches. To him who overcomes the world through believing that Jesus is the Son of God, I will give the privilege of eating *some* of the hidden manna, and I will give him a white stone with a new name engraved on it that no one knows except the one who receives it.'

Verses 18-19
Letter to Thyatira

[18] And to the angel of the church in Thyatira write: The Son of God, the One whose eyes are like a fiery flame, and His feet are like fine bronze, says: [19] 'I know your works—your love, faith, service, endurance, and that your works of late are greater than the first.

[18] And
  to the angel
    of the church
    in Thyatira
    write:
      The Son of God,
        the One whose eyes are like a fiery flame,
        and His feet are like fine bronze,
      says:
        [19] 'I know your works
        your love,
        faith,
        service,
        endurance,
        and that your works
          of late
          are greater than the first.

Verse: 18

[18] And to the angel of the church in Thyatira write: The Son of God, the One whose eyes are like a fiery flame, and His feet are like fine bronze, says:

angel of the church – this is not referring to a spiritual angel. It is referring to the leader of the church to take this message to the church.

Thyatira – odor of affliction – a colony of Macedonia Greeks, situated between Sardis and Pergamos on the river Lycus; its inhabitants gained their living by traffic and the art of dyeing in purple

Now comes the letter to the church in Thyatira. Jesus draws their attention to the fact that He is the Son of God.

"Eyes like a fiery flame" are ready to burn away any disguise for sin or wrongdoing the church might be trying to hide. They are only deceiving themselves.

Feet "like fine bronze" means there is no contamination in them. He was totally free from sin when He was on earth therefore, he is able to bring judgment on sin.

Verse: 19

[19] 'I know your works – your love, faith, service, endurance, and that your works of late are greater than the first.

service – service, ministering, especially of those who execute the commands of others; of those who by the command of God proclaim and promote religion among men

endurance – steadfastness, constancy, endurance; in the NT the characteristic of a man who is not swerved from his deliberate purpose and his loyalty to faith and piety by even the greatest trials and sufferings; patiently, and steadfastly; a patient, steadfast waiting for; a patient enduring, sustaining, perseverance

Jesus knew a lot of good things the church at Thyatira was doing. They were apparently ministering for the Lord.

Greek Paraphrase of Verses: 18-19

"And to the divine messenger of the church in Thyatira write: "These are the words of the Son of God, who has eyes that flash like a fiery flame in righteous judgment, and whose feet are like polished white-hot bronze: 'I know what you do, your love, faith, service and patient endurance, and that the last things you do are more numerous and greater than the first.

Verse 20

[20] But I have this against you, that you tolerate the woman Jezebel, who calls herself a prophetess to teach and mislead My slaves to commit immorality and to eat things sacrificed to idols.

²⁰ But
>
> I have this against you,
>> that you tolerate the woman
>>> Jezebel,
>>> who calls herself a prophetess
>>>> to teach and mislead My slaves
>>>>> to commit immorality
>>>>> and
>>>>> to eat things sacrificed to idols.

tolerate – to send away; of a husband divorcing his wife; to let go, let alone, let be; to disregard; to let go, give up a debt, forgive, to remit; to permit, allow, not to hinder, to give up a thing to a person; to leave, go way from one in order to go to another place; to desert wrongfully; to go away leaving something behind; to leave on dying, leave behind one; abandon, leave destitute (Different word from 2:2)

Jezebel – "chaste" – wife of Ahab, an impious and cruel queen who protected idolatry and persecuted the prophets; the symbolic name of a woman who pretended to be a prophetess, and who, addicted to antinomianism, claimed Christian liberty of eating things sacrificed to idols

But! Isn't there always a but? Jesus tells them that even though they are doing so many things right, He still has something against them.

There was a woman in the church (her name probably wasn't Jezebel) who claimed to be a prophetess but was teaching them to commit sexual immorality and to eat food that had been sacrificed to idols.

Greek Paraphrase of Verse: 20
But I have this against you, that you permit the woman Jezebel, who claims to be inspired by God, but she teaches and misleads My believers to commit acts of sexual immorality and to eat food sacrificed to idols.

Verse 21
²¹ I gave her time to repent, but she does not want to repent of her immorality.

²¹ I gave her time
> to repent,
>> but she does not want to repent
>> of her immorality.

repent – to change one's mind for better, heartily to amend with abhorrence of one's past sins

immorality – illicit sexual intercourse; adultery, fornication, homosexuality, lesbianism, intercourse with animals etc.; metaphorically the worship of idols; of the defilement of idolatry, as incurred by eating the sacrifices offered to idols

Jesus had already tried to get this woman to repent but she wouldn't. The implication here is that she will receive much harsher punishment because she'd leading others away from Christ.

Greek Paraphrase of Verse: 21
I gave her time to change her inner self and her sinful way of thinking, but she has no desire to repent of her immorality *and* refuses to do so.

Verse 22
22 Behold, I will throw her on a bed of sickness, and those who commit adultery with her into great tribulation, unless they repent of her ways.

22 Behold,
　　I will throw her on a bed
　　　of sickness,
　　　and those who commit adultery
　　　　with her
　　　　into great tribulation,
　　　　　unless they repent of her ways.

throw – to throw or let go of a thing without caring where it falls; to scatter, to throw, cast into to give over to one's care uncertain about the result; to pour, pour into of rivers; to pour out
bed of sickness – a small bed, a couch; a couch to recline on at meals; a couch on which a sick man is carried
tribulation – a pressing, pressing together, pressure; oppression, affliction, tribulation, distress, straits
repent – to change one's mind for better, heartily to amend with abhorrence of one's past sins

Now comes the punishment reserved just for her. She will be thrown into a bed of sickness which leads to physical death. It could possibly mean spiritual death as well.

In the statement above, Jesus was pronouncing judgment on her. But the ones who followed her teachings are thrown into great tribulation if they don't repent first.

Greek Paraphrase of Verse: 22
Listen carefully, I will throw her on a bed *of sickness,* and those who commit adultery with her I will put into great tribulation, unless they repent of her ways.

Verse 23

23 And I will kill her children, and all the churches will know that I am the One who searches the minds and hearts, and I will give to each of you according to your works.

23 And
 I will kill her children
  and all the churches will know
   that I am the One
    who searches the minds and hearts,
    and I will give to each
     of you
     according to your works.

This drastic punishment for the woman is to set an example to all the other churches that Jesus knows everything they do and that he will punish or reward them according to what they do.

Greek Paraphrase of Verse: 23
And I will kill her followers with pestilence, and all the churches will know without a doubt that I am the One who searches the innermost thoughts and purposes, and I will give to each one of you a reward or punishment according to your works.

Verses 24-25

24 But I say to the rest of you in Thyatira, who do not hold this teaching, who have not known the deep things of Satan—as they call them—I will not place any other burden on you. 25 hold on to what you have until I come.

24 But
 I say to the rest
  of you
  in Thyatira,
  who do not hold this teaching,
  who have not known the deep things of Satan
   as they call them
  I will not place any other burden on you.
  25 hold on to what you have
   until I come.

Verse: 24

24 But I say to the rest of you in Thyatira, who do not hold this teaching, who have not known the deep things of Satan—as they call them—I will not place any other burden on you.

Thyatira – "odor of affliction" – a colony of Macedonia Greeks, situated between Sardis and Pergamos on the river Lycus; its inhabitants gained their living by traffic and the art of dyeing in purple

Good news Thyatira! He is not going to punish the rest of them. He knew that not all the people in the church were following the woman and He wanted them to know they were safe from His wrath.

Verse: 25
25 hold on to what you have until I come.

hold – to have power, be powerful; to take hold of, take, seize; to keep carefully and faithfully; to continue to hold, to retain

So, now Jesus is giving them advice. Keep doing what you're doing until I come again. Isn't that what He is saying to all of us who are following Him?

Greek Paraphrase of Verses: 24-25
But to the rest of you in Thyatira, who do not hold this teaching, and have not explored and known the depths of Satan, as they call them, I will not place any other burden on you, except to hold tightly to what you have until I come.

Verses 26-28
26 The one who overcomes, and the one who keeps My works until the end, to him I will give authority over the nations—27 and he will shepherd them with an iron scepter, as the vessels of pottery are broken to pieces, as I also have received authority from My Father. 28 I will give him the morning star.

26 The one who overcomes,
    and the one who keeps My works
      until the end,
    to him I will give authority
      over the nations—
      27 and he will shepherd them
        with an iron scepter,
          as the vessels of pottery are broken to pieces,
          as I also have received authority from My Father.
    28 I will give him the morning star.

Verse: 26
26 The one who overcomes, and the one who keeps My works until the end, to him I will give authority over the nations—

overcomes – to conquer; to carry off the victory, come off victorious; when one is arraigned or goes to law, to win the case, maintain one's cause
keeps – to attend to carefully, take care of; to guard; to keep, one in the state in which he is; to observe; to reserve: to undergo something
works – business, employment, that which any one is occupied; that which one undertakes to do, enterprise, undertaking; any product whatever, anything accomplished by hand, art, industry, or mind
authority –physical and mental power; the power of authority (influence) and of right (privilege); the power of rule or government (the power of him whose will and commands must be submitted to by others and obeyed); the power of judicial decisions; one who possesses authority; a ruler, a human magistrate

Verse: 27
27 and he will shepherd them with an iron scepter, as the vessels of pottery are broken to pieces, as I also have received authority from My Father.

shepherd – (rule) – to feed, to tend a flock, keep sheep; to rule, govern; of rulers; to furnish pasture for food; to nourish; to cherish one's body, to serve the body; to supply the requisites for the soul's need
scepter – (rod) – a staff, a walking stick, a twig, rod, branch; a rod with which one is beaten; a staff as used on a journey, or to lean upon, or by shepherds; with a rod of iron, indicates the severest, most rigorous rule; a royal scepter
authority –physical and mental power; the power of authority (influence) and of right (privilege); the power of rule or government (the power of him whose will and commands must be submitted to by others and obeyed); the power of judicial decisions; one who possesses authority; a ruler, a human magistrate

Psalm 2:9, "You will break them with a rod of iron. You will shatter them like pottery.

Jesus will still be the shepherd but instead of a staff, He will use an iron rod. He also reminds them that His authority comes from God the Father.

Verse: 28
28 I will give him the morning star.

Wow! Jesus is saying that those who overcome will receive a part of Him since he is the morning star.

Greek Paraphrase of Verses: 26-28
The one who overcomes the world through believing that Jesus is the Son of God and he who keeps doing the things that please Me until the very end, to him I will give authority and power over the nations; and he will shepherd *and* rule them with a rod of iron, as the earthen pots are broken to pieces, as I also have received authority and power to rule from My Father, I will give him the Morning Star.

Verse 29
²⁹ The one who has an ear, let him hear what the Spirit says to the churches. '

²⁹ The one who has an ear,
> let him hear
>> what the Spirit says
>>> to the churches.'

He ends with the same admonition to listen, understand and apply what He is saying to them.

Greek Paraphrase of Verse: 29
The one who has an ear, let him understand and do what the Spirit says to the churches.'

Chapter Three

Chapter Three is made up of letters to the last three of the seven churches. The churches are Sardis, Philadelphia and Laodicea.

Each church will be dealt with individually as John writes about them, but Jesus describes each one this way:

Sardis: The Spiritually Dead Church
Philadelphia: The Tried and Faithful Church
Laodicea: The Lukewarm Church

But He does attack each one as well:
Sardis about their hypocrisy
Philadelphia about hollow profession
Laodicea on apostasy

This is Christ's attitude to the Church in its final stage in the world.

Verse 1
Letter to Sardis

[1] "To the angel of the church in Sardis write: The One who has the seven spirits of God and the seven stars, says this: 'I know your works, that you have a reputation for being alive, but you are dead.

[1] "To the angel
    of the church
    in Sardis
    write:
      The One
        who has the seven spirits of God
          and the seven stars,
        says this:
          'I know your works,
            that you have a reputation for being alive,
            but you are dead.

Sardis – red ones – a luxurious city in Asia Minor, the capital of Lydia
works – business, employment, that which any one is occupied; that which one undertakes to do, enterprise, undertaking; any product whatever, anything accomplished by hand, art, industry, or mind
reputation – the word is name, but it means reputation (similar to someone having a good name)

Jesus starts out by drawing attention to the fact that He has the sevenfold Spirit of God as depicted in Isaiah 11:2

The Spirit of the LORD will rest on Him— a Spirit of wisdom and understanding, a Spirit of counsel and strength, a Spirit of knowledge and of the fear of the LORD.

Jesus doesn't waste time in telling them what's wrong with them. They look alive but they are actually dead. Wow!

Greek Paraphrase of Verse: 1
"To the divine messenger of the church in Sardis write: "These are the words of the One who has the seven Spirits of God and the seven stars: 'I know what you do, that you have a reputation for being alive, but in reality you are dead.

Verse 2
² Be alert and strengthen what remains, which is about to die, for I have not found your works complete in the sight of My God.

² Be alert and strengthen what remains,
　　which is about to die,
　　　for I have not found your works complete
　　　　in the sight of My God.

alert – to watch; give strict attention to, be cautious, active
strengthen – to make stable, place firmly, set fast, fix; to strengthen, make firm; to render constant, confirm, one's mind
remains – remaining, the rest; the rest of any number or class under consideration; with a certain distinction and contrast, the rest, who are not of a specific class or number; the rest of the things that remain
complete – to make full, to fill up, i.e. to fill to the full; to cause to abound, to furnish or supply liberally; to make complete in every particular, to render perfect
sight – in the presence of, before; of occupied place: in that place, which is before, or over against, opposite, any one and towards which another turns his eyes

The Christians at Sardis were depending on their past to keep them going but there was nothing left of that past. Christ is saying that all they've done so far is not enough. They need to keep on going and doing the right things.

Greek Paraphrase of Verse: 2
Be alert, strengthen and reaffirm what remains of your faithful commitment to Me, which is about to die, for I have not found anything that you have completed in the sight of My God *or* anything that meets His requirements.

Verse 3
³ Remember therefore, what you have received and heard; keep it and repent. Therefore, if you are not alert, I will come like a thief, and you will not know at what hour I will come to you.

³ Remember
   therefore,
   what you have received and heard;
     keep it and repent.
  Therefore,
  if you are not alert,
   I will come
    like a thief,
    and you will not know at what hour I will come to you.

remember – to be mindful of, to remember, to call to mind; to think of and feel for a person or thing; to hold in memory, keep in mind; to make mention of
alert – to watch; give strict attention to, be cautious, active

Repent! That's what Christ wants them to do. He uses His Second Coming as a warning for them to get ready and to stay ready.

They had once received the truths of the Gospel (good news) with joy. Now, He's not only reminding them of that but commanding them to return to that former joy.

Greek Paraphrase of Verse: 3
Therefore, remember and take to heart the lessons you have received and heard. Keep *and* obey them, and change your sinful way of thinking, and demonstrate your repentance with new behavior that proves a conscious decision to turn away from sin. Therefore, if you do not keep watching, I will come like a thief in the night, and you will not know at what hour I will come to you.

Verse 4
⁴ But you have a few people in Sardis who have not defiled their clothes, and they will walk with Me in white, for they are worthy.

⁴ But
  you have a few people
   in Sardis
  who have not defiled their clothes,
    and they will walk
     with Me
     in white,
      for they are worthy.
Sardis – red ones – a luxurious city in Asia Minor, the capital of Lydia
defiled – to pollute, stain, contaminate, defile; used in the New Testament of those who have not kept themselves pure from the defilements of sin, who have soiled themselves by fornication and adultery
worthy – weighing, having weight, having the weight of another thing of like value, worth as much

As always, there were a few exceptions, those who were living right, and Christ was going to reward them by allowing them to wear white and walk with Him. That would be great!

Greek Paraphrase of Verse: 4
But you still have a few people in Sardis who have not contaminated their character and personal integrity with sin, and they will walk with Me dressed in white, because they are worthy.

Verse 5
⁵ The one who overcomes will be clothed in white clothes, and I will never erase his name from the scroll of life, but I will acknowledge his name before My Father and before His angels.

⁵ The one who overcomes
    will be clothed in white clothes,
    and
    I will never erase his name
      from the scroll of life,
      but I will acknowledge his name
        before My Father
        and
        before His angels.

overcomes – to conquer; to carry off the victory, come off victorious; when one is arraigned or goes to law, to win the case, maintain one's cause
acknowledge – to say the same thing as another, i.e. to agree with, assent; to concede; not to refuse, to promise; not to deny; to confess; declare; to confess, i.e. to admit or declare one's self guilty of what one is accused of; to profess; to declare openly, speak out freely; to profess one's self the worshipper of one; to praise, celebrate

Jesus is making several promises now to all of those who will overcome. He's not just talking about the ones who were right with Him then, but also all of those who would get right with Him after this.

The best part of this is that Jesus said He would acknowledge their names before God the Father.

Greek Paraphrase of Verse: 5
The one who overcomes the world through believing that Jesus is the Son of God will be dressed in white clothing, and I will never take out his name from the Book of Life, and I will openly acknowledge his name before My Father and before His angels saying that he is one of Mine.

Verse 6
⁶ The one who has an ear, let him hear what the Spirit says to the churches.'

⁶ The one who has an ear,
    let him hear what the Spirit says
        to the churches.'

hear – in this context, it means to understand completely

    Again, Jesus is calling on all believers to listen, heed and do what the Spirit is saying to the churches.

Greek Paraphrase of Verse: 6
The one who has an ear, let him hear and heed what the Spirit says to the churches.'

Verses 7-8
Letter to Philadelphia
⁷ *And to the angel of the church in Philadelphia write: The holy One, the true One, the One who has the key of David, who opens and no one will close, and who closes, and no one opens, says:* ⁸ *'I know your works. Behold, because you have a little strength, have kept My word and have not denied My name and have put before you an open door which no one can close.*

⁷ And
  to the angel
    of the church
    in Philadelphia
    write:
      The holy One,
      the true One,
      the One
        who has the key of David,
        who opens and no one will close,
        and
        who closes and no one opens,
        says:
          ⁸ 'I know your works.
  Behold,
  because you have a little strength
    have kept My word
    and have not denied My name,
      and have put
        before you
        an open door
          which no one can close.

Verse: 7
7 And to the angel of the church in Philadelphia write: The holy One, the true One, the One who has the key of David, who opens, and no one will close, and who closes, and no one opens, says:

Philadelphia – brotherly love – a city of Lydia in Asia Minor, situated near the eastern base of Mount Tmolus, founded and named by the Pergamene king, Attalus II Philadelphus. After the death of Attalus III Philometor, 133 BC, it together with his entire kingdom came by his will under the jurisdiction of the Romans.

Now Jesus refers to Himself as the holy One, the true One and the One who has the key of David.
The key of David represents the authority of Christ's royal office.

Isaiah 22:22, I will place the key of the House of David on his shoulder; what he opens, no one can close; what he closes, no one can open.

He can close doors that no one can close, and He can open doors that no one can open.
Of all the churches Jesus was writing to, the church in the city of brotherly love was the one that was closer to the truth in all they did.

Verse: 8
8 'I know your works. Behold, because you have a little strength, have kept My word and have not denied My name and have put before you an open door which no one can close.

strength – dunamis – strength, power, ability (word we get dynamite from)

He starts out the same way as with the other churches, but this time Jesus is actually saying that He knows of their good works.
"Little strength" probably doesn't mean weak in the spirit. It probably means that they were very few and therefore not very powerful that way.
Therefore, Jesus is not withholding His name from them and He has opened a door for them that no one can close. That's great.

Greek Paraphrase of Verses: 7-8
"And to the divine messenger of the church in Philadelphia write: These are the words of the Holy One, the True One, He who has the key to the house of David, who opens and no one will be able to shut, and who shuts and no one will be able to open: I know what you do. Look, I have set before you an open door which no one is able to shut, for you have a little power, and have kept My word, and have not rejected or denied My name.

Verse 9

⁹ Behold, I will cause those of the synagogue of Satan, who say that they are Jews and are not, but lie—I will make them come and bow down at your feet, and they will know that I have loved you.

⁹ Behold,
>I will cause those
>>of the synagogue of Satan,
>>who say that they are Jews
>>>and are not, but lie—
>I will make them come and bow down
>>at your feet,
>>and they will know that I have loved you.

synagogue – a bringing together, gathering (as of fruits), a contracting; in the New Testament, an assembling together of men, an assembly of men; a synagogue

There was a serious conflict between the church at Philadelphia and the synagogue of the Jews.

So, Jesus is going to salve that little dispute. He's going to make the fake Jews bow down at their feet so that everyone will know that Jesus loves them.

Greek Paraphrase of Verse: 9
Behold, I will make *those* of the synagogue of Satan, who say that they are Jews and are not, but lie—I will make them come and bow down at your feet and *make them* know without a doubt that I have loved you.

Verse 10

¹⁰ Because you have kept My command to endure, I also will keep you from the hour of testing, that is about to come over the whole world, to test those who live on the earth.

¹⁰ Because
>you have kept My command
>>to endure,
>I also will keep you
>>from the hour of testing,
>>>that is about to come
>>>>over the whole world,
>>>to test those
>>>>who live on the earth.

kept – to attend to carefully, take care of; to guard; to keep, one in the state in which he is; to observe; to reserve: to undergo something
command – here it basically means what He told them to do – literally "what I told you to do"

58

endure – steadfastness, constancy, endurance; in the NT the characteristic of a man who is not swerved from his deliberate purpose and his loyalty to faith and piety by even the greatest trials and sufferings; patiently, and steadfastly; a patient, steadfast waiting for; a patient enduring, sustaining, perseverance

testing – an experiment, attempt, trial, proving; the trial of man's fidelity, integrity, virtue, constancy; an enticement to sin, temptation; an internal temptation to sin

What did Jesus mean when He said He would keep them "from the hour of testing?" Remember, this verse needs to be looked at from an end-time perspective, for Jesus said, "I am coming quickly" in verse 11.

One theory is that He is telling them they will be present during the tribulation, but He will protect them from it.

Another theory is that He is telling them that they will be removed before the tribulation.

Either one, the church at Philadelphia will not be harmed during the tribulation.

Greek Paraphrase of Verse: 10

Because you have kept the My command to persevere, I will keep you safe from the hour of temptation, that *hour,* which is about to come on the whole world, to test those who live on the earth.

Verse 11

¹¹ I am coming quickly. Hold on to what you have, so that no one will take your crown.

¹¹ I am coming quickly.
  Hold on
    to what you have,
    so that no one will take your crown.

hold – to have power, be powerful; to take hold of, take, seize; to keep carefully and faithfully; to continue to hold, to retain

The KJV translates "no one" as "man" which leads some to a different interpretation of this verse. The emphasis is that the crown is theirs and no one can take it away from them as long as they hold on to what they had been doing.

The warning at the beginning of this verse is meant for others more than for the church at Philadelphia. Still, they needed to know that they couldn't take time off from obeying God's word.

Greek Paraphrase of Verse: 11
I am coming quickly. Hold tight to what you have, so that no one will be able to take your crown by leading you to renounce the faith.

Verse 12
12 The one who overcomes, I will make him a pillar in the temple of My God, and he will never go out again. I will write on him the name of My God, and the name of the city of My God, the new Jerusalem, which comes down out of heaven from My God, and My new name.

12 The one who overcomes,
 I will make him a pillar
  in the temple of My God,
  and he will never go out again.
 I will write on him the name of My God,
  and the name of the city
   of My God,
   the new Jerusalem,
   which comes down
    out of heaven
    from My God,
  and My new name.

overcomes – to conquer; to carry off the victory, come off victorious; when one is arraigned or goes to law, to win the case, maintain one's cause
pillar – a pillar; a column; pillars of fire, i.e. flames rising like pillars; a prop or support

 For all those who faithfully follow Jesus, He will place them in a place of high honor, a place that will be stable and permanent in the inner sanctuary, the Holy of Holies.

Greek Paraphrase of Verse: 12
He who is victorious over the world through believing that Jesus is the Son of God, I will make him a pillar in the temple of My God, and he will definitely never be put out of it again. I will write on him the name of My God, and the name of the city of My God, the new Jerusalem, which will descend out of heaven from My God, and My new name.
Verse 13
13 The one who has an ear, let him hear what the Spirit says to the churches.'

13 The one who has an ear,
 let him hear
  what the Spirit says to the churches.'

 One more time, Jesus reminds everyone that this promise is for anyone who will hear it in all the churches of all times.

Greek Paraphrase of Verse: 13
The one who has an ear, let him understand and do what the Spirit says to the churches.'

Verses 14-15
Letter to Laodicea
14 To the angel of the church in Laodicea write: The Amen, the faithful and true Witness, the Beginning of the creation of God, says: 15 'I know your works, that you are neither cold nor hot. I wish that you were cold or hot.

14 To the angel
　　of the church
　　in Laodicea
　　write:
　　　　The Amen,
　　　　the faithful and true Witness,
　　　　the Beginning of the creation
　　　　　of God,
　　　　　says:
　　　　　　15 'I know your works,
　　　　　　　that you are neither cold nor hot.
　　　　　　　I wish that you were cold or hot.

Verse: 14
14 To the angel of the church in Laodicea write: The Amen, the faithful and true Witness, the Beginning of the creation of God, says:

Laodicea – "justice of the people" – a city of Phrygia, situated on the river Lycus not far from Colosse. It was destroyed by an earthquake in 66 A.D. and rebuilt by Marcus Aurelius. It was the seat of the Christian church.
Amen – verily, amen; at the beginning of a discourse - surely, truly, of a truth; at the end - so it is, so be it, may it be fulfilled. It was a custom, which passed over from the synagogues to the Christian assemblies, that when he who had read or discoursed, had offered up solemn prayer to God, the others responded Amen, and thus made the substance of what was uttered their own.
faithful –trusty, faithful; of persons who show themselves faithful in the transaction of business, the execution of commands, or the discharge of official duties; one who can be relied on; easily persuaded; believing, confiding, trusting

Now, we're moving on to the church in Laodicea, the last of the seven churches.
Here, Jesus gives Himself three more names;
1. The Amen which literally means truly. He is the true God.

2. The faithful and true Witness. He is witness to the Father, the truth and to His own nature and being as the unique Son of God.

3. The Beginning of the creation of God. He is not only the beginning of creation but the origin, first cause and ruler of all of God's creation.

Verse: 15

[15] *'I know your works, that you are neither cold nor hot. I wish that you were cold or hot.*

I think this implies that the Laodiceans had forgotten who Jesus really is and why He died. They were neither hot nor cold, so Jesus is really blasting them. He even says that He wished they were one or the other.

Greek Paraphrase of Verses: 14-15

"To the divine messenger of the church in Laodicea write: "These are the words of the Amen, the trusted, faithful and true Witness, the Beginning and Origin of God's creation: 'I know what you do, that you are neither invigorating and refreshing nor healing and beneficial. I wish that you were one or the other.

Verse 16

[16] *So, because you are lukewarm, and neither hot nor cold, I will spit you out of My mouth.*

[16] So,
>   because you are lukewarm,
>   and neither hot nor cold,
>   I will spit you out of My mouth.

They were basically ignoring Jesus. That didn't set well with Him. He told them he would just throw them away.

Greek Paraphrase of Verse: 16

So, because you are spiritually useless, and neither hot nor cold, I will spit you out of My mouth rejecting you with disgust.

Verse 17

[17] *Because you say, "I am rich, and have become wealthy, and need nothing," and you do not know that you are wretched, pitiful, poor, blind, and naked,*

[17] Because you say,
>   "I am rich,
>   and have become wealthy,
>   and need nothing,
>   and you do not know
>   that you are wretched,

      pitiful,
      poor,
       blind,
      and naked,

wretched – enduring toils and troubles; afflicted, wretched
pitiful – to pitied, miserable

Why were the Laodiceans lukewarm?

One way is because of their prosperity. They had all they thought they needed and therefore they didn't need Jesus.

The other one is that they had deceived themselves into thinking they were spiritual. They even considered themselves more spiritual than others. Therefore, they thought they didn't need anything.

Greek Paraphrase of Verse: 17
Because you say, "I am rich, and have prospered *and* grown wealthy, and need nothing," and you do not know that you are wretched, miserable, poor, blind and naked without hope and in great need,

Verse 18
18 I advise you to buy from Me gold refined in the fire so that you may be rich, and white clothes so that you may be dressed, and your shameful nakedness will not be revealed, and eye salve to anoint your eyes so that you may see.

18 I advise you to buy
    from Me
    gold refined in the fire
      so that you may be rich,
    and
    white clothes
      so that you may be dressed,
        and your shameful nakedness
          will not be revealed,
    and eye salve
      to anoint your eyes
      so that you may see.

advise – to give counsel; to take counsel with others, take counsel together, to consult, deliberate
refined – to burn with fire, to set on fire, kindle; to be incensed, indignant; full of fire, fiery, ignited
shameful – the confusion of one who is ashamed of anything, sense of shame; ignominy, disgrace, dishonor; a thing to be ashamed of
anoint – to rub in, besmirch, anoint; to anoint one's self

revealed – to make manifest or visible or known what has been hidden or unknown, to manifest, whether by words, or deeds, or in any other way; make actual and visible, realized; to make known by teaching; to become manifest, be made known; expose to view, make manifest, to show one's self, appear; to become known, to be plainly recognized, thoroughly understood who and what one is

The gold represents faith. God wants believers to be rich in faith.

The white clothing represents the triumph of righteousness. Dressed in white clothes, they would show others that they were righteous.

Then, the eye salve is to be used so they can see their true condition that has been blinded by their wealth.

Greek Paraphrase of Verse: 18
I advise you to buy gold that has been heated red hot *and* refined by fire from Me so that you may become *truly* rich and dressed in righteous white clothes so that the shame of your nakedness will not be seen, and have *healing* salve to put on your eyes so that you may see.

Verse 19
19 As many as I love, I rebuke and discipline. So be earnest and repent.

19 As many as I love,
    I rebuke and discipline.
So
be earnest and repent.

rebuke – to convict, refute, confute; generally, with a suggestion of shame of the person convicted; by conviction to bring to the light, to expose; to find fault with, correct; to call to account, show one his fault, demand an explanation; by deed; to chasten, to punish
discipline – to train children; to be instructed or taught or learn; to cause one to learn; to chastise or castigate with words, to correct; of those who are molding the character of others by reproof and admonition
earnest – to burn with zeal; to be heated or to boil with envy, hatred, anger; in a good sense, to be zealous in the pursuit of good; to desire earnestly, pursue; to envy
repent – to change one's mind for better, heartily to amend with abhorrence of one's past sins

Just the fact that Jesus rebuked and disciplined the Laodiceans showed that He Still loved them.

The Greek word translated 'rebuke' includes the idea of convicting and declaring someone guilty. So, if they are 'earnest' which means to desire something, they will come back in God's favor.

Greek Paraphrase of Verse: 19
Those I dearly and tenderly love; I rebuke and discipline showing them their faults and instructing them. So be enthusiastic and change your old way of thinking, your sinful behavior and seek God's will.

Verse 20
[20] Behold, I stand at the door and knock. If anyone hears My voice and opens the door, I will come in to him and will dine with him, and he with Me.

[20] Behold,
   I stand at the door and knock.
     If anyone hears My voice
       and opens the door,
         I will come in to him
         and
         will dine with him,
           and he with Me.

    This verse gives Christ's final words to the church in Laodicea and it's another wonderful demonstration of His love.
    Because of His love, he rebuked and disciplined the church. Because of His love, He stands at their door knocking and waiting for them to let Him in. Then He will go in and fellowship with them.

Greek Paraphrase of Verse: 20
Behold, I stand at the door of the church and *continually* knock. If anyone hears My voice and opens the door, I will come in and eat with him thus restoring him, and he will eat with Me.

Verse 21
[21] The one who overcomes, I will give him the right to sit down with Me on My throne, as I also overcame and sat down with My Father on His throne.
[21] The one who overcomes,
   I will give him the right to sit down
     with Me
     on My throne,
     as I also overcame and sat down
       with My Father
       on His throne.

overcomes – to conquer; to carry off the victory, come off victorious; when one is arraigned or goes to law, to win the case, maintain one's cause

right – give, give out, hand over, entrust, give back, give up; to give; to bestow a gift; to grant, give to one asking, let have; to supply, furnish, necessary things; to grant or permit one; to commission

This verse is basically a conclusion to the whole collection of letters to the seven churches.

Christ is saying to all seven churches at once that if they overcome (conquer), He will give them the same right He has, that of sitting down with Him and the Father.

Greek Paraphrase of Verse: 21
The one who overcomes the world through believing that Jesus is the Son of God, I will grant to him the privilege of sitting beside Me on My throne, as I also overcame and sat down beside My Father on His throne.

Verse 22
²² The one who has an ear, let him hear what the Spirit says to the churches.'"

²² The one who has an ear,
   let him hear
      what the Spirit says
         to the churches.'"

This verse repeats what He said at the end of the letters to all seven churches.

Greek Paraphrase of Verse: 22
The one who has an ear, let him understand *and* do what the Spirit says to the churches.'"

Chapter Four

This chapter begins the series of visions about future events. It also introduces the symbolical descriptions which were intended to cheer up those to whom the book was first sent.

It is intended to give all believers in all ages assurance that the gospel will finally triumph.

There are several different interpretations of these visions.

Some say that all that is described was only supposed to be the mind, with no visible happening.

Others say that what John saw was given to him so he could copy them.

Still others say that everything John was told, and saw was only in his imagination.

Regardless of all that, what John sees is the throne of God in heaven surrounded by twenty-four elders. They all join in giving glory to God.

Verse 1
The Throne Room of Heaven
¹ After this, I looked, and behold, a door standing open in heaven, and the first voice that I had heard, speaking to me like a trumpet said, "Come up here, and I will show you what must take place after this."

¹ After this,
  I looked,
    and behold,
    a door standing open
      in heaven,
      and the first voice
        that I had heard,
        speaking to me like a trumpet
        said,
          "Come up here,
            and I will show you
              what must take place
                after this."

'After this' indicates that some time has passed since the last verse of Chapter 3.

Apparently, John did not see one continuous vision. There were many and there were probably days between each one.

So, now we see a change in scene as well as a change in time. John saw a door standing open in heaven. The voice that came out of it, like a trumpet, told John to come up there so the voice could reveal the future to him.

Greek Paraphrase of Verse: 1
After this I looked, and behold, a door was standing open in heaven! And the first voice I heard, was speaking to me like *the sound* of a war trumpet, "Come up here, and I will show you what must take place after these things."

Verse 2
2 Immediately, I was in the Spirit, and behold, a throne was sitting in heaven, and One sitting on the throne.

2 Immediately,
  I was in the Spirit,
    and behold,
    a throne was sitting
      in heaven,
      and One sitting on the throne.

John says he was caught up in the Spirit four times in the book of Revelation: 1:10, 4:2, 17:3 and 21:10.

This statement means that the Holy Spirit was giving him a vision. The Holy Spirit was showing him situations and events he could not have seen with mere human eyesight. All true prophecy comes from God through the Holy Spirit.

Peter 1:20-21, For He was known before the foundation of the world, but was revealed in these last times for your sake who through Him are believers in God, who raised Him from the dead and gave Him glory, so that your faith and hope are in God.

Then he saw a throne and it had to be God the Father sitting on it.

Greek Paraphrase of Verse: 2
All of a sudden, I was in special communication with the Spirit, and behold, a throne sat in heaven, with One seated on the throne.

Verse 3
3 And the one sitting looked like a jasper and carnelian. There was a rainbow around the throne that looked like an emerald.

3 And
  the one sitting
    looked like a jasper and carnelian.
  There was a rainbow
    around the throne
    that looked like an emerald.

jasper – jasper, a precious stone of various colors (for some are purple, others blue, others green, and others the color of brass)
carnelian – a Sardis, a precious stone of which there are two types, the former is called a carnelian (because flesh colored) and the latter a sardis

John is not describing God, only the brilliance and fiery red presence that glowed with the red of carnelian.

The beautiful description continues with the rainbow. Not only is the rainbow beautiful but it also serves to remind us of God's promises.

Greek Paraphrase of Verse: 3
And He who sat there appeared like the crystalline sparkle of a jasper stone and the fiery redness of a carnelian stone, and around the throne was a rainbow that was the color of an emerald.

Verse 4
⁴ Around the throne, were twenty-four thrones, and on the thrones, I saw twenty-four elders sitting, dressed in white clothes with golden crowns on their heads.

⁴ Around the throne,
    were twenty-four thrones,
        and on the thrones, I saw twenty-four elders
            sitting,
            dressed in white clothes
                with golden crowns on their heads.

elders – elder, of age; the elder of two people; advanced in life, an elder, a senior; forefathers; a term of rank or office; among the Jews; members of the great council or Sanhedrin (because in early times the rulers of the people, judges, etc., were selected from elderly men); among the Christians, those who presided over the assemblies (or churches) The NT uses the term bishop, elders, and presbyters interchangeably; the twenty-four members of the heavenly court seated on thrones around the throne of God

In a circle around God's throne were the thrones of 24 elders. Elders was the title given to the leaders of the early church.

Some have suggested they were angels but nowhere else in the Bible are angels called elders.

The fact that they have golden crowns, the symbol of victory, might mean that they are those who have been rewarded as Jesus told John. They sit at the side of God the Father.

Trennis E. Killian

Greek Paraphrase of Verse: 4
Twenty-four other thrones were surrounding the throne and seated on the thrones were twenty-four elders dressed in white clothing, with golden crowns on their heads.

Verse 5
⁵ From the throne came flashes of lightning, rumblings, and thunder. And there were seven lamps of fire burning before the throne, which are the seven Spirits of God.

⁵ From the throne came
    flashes of lightning
    rumblings,
    and thunder.
  And
  there were seven lamps
    of fire
    burning before the throne,
    which are the seven Spirits of God.

    Lightnings, thundering, and voices coming from the throne are like the Old Testament expressions of God speaking.
    The seven lamps of fire represent the seven Spirits of God.

    Isaiah 11:2, The Spirit of the LORD will rest on Him— a Spirit of wisdom and understanding, a Spirit of counsel and strength, a Spirit of knowledge and of the fear of the LORD.

Greek Paraphrase of Verse: 5
From the throne came flashes of lightning and the rumbling sounds of thunder. Seven lamps of fire were burning in front of the throne, which are the seven Spirits of God.

Verse 6
⁶ Before the throne, was something like a sea of glass, like crystal. In the center, and around the throne were four living creatures full of eyes in front and back.

⁶ Before the throne,
    was something like a sea of glass,
      like crystal.
  In the center,
    and around the throne
    were four living creatures
      full of eyes
        in front and back.

We need to remember that all the miraculous and wonderful things John sees, he only describes them in human terms. Therefore, I feel that his description falls short of the magnificence of all that he saw.

There are all kinds of parallels drawn between the 'sea of glass' and Old Testament happenings. But I don't really see all that. What I do see is the sea of glass or whatever it is only serves to separate Creator from His creation.

The four living creatures could be similar to the seraphim with God in Isaiah Chapter 6.

Isaiah 6:2, Seraphim were standing above Him; each one had six wings: with two he covered his face, with two he covered his feet, and with two he flew.

Or maybe they were like the cherubim that the descriptions in verse 7 depict.

Greek Paraphrase of Verse: 6
In front of the throne there was something like a sea *or* large expanse of glass, like the clearest crystal. In the center and around the throne were four living creatures who were full of eyes in front and behind seeing everything and knowing everything around them.

Verse 7
⁷ The first creature was like a lion, the second living creature like a calf, the third living creature had a face like that of a man, and the fourth living creature was like a flying eagle.

⁷ The first creature was like a lion,
    the second living creature like a calf,
    the third living creature had a face like that of a man,
    and the fourth living creature was like a flying eagle.

The way the living creatures is described is similar to the Old Testament, especially from the description of the cherubim in Ezekiel. They are first mentioned as guardians of the road to the Garden of Eden in Genesis 3:24. There are many more such references in the Old Testament.

Greek Paraphrase of Verse: 7
The first living creature was like a lion, the second creature like an ox calf, the third living creature had the face of a man, and the fourth living creature was like a flying eagle.

Verse 8
⁸ Each of the four living creatures had six wings, were full of eyes around and inside. Day and night, they never stop saying, "Holy, holy, holy is the Lord God, the Almighty, Who was, Who is, and Who is to come."
⁸ Each of the four living creatures had six wings,
    were full of eyes
      around and inside.
  Day and night, they never stop saying,
    "Holy, holy, holy is the Lord God,
      the Almighty,
      Who was,
      Who is,
      and Who is to come."

Each of the living creatures had to be a strange sight to John but their significance is that they were constantly praising God.

Greek Paraphrase of Verse: 8
Each of the four living creatures had six wings, were full of eyes all over within and underneath their wings. Day and night, they never stop saying, "Holy, holy, holy is the Lord God, the Almighty, the Omnipotent, the Ruler of all, Who was and Who is and Who is to come the unchanging, eternal God."

Again, the living creatures each had six wings like the seraphim in Isaiah Chapter 6.

Calling out holy three times is to emphasize God's supreme holiness. Holiness in the Bible is always two times. Three times is placing extra emphasis on His holiness.

The last part of this verse is similar to Revelation 1:4 and 8 when Jesus used it to describe Himself.

Verses 9-11
⁹ And when the living creatures give glory, honor, and thanks to the One sitting on the throne, to the One Who lives forever and ever, ¹⁰ the twenty-four elders will fall down before the One sitting on the throne, and will worship the One who lives forever and ever, and will cast their crowns before the throne, saying, ¹¹ "Worthy are You, our Lord and our God, to receive glory and honor and power, because You created all things, and because of Your will they exist and were created."

⁹ And
  when the living creatures give
    glory,
    honor,
    and
    thanks
      to the One sitting on the throne,

to the One Who lives forever and ever,
[10] the twenty-four elders will fall down
before the One sitting on the throne,
and will worship the One
who lives forever and ever,
and will cast their crowns before the throne,
saying,
[11] "Worthy are You,
our Lord
and our God,
to receive glory
and honor
and power,
because You created all things,
and
because of Your will they exist and were created."

Verse: 9

[9] And when the living creatures give glory, honor, and thanks to the One sitting on the throne, to the One Who lives forever and ever,

when – here it means from time to time, over and over again

Therefore, the praise of the living creatures is probably not continuous on the same level.

Verse: 10

[10] the twenty-four elders will fall down before the One sitting on the throne, and will worship the One who lives forever and ever, and will cast their crowns before the throne, saying,

elders – elder, of age; the elder of two people; advanced in life, an elder, a senior; forefathers; a term of rank or office; among the Jews; members of the great council or Sanhedrin (because in early times the rulers of the people, judges, etc., were selected from elderly men); among the Christians, those who presided over the assemblies (or churches) The NT uses the term bishop, elders, and presbyters interchangeably; the twenty-four members of the heavenly court seated on thrones around the throne of God

Every time the living creatures break out with their praising of God, the twenty-four elders fall down to worship Him. They also show their submission to God by throwing their crowns in front of the throne of God.

Verse: 11

[11] "Worthy are You, our Lord and our God, to receive glory and honor and power, because You created all things, and because of Your will they exist and were created."

Worthy – weighing, having weight, having the weight of another thing of like value, worth as much
honor – a valuing by which the price is fixed; of the price itself; honor which belongs or is shown to one; deference, reverence
power – strength, power, ability (word we get dynamite from)

They are acknowledging that God the Creator is worthy of their praise, the glory, honor and power He has. Without Him there is nothing, period.

Greek Paraphrase of Verses: 9-11
Whenever the living creatures give glory, honor and thanksgiving to the One who sits on the throne, to the One Who lives forever and ever, the twenty-four elders fall down before the One sitting on the throne, and they worship the One who lives forever and ever, and they will throw down their crowns before the throne, saying, "Worthy are You, our Lord and our God, to receive the glory, honor and power; because You created all things, and because of Your will they exist, and were created and brought into being."

Chapter Five

This chapter includes the vision of the seven sealed books. Christ is seen in His Kingly character. Angels, elders and living creatures exalt the Lamb who is King.

Christ, Who as the Lamb of God was slain and rejected by men, will be established as the Lion of the tribe of Judah, breaking the seals of God's wrath against sinners upon the earth.

Verse 1
The Lamb Takes the Scroll
¹ I saw in the right hand of the One sitting on the throne a scroll written inside and on the back, sealed with seven seals.

¹ I saw
    in the right hand of the One sitting on the throne
    a scroll written inside and on the back,
      sealed with seven seals.

There are two different views on the scroll and the seven seals.

One is that the scroll is rolled up and all seven seals are spread out along it to keep it closed. Therefore, all seven seals would have to be broken in order to open it.

The other view is that each seal opens a different part of the scroll.

The one thing all agree on is that this scroll is of great importance and significance.

Greek Paraphrase of Verse: 1
I saw in the right hand of the One who was seated on the throne a scroll written on the inside and on the back, closed and sealed with seven seals.

Verse 2
² I saw a mighty angel proclaiming in a loud voice, "Who is worthy to open the scroll and break its seals?"

² I saw a mighty angel
    proclaiming
      in a loud voice,
      "Who is worthy
        to open the scroll
          and break its seals?"

mighty – strong, mighty; strong either in body or in mind; strong, violent, forcibly uttered, firm, sure

worthy – weighing, having weight, having the weight of another thing of like value, worth as much

Some think this angel is Gabriel whose name can mean either "man of God," "strength of God" or "mighty one of God."

Part of the reason for thinking this is that Gabriel was the angel who ordered Daniel to close and seal his book in Daniel 12:4.

The big question here is, who is worthy to open the scroll and break the seals. Is it John?

Greek Paraphrase of Verse: 2
I saw a mighty angel announcing with a loud voice, "Who is worthy, having the authority and virtue to open the scroll and to break its seals?"

Verse 3
³ But no one in heaven or on the earth or under the earth was able to open the scroll or to look in it.

³ But
  no one
    in heaven
    or on the earth
    or under the earth
    was able to open the scroll
      or to look in it.

able – to be able, have power whether by virtue of one's own ability and resources, or of a state of mind, or through favorable circumstances, or by permission of law or custom; to be able to do something; to be capable, strong and powerful

This is the same phrase that Paul wrote in:
Philippians 2:10, so that at the name of Jesus every knee should bow, of those who are in heaven and on earth and under the earth,

This means that no created being is worthy to claim the Kingdom or take care of the future of the world.

Greek Paraphrase of Verse: 3
But no one in heaven or on the earth or under the earth in Hades, the realm of the dead was able to open the scroll or look into it.

Verse 4
⁴ And I wept and wept because no one was found worthy to open the scroll or to look in it.

⁴ And
    I wept and wept
       because no one was found worthy
         to open the scroll
           or to look in it.

worthy – weighing, having weight, having the weight of another thing of like value, worth as much

    Recognizing the importance of the revelation contained in the scroll, John couldn't stop crying. What would the people do if they couldn't open the scroll?

    This scroll is different from any prophesy of the Old Testament. God always provided some way for the prophets to know what He wanted them to do.

Greek Paraphrase of Verse: 4
And I began to weep greatly because no one was found worthy to open the scroll or to look into it.

Verse 5
⁵ *Then one of the elders said to me, "Stop weeping. Behold, the Lion that is from the tribe of Judah, the Root of David, overcame so as to open the scroll and its seven seals."*

⁵ Then
  one of the elders
    said
      to me,
      "Stop weeping.
      Behold,
        the Lion
          that is from the tribe of Judah,
          the Root of David,
          overcame so as to open the scroll and its seven seals."

elders – elder, of age; the elder of two people; advanced in life, an elder, a senior; forefathers; a term of rank or office; among the Jews; members of the great council or Sanhedrin (because in early times the rulers of the people, judges, etc., were selected from elderly men); among the Christians, those who presided over the assemblies (or churches) The NT uses the term bishop, elders, and presbyters interchangeably; the twenty-four members of the heavenly court seated on thrones around the throne of God
overcame – to conquer; to carry off the victory, come off victorious; when one is arraigned or goes to law, to win the case, maintain one's cause

As John continued to cry, one of the elders came and told him to stop crying. There was One who would break the seals and read the scroll.

Notice the beautiful names or titles given to Jesus here.

The Lion of Judah and the Root of David both point to Jesus as the only One who could break the seals and open the scroll.

Greek Paraphrase of Verse: 5

Then one of the twenty-four elders said to me, "Stop weeping! Look closely, the Lion of the tribe of Judah, the Root of David, has overcome and conquered! He can open the scroll and break its seven seals."

Verse 6

6 Then I saw a Lamb, as if slain, standing between the throne and the four living creatures and among the elders. He had seven horns and seven eyes, which are the seven Spirits of God, sent into all the earth.

6 Then I saw a Lamb,
> as if slain,
> standing
>> between the throne and the four living creatures
>> and
>> among the elders.
> He had seven horns and seven eyes,
>> which are the seven Spirits
>>> of God,
>>> sent into all the earth.

When John looked, he didn't see a lion, but a Lamb that still had the marks of being slain.

The sevenfold Spirit which in the previous chapter burned as seven lamps of fire before the throne had now become the One to take the wisdom and power of the Lamb into all the earth.

Greek Paraphrase of Verse: 6

Then I saw a Lamb bearing scars and wounds as if it had been slain, standing with the four living creatures and among the elders. He had seven horns of complete power and seven eyes of complete knowledge which are the seven Spirits of God, who have been sent into all the earth.

Verse 7

7 He came and took the scroll out of the right hand of the One sitting on the throne.

7 He came and took the scroll
> out of the right hand
>> of the One sitting on the throne.

The Lamb with the seven horns and seven eyes took the scroll out of the One on the throne. It is considered to be the legal act of giving authority to reign on this earth.

Greek Paraphrase of Verse: 7
He came and took the scroll from the right hand of the One who sat on the throne.

Verse 8
The Lamb Is Worthy
8 When He took the scroll, the four living creatures and the twenty-four elders fell down before the Lamb. Each had a harp and golden bowls full of incense, which are the prayers of the saints.

8 When He took the scroll,
the four living creatures
and
the twenty-four elders
fell down before the Lamb.
Each had a harp and golden bowls
full of incense,
which are the prayers of the saints.

harp – a stringed instrument, harp, lyre (this word is the root word for our word guitar)

Up until this point, all the worship was of the One on the throne, God the Father. But now, since the Lamb took the scroll, everyone turns to Him and worships Him.

Previously, the twenty-four elders had presented their crowns in worship but now they worshiped the Lamb with a harp and incense which are called the prayers of the saints.

The use of this type of harp indicates a different sound from the normal harp.

The bowls of incense, which was always burned before worship, represent the fact that the scroll had to be opened and the judgments of the tribulation had to take place before the prayers of the saints could be answered.

Greek Paraphrase of Verse: 8
When He had taken the scroll, the four living creatures and the twenty-four elders fell down before the Lamb, each one holding a harp and golden bowls full of fragrant incense, which are the prayers of the saints, God's people.

Verse 9
⁹ And they sang a new song, saying, "You are worthy to take the scroll and open its seals; for You were slain, and purchased men for God with Your blood from every tribe and language and people and nation.

⁹ And they sang a new song,
    saying,
      "You are worthy
        to take the scroll and open its seals;
        for You were slain,
          and purchased men
          for God
            with Your blood
            from every tribe and language
            and people and nation.

worthy – weighing, having weight, having the weight of another thing of like value, worth as much
tribe – a tribe; in the NT all the persons descending from one of the twelve sons of the patriarch, Jacob; a nation, people
nation – a multitude (whether of men or of beasts) associated or living together; a company, troop, swarm; a multitude of individuals of the same nature or genus; in the OT, foreign nations not worshipping the true God, pagans, Gentiles; Paul uses the term for Gentile Christians

    They sang a new song to the Lamb which emphasized Jesus' role in the redemption of the lost.
    It is clear here that Jesus died for all, "every tribe, language, people and nation." That pretty much covers all the earth.

Greek Paraphrase of Verse: 9
And they sang a new song of glorious redemption, saying, "You are worthy and deserving to take the scroll and to break its seals; for You were slain, sacrificed and with Your blood You purchased *men* for God from every tribe, language, people and nation.

Verse 10
¹⁰ You have made them to be a kingdom and priests to our God, and they will reign on the earth."
¹⁰ You have made them
    to be a kingdom and priests
      to our God,
      and they will reign on the earth."

    In verses 9 and 10 we have two of those differences between the Textus Receptus (KJV) and the Nestle Aland (modern translations).
    The KJV has 'us' instead of 'them.' It also has 'we" instead of 'they.'

This would change the interpretation of this verse. KJV = the twenty-four elders are redeemed people. Otherwise, the interpretation is not clear as to who they are.

Greek Paraphrase of Verse: 10
"You have made them to be a kingdom of royal subjects and priests to our God, and they will reign on the earth."

Verses 11-12
[11] Then I looked and heard the voices of many angels around the throne, and the living creatures and the elders. Their number was thousands of thousands, [12] saying with a loud voice, "Worthy is the Lamb who was slain to receive power and riches and wisdom and strength and honor and glory and blessing."

[11] Then
  I looked
    and heard the voices
      of many angels
      around the throne,
        and the living creatures
        and the elders.
        Their number was thousands of thousands,
      [12] saying
      with a loud voice,
      "Worthy is the Lamb
        who was slain to receive
          power
          and riches
          and wisdom
          and strength
          and honor
          and glory
          and blessing."

Verse: 11
[11] Then I looked and heard the voices of many angels around the throne, and the living creatures and the elders. Their number was thousands of thousands,

many – the Greek word means ten thousand

Now, we have thousands of angels joining the twenty-four elders and the four living creatures in chorus bringing to a climax this part of John's vision.

Verse: 12

12 saying with a loud voice, "Worthy is the Lamb who was slain to receive power and riches and wisdom and strength and honor and glory and blessing."

power – dunamis – strength, power, ability (word we get dynamite from)
wisdom – wisdom, broad and full of intelligence; used of the knowledge of very diverse matters; the wisdom which belongs to men; the varied knowledge of things human and divine, acquired by acuteness and experience, and summed up in maxims and proverbs; the science and learning; supreme intelligence, such as belongs to God; the wisdom of God as evinced in forming and executing counsels in the formation and government of the world and the scriptures
strength – ability, force, strength, might

The angels were singing a different song from the song of redemption the elders had been singing. They can't sing the song of the redeemed, but they can sing praises to the Lamb.

The seven different things the Lamb was to receive: power, riches, wisdom, strength, honor, glory and blessing all point to the fact that He is worthy and no one else is.

Greek Paraphrase of Verses: 11-12
Then I looked, and I heard the voices of many angels around the throne and the voices of the living creatures and the elders. They numbered in the thousands of thousands, innumerable, saying in loud voices, "Worthy and deserving is the Lamb that was sacrificed to receive power, riches, wisdom, might, honor, glory and blessing."

Verse 13

13 And every creature in heaven, on the earth, under the earth, on the sea, and all things in them, I heard saying, "To Him who sits on the throne, and to the Lamb be praise, honor, glory, and dominion forever and ever."

13 And
   every creature
     in heaven,
     on the earth,
     under the earth,
     on the sea,
      and all things in them,
   I heard saying,
    "To Him
      who sits on the throne,

and
to the Lamb
  be praise,
    honor,
    glory,
    and dominion
    forever and ever."

dominion – force, strength; power, might: mighty with great power; a mighty deed, a work of power; dominion

Basically, all creatures everywhere gave Him all the praise, honor, glory and dominion, not just then but always.

Greek Paraphrase of Verse: 13
And I heard every created thing that is in heaven or on earth or under the earth in Hades, the realm of the dead or on the sea, and everything that is in them, saying together, "To Him who sits on the throne, and to the Lamb, be praise, blessing, honor, glory and dominion forever and ever."

Verse 14
14 The four living creatures were saying, "Amen," and the elders fell down and worshiped.

14 The four living creatures were saying,
  "Amen,"
    and the elders fell down and worshiped.

Finally, the four living creatures add their final word to all that was said before. Then the elders fell down and worshiped.

Greek Paraphrase of Verse: 14
The four living creatures kept saying, "Amen," and the elders fell down and worshiped Him who lives forever and ever.

Chapter Six

The opening of the seals.

The opening of the first seal brought the white horse of victory. The second seal brought the red horse taking away peace. The third seal brought the black horse and the famine. The fourth seal brought the pale green horse with Death ridding on it. The fifth seal showed John the souls of men under the altar who had been slain because of their testimony. The opening of the sixth seal brought the earthquake, the darkening of the sun and caused the moon and the stars to fall.

The seventh seal isn't opened until Chapter Eight.

It won't be good for those living on the earth in the days of the Tribulation. The wrath of God will be poured out on the earth to cleanse it for the last time.

There will be wars, famines, plagues and earthquakes causing fear among all those living.

Verse 1
The First Seal on the Scroll
¹ Then I saw the Lamb open one of the seven seals, and I heard one of the four living creatures saying with a voice like thunder, "Come!"

¹ Then
  I saw the Lamb open one of the seven seals,
    and
  I heard one of the four living creatures
    saying
      with a voice like thunder,
      "Come!"

John is still spiritually in heaven looking at all that Christ wants him to see. The Lamb is on the throne opening the seven seals.

This begins the first of three seven-part judgments. The trumpets in Chapters 8 and 9 and the bowls in Chapter 16 are the other two.

As Christ the Lamb opens each seal, He sets events in motion which will bring about the end of human history. This scroll is not completely opened until the seventh seal is broken in Revelation 8:1.

The contents of the scroll reveal the depravity of men and show God's authority over all the events of human history.

Greek Paraphrase of Verse: 1
Then I saw as the Lamb broke one of the seven seals of the scroll initiating the judgments, and I heard one of the four living creatures calling out as with a voice like thunder, "Come."

Verse 2
² I looked, and behold, a white horse, and the one sitting on it had a bow, and a crown was given to him, and he went out conquering and to conquer.

² I looked,
    and behold,
        a white horse,
           and the one
                sitting on it
                had a bow,
                and a crown was given to him,
                and he went out conquering and to conquer.

Conquerors usually rode white horses to symbolize their triumph.

The Bible doesn't tell us who the one on the white horse is but there are at least two different theories.

1. Christ Himself.

I agree with most in saying no to that one since Christ, the Lamb, is the one breaking the seals that allow John to see the white horse and its rider.

2. The Antichrist

Maybe but I think that wherever else the Antichrist appears, it's clear who he is.

Greek Paraphrase of Verse: 2
I looked, and behold, a white horse of victory whose rider carried a bow, and a crown of victory was given to him, and he rode forth conquering and to conquer.

Verse 3
The Second Seal
³ When He opened the second seal, I heard the second living creature saying, "Come."

³ When He opened the second seal,
    I heard the second living creature saying,
        "Come."

This is another one of those differences between the Textus Receptus (KJV) and the Nestle Aland (modern translations). The TR has "Come and see." Whether it is there or not, I think it is implied, nevertheless.

Greek Paraphrase of Verse: 3
When the Lamb broke the second seal, I heard the second living creature calling out, "Come."

Verse 4
⁴ And another horse went out, a red one, and the one sitting on it was
empowered to take peace from the earth, so that men would slay one another.
And a great sword was given to him.

⁴ And
  another horse went out,
    a red one,
    and the one
      sitting on it was empowered
        to take peace
          from the earth,
          so that men would slay one another.
      And
      a great sword was given to him.

empowered – up; to give; to bestow a gift; to grant, give to one asking, let
have; to supply, furnish, necessary things; to grant or permit one; to
commission

The other three horses are each a different color. Each one represents a
different judgment of God.
  Red = warfare and bloodshed
  Black = famine
  Pale green = death

Some think the rider on the red horse is the Antichrist's cohort, the false
prophet.
I think, though, that he is the personification of war or of the lust for war
and the great sword is a symbol of war's destruction.
Note for later on. He doesn't actually kill anyone. He just takes peace
from the earth causing everyone to kill each other.

Greek Paraphrase of Verse: 4
And another horse came out, a fiery red like bloodshed and its rider was
empowered to take peace from the earth, so that men would kill one
another. And a great sword of war and violent death was given to him.

Verse 5
The Third Seal
⁵ When He opened the third seal, I heard the third living creature saying,
"Come." I looked, and behold, a black horse, and the one sitting on it had a
pair of scales in his hand.

⁵ When He opened the third seal,
  I heard the third living creature saying,
    "Come."

I looked,
  and behold,
    a black horse,
      and the one
        sitting on it
        had a pair of scales in his hand.

scales – a yoke; a yoke that is put on draught cattle; metaphorically, used of any burden or bondage as that of slavery; a balance, pair of scales

Again, the KJV has "Come and see."
Black has always represented evil, suffering and hunger. The scales may represent the careful weighing out of food and maybe even general rationing because of the famine.

Greek Paraphrase of Verse: 5
When the Lamb broke open the third seal, I heard the third living creature calling out, "Come." I looked, and behold, a black horse of famine and the rider had a balance in his hand.

Verse 6
6 And I heard something like a voice among the four living creatures saying, "A quart of wheat for a denarius, and three quarts of barley for a denarius— but do not damage the oil and the wine."

6 And
  I heard something
    like a voice
    among the four living creatures
      saying,
        "A quart of wheat
          for a denarius,
        and
        three quarts of barley
          for a denarius—
          but do not damage the oil and the wine."

quart – (the word is 'measure') a choenix, a dry measure, containing four cotylae or two setarii (less than our quart, one liter) (or as much as would support a man of moderate appetite for a day)
denarius – "containing ten" – A Roman silver coin in NT time. It took its name from it being equal to ten "asses", a number after 217 B.C. increased to sixteen (about 3.898 grams or .1375 oz.). It was the principal silver coin of the Roman empire. From the parable of the laborers in the vineyard, it would seem that a denarius was then the ordinary pay for a day's wages.

damage – to act unjustly or wickedly, to sin; to be a criminal, to have violated the laws in some way; to do wrong; to do hurt; to do some wrong or sin in some respect; to wrong someone, act wickedly towards him; to hurt, damage, harm

This verse is basically telling about how bad times will be. There will be famine and a person would have to work for a whole day just to put half as much food on the table as would be needed.

The last line, "do not damage the oil and the wine." Seems to mean that even something as everyday back then would become a luxury that only rich people could afford.

Greek Paraphrase of Verse: 6
And I heard *something* like a voice in the middle of the four living creatures saying, "A quart of wheat for a day's wages, and three quarts of barley for a day's wages but do not damage the oil and the wine."

Verse 7
The Fourth Seal
[7] *When the He opened the fourth seal, I heard the voice of the fourth living creature saying, "Come."*

[7] When the He opened the fourth seal,
   I heard the voice
     of the fourth living creature
     saying,
      "Come."

creature – a living being; an animal, brute, beast

Again, the newer manuscripts which the KJV is based on has, "Come and see."

Also, again, this doesn't really change anything. Whether it is there or not, it is implied.

Each of the living creatures opened a different seal with a new vision for John.

Greek Paraphrase of Verse: 7
When the Lamb broke open the fourth seal, I heard the voice of the fourth living creature calling out, "Come."

Verse 8
[8] *I looked, and behold, a pale green horse, and the one sitting on it was named Death, and Hades was following him. Authority was given to them over a fourth of the earth, to kill with sword, with famine, with pestilence, and by the wild animals of the earth.*

[8] I looked,
> and behold,
>> a pale green horse,
>>> and the one
>>>> sitting on it
>>>> was named Death,
>>>>> and Hades was following him.
> Authority was given
>> to them
>> over a fourth of the earth,
>> to kill with sword,
>>> with famine,
>>> with pestilence,
>>> and by the wild animals of the earth.

Hades – name Hades or Pluto, the god of the lower regions; Orcus, the nether world, the realm of the dead; later use of this word: the grave, death, hell
authority – physical and mental power; the power of authority (influence) and of right (privilege); the power of rule or government (the power of him whose will and commands must be submitted to by others and obeyed); the power of judicial decisions; one who possesses authority; a ruler, a human magistrate
pestilence – the death of the body; that separation (whether natural or violent) of the soul and the body by which the life on earth is ended

This horse stands for pestilence and death with Death sitting on it and Hades following it.

The timing on these events is not clear but most think it will probably at the beginning of the second half of the tribulation and one-fourth of the earth's population will die.

Greek Paraphrase of Verse: 8
I looked, and behold, a pale greenish gray horse representing death and pestilence, and its rider's name was Death, and Hades the realm of the dead was following with him. They were given authority *and* power over a fourth of the earth, to kill with the sword and with famine, plague and by the wild animals of the earth.

Verse 9
The Fifth Seal
[9] *When He opened the fifth seal, I saw under the altar the souls of those who had been slain because of the word of God, and because of the testimony they had maintained.*

⁹ When He opened the fifth seal,
    I saw
      under the altar
      the souls of those
        who had been slain
          because of the word of God,
          and
          because of the testimony they had maintained.

maintained – to have, to hold; own, possess; to be closely joined to a person or a thing

With this fifth seal, John's attention is drawn away from visions of what is going to happen on the earth. What he does see is those who have been martyred for their faith and they're under the altar. They apparently remained faithful unto death.

Greek Paraphrase of Verse: 9
When the Lamb broke open the fifth seal, I saw underneath the altar the souls of those who had been slaughtered because of the word of God, and because of the testimony which they had maintained out of loyalty to Christ.

Verse 10
¹⁰ They cried out with a loud voice, saying, "O Lord, holy and true, how long until You judge and avenge our blood from those who live on the earth?"

¹⁰ They cried out
    with a loud voice,
    saying,
      "O Lord,
        holy and true,
        how long until You judge and avenge our blood
          from those
            who live on the earth?"

judge – separate, distinguish, decide between, judge, think, approve, resolve, determine, give judgment, decide, condemn, punish
avenge – to vindicate one's right, do one justice; to protect, defend, one person from another; to avenge a thing; to punish a person for a thing

The martyrs are crying out to God to avenge their blood. How long will it be before He does?

Notice how their appeal includes praises of His name. They call him Lord and that He is holy and true.

This was referred to in:

2 Thessalonians 1:4-8, Therefore, we ourselves boast about you among God's churches—about your endurance and faith in all the persecutions and afflictions you endure. ⁵ It is a clear evidence of God's righteous judgment that you will be counted worthy of God's kingdom, for which you also are suffering, ⁶ since it is righteous for God to repay with affliction those who afflict you ⁷ and to reward with rest you who are afflicted, along with us. This will take place at the revelation of the Lord Jesus from heaven with His powerful angels, ⁸ taking vengeance with flaming fire on those who don't know God and on those who don't obey the gospel of our Lord Jesus.

Greek Paraphrase of Verse: 10
They cried in a loud voice, saying, "O Lord, holy and true, how long now before You will sit in judgment and avenge our blood on those unregenerate ones who live on the earth?"

Verse 11
¹¹ And each of them was given a white robe, and they were told to rest for a little while longer, until the number of their fellow slaves and their brothers who were to be killed as they had been, would be completed.

¹¹ And
  each
    of them
    was given a white robe,
      and they were told to rest
        for a little while longer,
      until the number
        of their fellow slaves
        and their brothers
        who were to be killed
          as they had been,
          would be completed.

The martyrs were basically told that the timing wasn't right yet. They were given white robes and told to rest until the rest of the people like them were killed and that phase would be completed.

Greek Paraphrase of Verse: 11
Then they were each given a white robe, and they were told to rest and wait quietly for a little while longer, until the number of their fellow servants and their brothers and sisters who were to be killed even as they had been, would be completed.

Verses 12-13
The Sixth Seal
¹² When He opened the sixth seal, I looked and there was a great earthquake, and the sun became black as sackcloth made of hair, and the whole moon became like blood, ¹³ and the stars of the heaven fell to the earth as a fig tree drops its unripe figs when shaken by a strong wind.

¹² When He opened the sixth seal,
   I looked
and
there was a great earthquake,
and
the sun became black
   as sackcloth made of hair,
and
the whole moon became like blood,
¹³ and
the stars
   of the heaven
   fell to the earth
      as a fig tree drops its unripe figs
         when shaken by a strong wind.

Verse: 12
¹² When He opened the sixth seal, I looked and there was a great earthquake, and the sun became black as sackcloth made of hair, and the whole moon became like blood,

sackcloth – a sack; a receptacle for holding or carrying various things, as money, food, etc.; a course cloth, a dark course stuff made especially from the hair of animals

Now, John looks back at the earth where things are getting really bad. These are the signs of the end of the age as prophesied in both the Old and New Testaments.
   See: Isaiah 34:4; Joel 2:31; Mark 13:24-25

Verse: 13
¹³ and the stars of the heaven fell to the earth as a fig tree drops its unripe figs when shaken by a strong wind.
unripe fig – an unripe fig which grows during the winter, yet does not come to maturity but falls off in the spring
shaken – to shake, agitate, cause to tremble; of men, to be thrown into a tremor, to quake for fear; metaphorically to agitate the mind

Most think the stars falling are basically showers of meteorites. When a fig is green, it is hard and heavy and therefore falls heavily when wind or some other disturbance such as an earthquake makes it fall before it should.

Greek Paraphrase of Verses: 12-13
When the Lamb broke open the sixth seal, I looked and there was a great earthquake, and the sun became black as sackcloth made of hair, and the whole moon became like blood, and the stars of the sky fell to the earth, like a fig tree drops its late unripe figs when shaken by a strong wind.

Verse 14
14 The sky was split apart like a scroll when it is rolled up, and every mountain and island was moved out of their places.

14 The sky was split apart
    like a scroll
      when it is rolled up,
      and every mountain and island was moved out of their places.

    The Old Testament Israelites thought the heavens looked like a tent spread out above the earth (Psalm 104:2; Isaiah 40:22).
    These happenings are all John's attempt to describe everything being tossed around, rearranged and even destroyed.
    No one and nothing would be safe from this event.

Greek Paraphrase of Verse: 14
The sky was split and separated from the land and rolled up like a scroll, and every mountain and island was dislodged *and* moved out of their places.

Verse 15
15 Then the kings of the earth, the great men, the commanders, the rich, the strong, and every slave and free man hid in the caves and among the rocks of the mountains.

15 Then
    the kings
      of the earth,
    the great men,
    the commanders,
    the rich,
    the strong,
    and
    every slave
      and free man
      hid

in the caves
and among the rocks
of the mountains.

kings – leader of the people, prince, commander, lord of the land, king
great men – the grandees, magnates, nobles, chief men of a city or a people
or of the associates or courtiers of a king
commanders – a chiliarch, the commander of a thousand soldiers; the
commander of a Roman cohort (a military tribunal); any military commander
strong – strong, mighty; strong either in body or in mind; strong, violent,
forcibly uttered, firm, sure

The first part of this verse is simply a dramatic if not poetic way of saying
everyone living on the earth at that time. It was so bad, they all fled to the
caves on the mountainsides.

Greek Paraphrase of Verse: 15
**Then the kings of the earth, the great men, the military commanders, the
wealthy, the strong and everyone, whether slave or free man, hid
themselves in the caves and among the rocks of the mountains.**

Verses 16-17
*[16] And they said to the mountains and to the rocks, "Fall on us and hide us
from the face of the One sitting on the throne, and from the wrath of the Lamb,
[17] because the great day of their wrath has come, and who is able to stand?"*

[16] And
they said
to the mountains
and to the rocks,
"Fall on us and hide us
from the face
of the One sitting on the throne,
and
from the wrath of the Lamb,
[17] because the great day
of their wrath
has come,
and who is able to stand?"

Verse: 16
*[16] And they said to the mountains and to the rocks, "Fall on us and hide us
from the face of the One sitting on the throne, and from the wrath of the Lamb,*

wrath – anger, the natural disposition, temper, character; movement or
agitation of the soul, impulse, desire, any violent emotion, but especially

anger; anger, wrath, indignation; anger exhibited in punishment, hence used for punishment itself

They become desperate then start to bemoan their situation. There is nowhere they can go to get away from all the destruction. They attribute it all to God, the One on the throne, and to Christ, the Lamb.

Notice they are praying to the mountains and the rocks, not to God.

Verse: 17
¹⁷ because the great day of their wrath has come, and who is able to stand?"

wrath – anger, the natural disposition, temper, character; movement or agitation of the soul, impulse, desire, any violent emotion, but especially anger; anger, wrath, indignation; anger exhibited in punishment, hence used for punishment itself

All the people who had ignored all the warnings of the coming judgment are now experiencing it.

"Who is able to stand?" The answer is simple, nobody.

Greek Paraphrase of Verses: 16-17
And they called to the mountains and the rocks, "Fall on us and hide us from the face of the One who is sitting on the throne, and from the righteous wrath *and* indignation of the Lamb, because the great day of their wrath, vengeance *and* retribution has come, and who is able to face God and stand before the wrath of the Lamb?"

Chapter Seven

This chapter takes a break in the action. In fact, the seventh seal isn't opened until Chapter Eight.

John saw four angels at the four corners of the earth, holding back the four winds of the earth.

During this time of trouble all over the earth, there will be a group of repentant Israelites who will be sealed to preserve them, and a large number of Gentiles until Christ comes.

Verse 1
The Sealed of Israel
¹ After this, I saw four angels standing at the four corners of the earth, holding back the four winds of the earth, so that no wind could blow on the earth or on the sea or on any tree.

¹ After this,
  I saw four angels
    standing at the four corners of the earth,
    holding back the four winds of the earth,
      so that no wind could blow on the earth
        or on the sea
        or on any tree.

holding – to have power, be powerful; to take hold of, take, seize; to keep carefully and faithfully; to continue to hold, to retain

Between the sixth and seventh seals, John writes about two visions he had. 'After these things' means after the visions that came with the opening of the sixth seal.

This is a calm before the storm. The four angels are keeping the winds from blowing therefore giving calm, at least weather wise.

'The four corners of the earth' does not imply that the Bible is saying the earth is square or flat. Four corners of the earth even today usually means the four different directions.

Greek Paraphrase of Verse: 1
After this I saw four angels stationed at the four corners of the earth, holding back the four winds of the earth, so that no wind would blow on the earth, the sea or on any tree.

Verses 2-3
² And I saw another angel coming up from the east, having the seal of the living God. He cried out with a loud voice to the four angels who were

empowered to harm the earth and the sea, ³ *saying, "Do not harm the earth or the sea or the trees until we seal the slaves of our God on their foreheads."*

² And
  I saw another angel
    coming up from the east,
    having the seal of the living God.
    He cried out
      with a loud voice
      to the four angels
        who were empowered to harm the earth and the sea,
        ³ saying,
          "Do not harm the earth
            or the sea
            or the trees
            until we seal the slaves
              of our God
              on their foreheads."

Verse: 2

² *And I saw another angel coming up from the east, having the seal of the living God. He cried out with a loud voice to the four angels who were empowered to harm the earth and the sea,*

empowered – give, give out, hand over, entrust, give back, give up; to give; to bestow a gift; to grant, give to one asking, let have; to supply, furnish, necessary things; to grant or permit one; to commission
harm – to act unjustly or wickedly, to sin; to be a criminal, to have violated the laws in some way; to do wrong; to do hurt; to do some wrong or sin in some respect; to wrong someone, act wickedly towards him; to hurt, damage, harm

John saw a fifth angel but where was he coming from? There is some confusion here for the Greek word is 'sun,' but John doesn't say the angel was coming from the sun. He does say that it's coming from the direction of the rising sun. In other words, the east.

This angel is different in that he has the God's seal and he calls out to the other four angels. This verse says that the four angels have the power to harm the earth and sea.

Verse: 3

³ *saying, "Do not harm the earth or the sea or the trees until we seal the slaves of our God on their foreheads."*

Now, this angel is telling the other four who have the power to harm the earth and seas not to do so. But he tells them to wait until they get a chance to place the mark on the foreheads of the servants/slaves of God.

Greek Paraphrase of Verses: 2-3
Then I saw another angel coming up from the rising of the sun, holding the seal of the living God. He called out with a loud voice to the four angels who were granted the authority and power to harm the earth and the sea, saying, "Do not harm the earth nor the sea nor the trees until we mark with a seal on their foreheads the bond-servants of our God."

Verses 4-8
⁴ And I heard the number of those who were sealed, 144,000 sealed from every tribe of the sons of Israel:
⁵ 12,000 from the tribe of Judah,
12,000 from the tribe of Reuben,
12,000 from the tribe of Gad,
⁶ 12,000 from the tribe of Asher,
12,000 from the tribe of Naphtali,
12,000 from the tribe of Manasseh,
⁷ 12,000 from the tribe of Simeon,
12,000 from the tribe of Levi,
12,000 from the tribe of Issachar,
⁸ 12,000 from the tribe of Zebulun,
12,000 from the tribe of Joseph,
12,000 were sealed from the tribe of Benjamin.

⁴ And
  I heard the number
    of those who were sealed,
    144,000 sealed from every tribe of the sons of Israel:
      ⁵ 12,000 from the tribe of Judah,
      12,000 from the tribe of Reuben,
      12,000 from the tribe of Gad,
      ⁶ 12,000 from the tribe of Asher,
      12,000 from the tribe of Naphtali,
      12,000 from the tribe of Manasseh,
      ⁷ 12,000 from the tribe of Simeon,
      12,000 from the tribe of Levi,
      12,000 from the tribe of Issachar,
      ⁸ 12,000 from the tribe of Zebulun,
      12,000 from the tribe of Joseph,
      12,000 were sealed from the tribe of Benjamin.

Israel – "he shall be a prince of God" the name given to the patriarch Jacob (and borne by him in addition to his former name); the family or descendants of Israel, the nation of Israel

Judah – Judah or Judas = "he shall be praised" – the fourth son of Jacob; an unknown ancestor of Christ; a man surnamed the Galilean, who at the time of the census of Quirinus, excited the revolt in Galilee; a certain Jew of Damascus; a prophet surnamed Barsabas, of the church at Jerusalem; the apostle who was surnamed Lebbaeus or Thaddaeus; the half-brother of Jesus, and according to opinion wrote the Epistle of Jude; Judas Iscariot, the apostle who betrayed Jesus

Reuben – "behold a son" Jacob's firstborn child by Leah

Gad – "a troop" the seventh son of the patriarch Jacob, by Zilpah, Leah's maid

Asher – "blessed" the eighth son of Jacob

Naphtali – "wrestling" was the sixth son of Jacob, the second child borne to him by Bilhah, Rachel's slave. His posterity formed the tribe of Naphtali.

Manasseh – "forgetting" the first-born son of Joseph; the son of Hezekiah, king of Judah

Simeon – "harkening" the second son of Jacob by Leah; one of Abraham's descendants; the one who took the infant Jesus in his arms in the temple; a teacher at the church of Antioch; the original name of Peter the apostle

Levi – "joined" the third son of the patriarch Jacob by his wife Leah, the founder of the tribe of Israelites which bears his name; the son of Melchi, one of Christ's ancestors; the son of Simeon, an ancestor of Christ

Issachar – "reward" the ninth son of Jacob and the fifth of Leah

Zebulun – the tenth of the sons of Jacob; the tribe of Zebulun

Joseph – "let him add" the patriarch, the eleventh son of Jacob; the son of Jonan or Jonam, one of the ancestors of Christ, (Luke 3:30); the son of Judah or Judas; better Joda another ancestor of Jesus, (Luke 3:26); the son of Mattathias, another ancestor of Christ (Luke 3:24); the husband of Mary, the mother of Jesus; a half-brother of Jesus (Matthew 13:55; Joseph of Arimathea, a member of the Sanhedrin, who favored Jesus; Joseph surnamed Barnabas (Acts 4:36);Joseph called Barsabas and surnamed Justus (Acts 1:23

Benjamin – "son of the right hand" or, "son of good fortune" Jacob's twelfth son; the tribe of Benjamin

Those to be sealed were 144,000 in number. Every tribe is represented here. There were 12,000 from each of the twelve tribes of Israel.

Greek Paraphrase of Verses: 4-8
And I heard how many were sealed, a hundred and forty-four thousand; twelve thousand sealed from each tribe of the sons of Israel: Twelve thousand were sealed from the tribe of Judah, twelve thousand from the tribe of Reuben, twelve thousand from the tribe of Gad, twelve thousand from the tribe of Asher, twelve thousand from the tribe of Naphtali, twelve thousand from the tribe of Manasseh, twelve thousand from the tribe of Simeon, twelve thousand from the tribe of Levi, twelve thousand from the tribe of Issachar, twelve thousand from the tribe of Zebulun,

twelve thousand from the tribe of Joseph, and twelve thousand from the tribe of Benjamin were sealed (marked, redeemed, protected).

Verse 9
The Great Multitude

⁹ After this, I looked, and behold, a great multitude which no one could count, from every nation and all tribes and peoples and languages, standing before the throne and before the Lamb, clothed in white robes, with palm branches in their hands.

⁹ After this,
>I looked,
>>and behold,
>>a great multitude
>>>which no one could count,
>>>from every nation
>>>>and all tribes
>>>>and peoples
>>>>and languages,
>>>standing before the throne
>>>>and before the Lamb,
>>>>clothed in white robes,
>>>>with palm branches in their hands.

This is the second vision between the sixth and seventh seals. The scene changes from earth back to heaven.

The multitude John saw before the throne had to be different from the 144,000 since every nation, tribe and language on earth was represented. The 144,000 was only from Israel.

Since they were already clothed in white robes, they were among those counted as righteous. The palm branches in their hands symbolize victory and show they share in His triumph.

Greek Paraphrase of Verse: 9
After these things, I looked, and this is what I saw, a vast multitude which no one could count, gathered from every nation and from all the tribes and peoples and languages of the earth, standing in front of the throne and the Lamb, who were dressed in white robes, with palm branches in their hands;

Verse 10

¹⁰ And they cried out with a loud voice, saying, "Salvation to our God the One sitting on the throne, and to the Lamb."

¹⁰ And
    they cried out
      with a loud voice,
      saying,
        "Salvation to our God
          the One sitting on the throne,
          and to the Lamb."

Salvation – deliverance, preservation, safety, salvation; deliverance from the molestation of enemies; of Messianic salvation

"Salvation to our God" is an expression from Hebrew which means salvation belongs to the Lord (Jehovah).

They were full of joy because they knew where their salvation came from.

Greek Paraphrase of Verse: 10
And they cried out in a loud voice, saying, "Salvation belongs to our God who is seated on the throne, and to the Lamb."

Verses 11-12
¹¹ All the angels stood around the throne, the elders, and the four living creatures, and they fell on their faces before the throne and worshiped God, ¹² saying, "Amen. Blessing and glory and wisdom and thanksgiving and honor and power and might, be to our God forever and ever. Amen."

¹¹ All the angels stood
    around the throne,
      the elders,
      and the four living creatures,
      and they fell on their faces
        before the throne
        and worshiped God,
        ¹² saying,
          "Amen.
          Blessing
            and glory
            and wisdom
            and thanksgiving
            and honor
            and power
            and might,
          be to our God
            forever and ever.
Amen."

Verse: 11
[11] All the angels stood around the throne, the elders, and the four living creatures, and they fell on their faces before the throne and worshiped God,

Thousands of angels (created beings who have never sinned) are around the throne not only beyond the 24 elders and the four living creatures but also beyond the 144,000 and the righteous from all the nations. All of those who have sinned but have been redeemed are ahead of the angels. Interesting!

Verse: 12
[12] saying, "Amen. Blessing and glory and wisdom and thanksgiving and honor and power and might, be to our God forever and ever. Amen."

Blessing – praise, laudation, panegyric: of Christ or God; fine discourse, polished language; an invocation of blessing, benediction; in a bad sense, language artfully adapted to captivate the hearer: fair speaking, fine speeches
glory – splendor, brightness; of the moon, sun, stars; magnificence, excellence, preeminence, dignity, grace; majesty; a thing belonging to God
wisdom – wisdom, broad and full of intelligence; used of the knowledge of very diverse matters; the wisdom which belongs to men; the varied knowledge of things human and divine, acquired by acuteness and experience, and summed up in maxims and proverbs; the science and learning; supreme intelligence, such as belongs to God; the wisdom of God as evinced in forming and executing counsels in the formation and government of the world and the scriptures
honor – a valuing by which the price is fixed; of the price paid or received for a person or thing bought or sold; honor which belongs or is shown to one; of the honor which one has by reason of rank and state of office which he holds; deference, reverence
power – strength, power, ability (word we get dynamite from)
might – ability, force, strength, might

Them saying 'Amen' here is affirming the truth of what is being said. What follows is seven different types of praise. Then it is ended with 'amen' to put further emphasis on the truth of what was just said.

Greek Paraphrase of Verse: 11-12
All the angels were standing around the throne and the twenty-four elders and the four living creatures, and they fell to their faces before the throne and worshiped God, saying, "Amen! Blessing, glory, majesty, wisdom, thanksgiving, honor, power and might belong to our God forever and ever. Amen."

Verse 13
[13] Then one of the elders answered, saying to me, "Who are these clothed in the white robes, and where did they come from?"

¹³ Then
> one of the elders answered,
>> saying
>>> to me,
>>>> "Who are these
>>>>> clothed in the white robes,
>>>>> and where did they come from?"

The elder is asking John a rhetorical question, one in which he already knows the answer and expects John to know too? Verse 14 proves that point.

Greek Paraphrase of Verse: 13
Then one of the elders answered, saying to me, "Who are these who are dressed in the long white robes, and from where did they come?"

Verse 14
¹⁴ I said to him, "Sir, you know." And he said to me, "These are the ones coming out of the great tribulation, and they have washed their robes and made them white in the blood of the Lamb.

¹⁴ I said
> to him,
> "Sir,
> you know."
>> And he said
>>> to me,
>>>> "These are the ones coming out of the great tribulation,
>>>>> and they have washed their robes
>>>>> and made them white
>>>>>> in the blood of the Lamb.

tribulation – a pressing, pressing together, pressure; oppression, affliction, tribulation, distress, straits

John's answer was both polite and complete. These people have already been through the great tribulation and washed clean by the blood of the Lamb (Christ).

Greek Paraphrase of Verse: 14
I said to him, "My lord, you know the answer." And he said to me, "These are the people who are coming out of the great tribulation, and they have washed their robes and made them white in the blood of the Lamb because of His atoning sacrifice.

Verse 15
15 For this reason, they are before the throne of God, and they serve Him day and night in His temple. The One sitting on the throne will shelter them.

15 For this reason,
    they are before the throne of God,
    and
    they serve
       Him day and night
       in His temple.
  The One
    sitting on the throne
    will shelter them.

reason – through; of place: with; in, of time: throughout; during; by; by the means of; the ground or reason by which something is or is not done

Because they have been washed by the blood of the Lamb, they are now continually before the throne of God constantly serving Him.
He goes on to say that God will shelter them from any more harm.

Greek Paraphrase of Verse: 15
For this reason, they are standing before the throne of God and they serve Him in worship, day and night in His temple. The One who sits on the throne will spread His tabernacle over them and shelter and protect them with His presence.

Verses 16-17
16 They will hunger no longer, nor thirst anymore, nor will the sun beat down on them, nor any heat, 17 because the Lamb in the center of the throne will be their shepherd, and will guide them to springs of the living water, and God will wipe every tear from their eyes."

16 They will hunger no longer,
    nor thirst anymore,
    nor will the sun beat down on them,
      nor any heat,
  17 because the Lamb
    in the center of the throne
    will be their shepherd,
    and
    will guide them to springs of the living water,
    and
    God will wipe every tear from their eyes."

Verse: 16

16 They will hunger no longer, nor thirst anymore, nor will the sun beat down on them, nor any heat,

During the tribulation, they were hungry, thirsty and the sun was unbearable. No more! John is saying those things will not happen anymore.

Verse: 17

17 because the Lamb in the center of the throne will be their shepherd and will guide them to springs of the living water, and God will wipe every tear from their eyes."

Here is the reason for all those hardships going away. The Lamb! He will be their shepherd, the One who will look after them from now on. They will drink from the living water and there will be no more tears.

Greek Paraphrase of Verses: 16-17

They will hunger no longer, nor thirst anymore. Nor will the sun beat down on them, nor any scorching heat, because the Lamb who is in the center of the throne will be their Shepherd, and He will guide them to springs of the waters of life, and God will wipe every tear from their eyes giving them eternal comfort."

Chapter Eight

The opening of the seventh seal brings out the seven trumpets. Four of the trumpets announce judgment.

The first trumpet brings a shower of hail, fire and blood. The second one sounds, and a burning mountain is thrown into the sea. The third trumpet sounds and the great star Wormwood falls from heaven. The fourth trumpet sounds and the sun, moon and stars are struck.

Then three woes are denounced against all living on the earth because of the three angels who have not blown their trumpets yet.

Verse 1
The Seventh Seal
¹ When He opened the seventh seal, there was silence in heaven for about half an hour.

¹ When He opened the seventh seal,
> there was silence
> > in heaven
> > for about half an hour.

Now, we're ready for the seventh seal to be opened. Suddenly, all the music, the singing, the shouting around the throne stopped for about half an hour.

Silence was always used as a prelude to something great or terrible about to happen. It is the silence of expectation. But what was coming? This seal is an introduction to the trumpets which follow.

Greek Paraphrase of Verse: 1
When the Lamb broke open the seventh seal, there was silence in heaven for about half an hour in awe of God's impending judgment.

Verse 2
² And I saw the seven angels who stand before God, and seven trumpets were given to them.

² And
> I saw the seven angels
> > who stand before God,
> > and seven trumpets were given to them.

John now sees the seven angels which had been standing before the throne given the seven trumpets. These trumpets were probably straight silver trumpets like those used in the tabernacle (Numbers 10:2) and the temple (2 Chronicles 5:12). They were also used in battle (Numbers 10:1-10; 31:6; Hosea 5:8).

Greek Paraphrase of Verse: 2
Then I saw the seven angels who stand before God, and seven trumpets
were given to them.

Verse 3

3 Another angel, holding a golden censer, came and stood at the altar. He
was given much incense to offer with the prayers of all the saints on the
golden altar before the throne.

3 Another angel,
    holding a golden censer,
    came and stood at the altar.
    He was given much incense
      to offer
        with the prayers
        of all the saints
        on the golden altar
          before the throne.

censer – the gum exuding from a frankincense tree; a censer: a container in
which incense is burned

This is a different angel, not one of the seven. The censer was basically
a fire pan which would burn a large amount of incense. This implies that there
was a large number of prayers to be offered to God.

Greek Paraphrase of Verse: 3
Another angel came and stood at the altar. He had a golden censer, and
much incense was given to him, so that he might add it to the prayers of
all of God's people on the golden altar in front of the throne.

Verse 4

4 And the smoke of the incense, with the prayers of the saints, went up before
God from the angel's hand.

4 And
    the smoke
      of the incense,
      with the prayers
        of the saints,
    went up
      before God
      from the angel's hand.

There are two different theories as to this verse. One theory is that the incense symbolizes the prayers of the saints as in:

5:8, When He took the scroll, the four living creatures and the twenty-four elders fell down before the Lamb. Each had a harp and golden bowls full of incense, which are the prayers of the saints.

The other theory is that since the incense was given to this angel, it was mingled with the prayers of the saints.

Regardless, the angel's action shows that the prayers must come before God by way of the altar.

Greek Paraphrase of Verse: 4
And the smoke *and* fragrant aroma of the incense, with the prayers of God's people, ascended before God from the angel's hand.

Verse 5
[5] *Then the angel took the censer, filled it with fire from the altar, and threw it to the earth, and there were peals of thunder, rumblings, lightning, and an earthquake.*

[5] Then
  the angel took the censer,
    filled it with fire from the altar,
    and threw it to the earth,
      and there were
        peals of thunder,
        rumblings,
        lightning,
        and an earthquake.

The same fire on the altar that made the incense and the prayers of the saints acceptable to God was now poured out on the earth. Since the angle filled the censer, that indicates the severity of the coming judgments of God's wrath.

Remember, John is still in heaven when he hears the noises of the fire hitting the earth.

Greek Paraphrase of Verse: 5
Then the angel took the censer and filled it with fire from the altar, and hurled it to the earth, and there were peals of thunder, loud rumblings, sounds and flashes of lightning and an earthquake.

Verse 6
[6] *And the seven angels who had the seven trumpets prepared to blow them.*

⁶ And
    the seven angels
      who had the seven trumpets
        prepared to blow them.

Now, all the preparations have been made and the seven angels are ready to blow the seven trumpets and the plagues will follow.

Greek Paraphrase of Verse: 6
Then the seven angels who had the seven trumpets prepared themselves to sound them initiating the judgments.

Verse 7
The First Trumpet
⁷ *The first blew, and hail and fire, mixed with blood, were thrown to the earth. So, a third of the earth was burned up, a third of the trees were burned up, and all the green grass was burned up.*

⁷ The first blew,
    and hail and fire,
      mixed with blood,
      were thrown to the earth.
        So, a third of the earth was burned up,
        a third of the trees were burned up,
        and all the green grass was burned up.

The words used to describe the hail and fire mixed with blood is like what was used to describe the seventh plague God sent to Egypt through Moses in Exodus 9:13-35.

The major effect was the burning of one-third of all the greenery on the earth.

Greek Paraphrase of Verse: 7
The first angel sounded his trumpet, and there was a storm of hail and fire, mixed with blood, and it was hurled to the earth. So, a third of the earth was burned up, a third of the trees were burned up, and all the green grass was burned up.

Verses 8-9
The Second Trumpet
⁸ *The second angel blew his trumpet, and something like a great mountain burning with fire was thrown into the sea, and a third of the sea became blood, ⁹ and a third of the creatures in the sea died, and a third of the ships were destroyed.*

⁸ The second angel blew his trumpet,
　　and something like a great mountain
　　　burning with fire
　　　was thrown into the sea,
　　　　and a third of the sea became blood,
　　　　⁹ and a third of the creatures
　　　　　in the sea
　　　　　died,
　　　　and a third of the ships were destroyed.

Verse 8
⁸ The second angel blew his trumpet, and something like a great mountain burning with fire was thrown into the sea, and a third of the sea became blood,

First, fire on the land then fire in the sea. It sounds like a monstrous fireball being thrown into the sea causing one-third of the sea to turn into blood.

Verse 9
⁹ and a third of the creatures in the sea died, and a third of the ships were destroyed.

The fire and the blood kills one-third of all sea life and the fire destroys one-third of the ships on the sea.

Greek Paraphrase of Verses: 8-9
The second angel sounded his trumpet, and *something* like a great mountain blazing with fire was hurled into the sea, and a third of the sea was turned to blood, and a third of the living creatures that were in the sea died, and a third of the ships were destroyed.

Verse 10
The Third Trumpet
¹⁰ The third angel blew his trumpet, and a great star, burning like a torch, fell from heaven. It fell on a third of the rivers and springs of water.

¹⁰ The third angel blew his trumpet,
　　and a great star,
　　　burning like a torch,
　　　fell from heaven.
　　　　It fell on a third of the rivers and springs of water.
　　As John watched, the third angel blew his trumpet and a falling star streaked across the sky poisoning one-third of the rivers and springs. Apparently, this didn't directly affect anything on land.

Greek Paraphrase of Verse: 10
The third angel sounded his trumpet, and a great star fell from heaven, burning like a torch flashing across the sky. It fell on a third of the rivers and on the springs of fresh waters.

Verse 11
[11] The name of the star is Wormwood, and a third of the waters became wormwood. Many men died from the waters, because they were made bitter.

[11] The name of the star is Wormwood,
    and a third of the waters became wormwood.
    Many men died from the waters,
        because they were made bitter.

Wormwood – a woody shrub with a bitter aromatic taste

It is significant that this star is named Wormwood which is a shrub that looks nice but is very bitter. The star must have looked magnificent as it streaked across the sky, but it caused a bitter poison in one-third of the rivers and springs.

Greek Paraphrase of Verse: 11
The name of the star is Wormwood, and a third of the waters became wormwood. And many men died from the waters, because they had become poisonous.

Verse 12
The Fourth Trumpet
[12] The fourth angel blew his trumpet, and a third of the sun, a third of the moon, and a third of the stars were struck, so that a third of them would be darkened and a third of the day was without light, and likewise, the night.

[12] The fourth angel blew his trumpet,
    and a third of the sun,
    a third of the moon,
    and a third of the stars
      were struck,
        so that a third of them would be darkened
          and a third of the day was without light,
            and likewise, the night.

The first three trumpets affected the earth but the fourth one struck one-third of the sun, moon and stars.

Think of how that would affect the sun and the moon. Each one would only shine two-thirds of the time now. But the stars would be a little different. Depending on the rotation of the earth, the night sky would be affected accordingly. At worst, there would still be two-thirds of the stars shining. The rest of the time, there would be more up to even all of the night sky full of stars.

This is a strong example for how God controls not only the earth and all creatures in it, but He also controls the entire universe.

Greek Paraphrase of Verse: 12
Then the fourth angel sounded his trumpet, and a third of the sun, a third of the moon and a third of the stars were struck, so that a third of them would be darkened, a third of the daylight would not shine and the night would not shine in the same way.

Verse 13
13 Then I looked, and I heard an eagle flying in mid-heaven, saying with a loud voice, "Woe! Woe! Woe to those who live on the earth, because of the remaining trumpet blasts that the three angels are about to sound!"

13 Then I looked,
   and I heard an eagle flying
     in mid-heaven,
    saying
      with a loud voice,
      "Woe!
      Woe!
      Woe
        to those who live on the earth,
          because of the remaining trumpet blasts
            that the three angels are about to sound!"

Woe – great sorrow or distress

Now, we have another pause in the trumpets for John to tell us what he saw.

First, this is another one of those differences between the Textus Receptus (KJV) and the Nestle Aland (modern translations).

The TR has angel and the NA has eagle. The biggest significance is that the Greek word for eagle can also mean vulture. That could open up all sorts of other possibilities.

No matter what it was, the warning is what is important.

An angel/eagle/vulture flying (probably back and forth) in midheaven shouts more warnings to the earth.

Just the word the angel/eagle/vulture shouted should send chills down everyone's backs. He is saying they will have great sorrow and distress because of the remaining trumpet announcements.

Greek Paraphrase of Verse: 13
Then I looked, and I heard a solitary eagle flying in mid-heaven for all to see, saying with a loud voice, "Woe! Woe! Woe, great wrath is coming to those who live on the earth, because of the remaining blasts of the trumpets which the three angels are about to sound announcing ever greater judgments!"

Chapter Nine

The judgments of the fifth and sixth trumpets.

The fifth angel sounds his trumpet, and a star falls from heaven to earth and the bottomless pit is opened. The sixth angel sounds his trumpet and the four angels bound in the Euphrates are turned loose. The army of horsemen come and destroy 200 million people, but they still do not repent.

Verse 1
The Fifth Trumpet
¹ Then the fifth angel blew his trumpet, and I saw a star that had fallen from heaven to earth. The key of the bottomless pit was given to him.

¹ Then
   the fifth angel blew his trumpet,
     and I saw a star
      that had fallen from heaven to earth.
   The key of the bottomless pit was given to him.

The star that fell out of heaven is thought by most commentators to be a living being not a star. Thus, you can see how the key to the bottomless pit could be given to it/him.

Some other commentators think the fallen star is Satan and some others think it is one of Satan's demons.

Greek Paraphrase of Verse: 1
Then the fifth angel sounded his trumpet, and I saw a star an angelic being that had fallen from heaven to the earth. The key to the bottomless pit was given to him, the star-angel.

Verse 2
² He opened the bottomless pit, and smoke came up out of the pit like the smoke from a great furnace so that the sun and the air were darkened by the smoke from the pit.

² He opened the bottomless pit,
   and smoke came up
     out of the pit
     like the smoke from a great furnace
     so that the sun and the air were darkened
      by the smoke from the pit.

The being (whatever or whoever it may be) had to open the bottomless pit with the key given to him.

It's not clear whether the pit is locked to keep innocent people from falling in or to keep those already in there from escaping. Either one or even both could be possible.

The smoke coming out should indicate that there is a lot of fire in the pit. Is this Hades? Some think so but others think Hades and the pit are near each other maybe even connected but separate.

Jesus described it in:

Luke 16:23-24, In Hell, he lifted up his eyes, being in torment, and saw Abraham far away and Lazarus in his bosom. He cried out, 'Father Abraham, have mercy on me, and send Lazarus that he may dip the tip of his finger in water and cool my tongue, for I am suffering in this flame.

Greek Paraphrase of Verse: 2
He opened the bottomless pit, and smoke like from a great furnace flowed up out of the pit so that the sun and the sky were darkened by the smoke from the pit.

Verse 3
³ Then out of the smoke, locusts came upon the earth, and power was given them, as the scorpions of the earth have power.

³ Then
  out of the smoke,
    locusts came upon the earth,
      and power was given them,
        as the scorpions
          of the earth
          have power.

locusts – a locust, particularly that species which especially infests oriental countries, stripping fields and trees. Numberless swarms of them almost every spring are carried by the wind from Arabia into Palestine, and having devastated that country, migrate to regions farther north, until they perish by falling into the sea. The Orientals accustomed to feed upon locusts, either raw or roasted and seasoned with salt (or prepared in other ways), and the Israelites also were permitted to eat them.

power – physical and mental power; the power of authority (influence) and of right (privilege); the power of rule or government (the power of him whose will and commands must be submitted to by others and obeyed); the power of judicial decisions; one who possesses authority; a ruler, a human magistrate

The smoke came from the pit so therefore the locusts came from there too.

The belief is that the 'locusts' were not actual locusts as we know them. They were possibly demons released to devour the earth the way locusts do.

This is not like the locusts released on Egypt as punishment. These are much worse and will totally destroy everything anywhere they go.

Greek Paraphrase of Verse: 3
Then out of the smoke locusts came upon the earth, and power to hurt was given to them, like the power the scorpions of the earth have.

Verse 4
⁴ They were told not to harm the grass of the earth, nor any green thing, nor any tree, but only the men who do not have the seal of God on their foreheads.

⁴ They were told not to harm the grass
    of the earth,
    nor any green thing,
    nor any tree,
    but only the men
      who do not have the seal
        of God
        on their foreheads.

Here is further proof that they are not ordinary locusts which only destroy vegetation. Their mission will be to injure, hurt and damage human beings. But only those without the seal of God on their foreheads (the 144,000 mentioned before).

Greek Paraphrase of Verse: 4
They were told not to hurt the grass of the earth, nor any green thing, nor any tree, but to hurt only the people who do not have the seal of ownership and protection of God on their foreheads.

Verse 5
⁵ They were not permitted to kill anyone, but to torment for five months, and their torment was like the torment of a scorpion when it stings a man.

⁵ They were not permitted to kill anyone,
    but to torment
      for five months,
      and their torment was like the torment of a scorpion
        when it stings a man.

torment – to torture, a testing by the touchstone, which is a black siliceous stone used to test the purity of gold or silver by the color of the streak produced on it by rubbing it with either metal

More limitations are given to the locusts. They can't kill anyone, and their time on earth is limited.

They can only torment those they are sent to and they can only do it for five months.

Again, they are likened to scorpions in how they sting men.

Greek Paraphrase of Verse: 5
They were not permitted to kill anyone, but to torment and cause them extreme pain for five months, and their torment was like the torment from a scorpion when it stings a man.

Verse 6
⁶ In those days, men will seek death and will not find it. They will long to die, but death will flee from them.

⁶ In those days,
>men will seek death
>>and will not find it.
>>They will long to die,
>>>but death will flee from them.

All through the Old Testament there are many instances where someone was being tormented and wished to die.

Some even suggest that people were trying to commit suicide but were even unable to do that. I personally think that one might be a bit of a stretch, but who knows?

Greek Paraphrase of Verse: 6
In those days, men will seek death and will not find it. They will want to die to escape the pain but will discover that death escapes them.

Verse 7
⁷ The appearance of the locusts was like horses prepared for battle. On their heads appeared to be crowns like gold, and their faces were like the faces of men.

⁷ The appearance
>of the locusts
>was like horses prepared for battle.
>On their heads
>>appeared to be crowns like gold,
>>>and their faces were like the faces of men.

Joel 2:4 describes the locust plague like an army where they appear like horses. But Joel was talking about real locusts. This would also imply that the 'locusts' were very big.

Note that John says what they had on their heads appeared to be crowns like gold. This implies that they were not crowns and they were also not made from gold.

The same goes for the faces like faces of men. They were not men.

Greek Paraphrase of Verse: 7
The locusts resembled horses prepared *and* equipped for battle. On their heads appeared to be something like golden crowns, and their faces resembled human faces.

Verse 8
8 They had hair like the hair of women, and their teeth were like the teeth of lions.

8 They had hair like the hair of women,
 and their teeth were like the teeth of lions.

Again, every description is 'like' – like women's hair and like lions' teeth. John was simply describing what he saw in terms of what he knew.

The hair could be referring to the long antennae of locusts.

The lions' teeth would refer to destruction. They would be capable of tearing people apart with their teeth like lions even though the pain they render is like that of a scorpion sting.

Greek Paraphrase of Verse: 8
They had hair like women's hair, and their teeth were like lions' *teeth*.

Verse 9
9 They had breastplates like breastplates of iron, and the sound of their wings was like the sound of chariots, of many horses rushing into battle.

9 They had breastplates like breastplates of iron,
 and the sound
  of their wings
 was like the sound of chariots,
  of many horses rushing into battle.

breastplates – a breastplate or corset consisting of two parts and protecting the body on both sides from the neck to the middle

Now, John talks about how invincible these creatures will be. He describes them like flying, armored chariots making the same sound of many horses stampeding into battle.

The sound John describes is the noise their wings make as they fly. All of that would really be a frightening description to someone of that time period.

Greek Paraphrase of Verse: 9
They had scales like breastplates made of iron, and the whirring noise of their wings was like the thunderous noise of countless horse-drawn chariots charging at full speed into battle.

Verse 10
[10] They have tails and stingers like scorpions so that with their tails, they had the power to harm men for five months.

[10] They have tails and stingers
    like scorpions
    so that with their tails,
      they had the power
        to harm men
        for five months.

These demon locusts have stingers and are able to sting the same way a real scorpion does. Again, John mentions that they can only harm and not kill people and even that for only five months.

Greek Paraphrase of Verse: 10
They have tails and stingers like scorpions, so they have the power to hurt people for five months with their tails.

Verse 11
[11] They have as king over them, the angel of the abyss. His name in Hebrew is Abaddon, and in the Greek, he has the name Apollyon.

[11] They have
    as king over them,
    the angel of the abyss.
      His name
        in Hebrew
          is Abaddon,
      and
      in the Greek
        he has the name Apollyon.

abyss – Bottomless; unbounded; the abyss; the pit; the immeasurable depth; of Orcus, a very deep gulf or chasm in the lowest parts of the earth used as the common receptacle of the dead and especially as the abode of demons

Abaddon – "destruction" ruin; the place of destruction; the name of the angel-prince of the infernal regions, the minister of death and the author of havoc on the earth
Apollyon – "Destroyer" the angel of the bottomless pit, the Destroyer

> If they have a king over them, that proves that they're not real locusts.
> *Proverbs 30:27, locusts have no king, yet all of them march in ranks*
> Their king is the angel of the bottomless pit, the Destroyer.

Greek Paraphrase of Verse: 11
Their king over them, is the angel of the bottomless pit. His name in Hebrew is Abaddon which means destruction, and in Greek he is called Apollyon the destroyer–king.

Verse 12
12 The first woe has passed. Behold, two woes are still coming after this.

12 The first woe has passed.
    Behold,
        two woes are still coming
           after this.

    John's vision now moves to the end of the five months mentioned in the last few verses. The demon/locusts are now gone.
    The first of the three woes predicted in 8:13 by that flying angel is now over. But two more woes are coming, and it is implied that they will be worse than the first one.

Greek Paraphrase of Verse: 12
The first woe has passed. Behold, two more woes are still coming after these things.

Verses 13-14
The Sixth Trumpet
13 The sixth angel blew his trumpet, and I heard a voice from the four horns of the golden altar that is before God, 14 saying to the sixth angel who had the trumpet, "Release the four angels bound at the great river Euphrates."

13 The sixth angel blew his trumpet,
    and I heard a voice
        from the four horns
           of the golden altar
           that is before God,
        14 saying
           to the sixth angel
              who had the trumpet,

"Release the four angels bound at the great river Euphrates."

Verse 13
13 The sixth angel blew his trumpet, and I heard a voice from the four horns of the golden altar that is before God,

The second woe comes when the sixth angel blows his trumpet. The voice John hears is coming from the four points of the altar that stick out like horns.

Note here the difference in the description of the gold. The altar is not like gold, it is gold because it is in front of God.

Verse 14
14 saying to the sixth angel who had the trumpet, "Release the four angels bound at the great river Euphrates."

Euphrates – "the good and abounding river" a large, famous river which rises in the mountains of Armenia Major, flows through Assyria, Syria, Mesopotamia and the city of Babylon, and empties into the Gulf of Persia

In the Old Testament, God used the robber kings of the Euphrates valley to bring His judgment. Thus, the Euphrates River becomes a symbol of the spirit of conquest God uses to bring about His judgment.

Note that God's holy angels are never bound so the difference is readily apparent.

Greek Paraphrase of Verses: 13-14
Then the sixth angel sounded his trumpet, and I heard a solitary voice from the four horns of the golden altar which stands before God, saying to the sixth angel who had the trumpet, "Release the four angels who are bound at the great river Euphrates."

Verse 15
15 And the four angels who had been prepared for the hour, day, month and year, were released, to kill a third of mankind.

15 And
  the four angels
    who had been prepared
      for the hour,
        day,
        month
        and year,
    were released,
      to kill a third of mankind.

While the demon locusts could only torture people, these four angels were given the power to kill one-third of the entire population of the earth.

Notice that they had been prepared beforehand and were just waiting for this very moment.

Greek Paraphrase of Verse: 15
And the four angels who had been prepared for the appointed hour, day, month and year, were released to kill a third of mankind.

Verse 16
16 The number of the armies of the horsemen was two hundred million. I heard their number.

16 The number
> of the armies of the horsemen
> was two hundred million.
>> I heard their number.

As soon as the four angels were released, John saw a huge army of cavalry. His mentioning the fact that he heard their number shows that God wanted him to know exactly how many there were. Also, there is the fear factor. There has never been an army that large assembled in one place in the history of the world.

Greek Paraphrase of Verse: 16
The number of the armies of cavalry was two hundred million. I heard the number of them.

Verse 17
17 And this is how I saw the horses in the vision and those sitting on them had breastplates the color of fire and of hyacinth and of brimstone. The heads of the horses were like the heads of lions and fire and smoke and brimstone came from their mouths.

17 And
> this is how I saw the horses
>> in the vision
>> and those sitting on them had breastplates the color
>>> of fire
>>> and of hyacinth
>>> and of brimstone.
> The heads
>> of the horses
>> were like the heads of lions
>>> and fire
>>> and smoke
>>> and brimstone
>>>> came from their mouths.

saw – this word means to actually see with your eyes, yet John is seeing a vision

Hyacinth is a red color that almost looks black (much like blood in different light). And of course, brimstone was a fiery glowing red. So, the breastplates were basically three shades of red, all of which depicted fire and destruction.

John spends the most time describing the horses since they are the sources of destruction this time. They were able to tear apart like a lion. They spewed fire, smoke and brimstone from their mouths. That is a fearsome picture for sure.

Greek Paraphrase of Verse: 17
And this is how I saw the horses and their riders in my vision. T*he riders* had breastplates the color of fire, hyacinth and of brimstone. The heads of the horses looked like the heads of lions, and fire, smoke and burning sulfur came out of their mouths.

Verse 18
[18] A third of mankind was killed by these three plagues—by the fire, the smoke, and the sulfur that came from their mouths.

[18] A third of mankind was killed
    by these three plagues
    by the fire,
    the smoke,
        and the sulfur that came from their mouths.

John describes this as three plagues not just one. The fire burns the people, the smoke suffocates them and finally, the sulfur poisons them.

The use of fire, smoke and sulfur is similar to God's judgment on Sodom and Gomorrah in Genesis 19:24-28.

Greek Paraphrase of Verse: 18
A third of mankind was killed by these three plagues—by the fire, the smoke and the brimstone that came out of the mouths of the horses.
Verse 19
[19] For the power of the horses is in their mouths and in their tails, for their tails are like serpents and have heads, and with them they injure.

[19] For
    the power
      of the horses
      is in their mouths
      and in their tails,

for their tails
  are like serpents
  and have heads,
  and with them they injure.

power – physical and mental power; the power of authority (influence) and of right (privilege); the power of rule or government (the power of him whose will and commands must be submitted to by others and obeyed); the power of judicial decisions; one who possesses authority; a ruler, a human magistrate

  The emphasis of this verse is that the power of death is in the mouths of these horses whose heads are like lions. Also, they have power not only to kill but to torture, hurt and damage.

  They have the power to damage with their tails like scorpions. But their tails are not like scorpions. They have serpent heads on them. This implies much more damage and death.

Greek Paraphrase of Verse: 19
For the power of the horses to do harm is in their mouths and in their tails, for their tails are like serpents and have heads. It is with them that they do harm.

Verse 20
20 The rest of mankind, who were not killed by these plagues, did not repent of the works of their hands, not to worship demons and idols of gold, silver, brass, stone, and wood, which are not able to see, hear or walk.

20 The rest of mankind,
  who were not killed
    by these plagues,
    did not repent
      of the works of their hands,
      not to worship demons
        and idols of gold,
          silver,
          brass,
          stone,
          and wood,
          which are not able to see,
            hear
            or walk.

repent – to change one's mind for better, heartily to amend with abhorrence of one's past sins

Surprisingly, there still seems to be the opportunity for people to repent in the midst of all these plagues. But they didn't!

Isn't that sad that all of these plagues still couldn't get the people to repent? They were certainly hardened by then. Remember though, that all the Christians have been removed before all this started happening.

Greek Paraphrase of Verse: 20
The rest of mankind, who were not killed by these plagues, did not repent even then of the works of their hands, so as to cease worshiping and paying homage to the demons and the idols of gold, silver, bronze, stone and wood, which can neither see nor hear nor walk.

Verse 21
21 And they did not repent of their murders, their sorceries, their immorality, or of their thefts.

21 And
    they did not repent
      of their murders,
        their sorceries,
        their immorality,
        or of their thefts.

repent – to change one's mind for better, heartily to amend with abhorrence of one's past sins
sorceries – the use or the administering of drugs; poisoning; sorcery, magical arts, often found in connection with idolatry and fostered by it; metaphorically the deceptions and seductions of idolatry

As in Romans 1:24-32, those who turn away from God keep falling farther away from Him.

John just lists a few of their sins but we certainly get the idea.

Greek Paraphrase of Verse: 21
And they did not repent of their murders nor of their sorceries, drugs, intoxications nor of their sexual immorality nor their thefts.

Chapter Ten

This is another one of those chapters that is in between two parts of the same vision.

Another angel comes to John and when he speaks, the seven thunders speak. The angel swears that there will be no more time and he gives John a book or scroll and tells him to eat it.

Then John is told that he must prophesy again about many peoples, nations, tongues and kings.

Verses 1-3
The Mighty Angel and the Small Scroll

¹ I saw another mighty angel coming down from heaven, clothed with a cloud, with a rainbow over his head. His face was like the sun, and his legs were like pillars of fire, ² and he had a little scroll open in his hand. He placed his right foot on the sea and his left on the land, ³ and he cried out with a loud voice like a roaring lion. When he cried out, the seven thunders spoke.

¹ I saw another mighty angel
    coming down from heaven,
    clothed with a cloud,
    with a rainbow over his head.
    His face was like the sun,
    and
    his legs were like pillars of fire,
    ² and
    he had a little scroll open in his hand.
    He placed his right foot on the sea
        and his left on the land,
    ³ and
    he cried out
        with a loud voice
            like a roaring lion.
    When he cried out,
        the seven thunders spoke.

Verse: 1

¹ I saw another mighty angel coming down from heaven, clothed with a cloud, with a rainbow over his head. His face was like the sun, and his legs were like pillars of fire,

mighty - strong, mighty; strong either in body or in mind; strong, violent, forcibly uttered, firm, sure

There was a break between the sixth and seventh seals and now there is also a break between the sixth and seventh trumpets. There is a long pause this time since the seventh trumpet isn't blown until Revelation 11:15.

In the first vision John saw another strong, mighty angel coming out of heaven. The word 'another' implies that this angel has not appeared before.

Since John saw the angel coming out of heaven, then John was on earth this time, not in heaven.

This angel is unusual. The first part of his description is rather soft. He is wearing a cloud and a rainbow is on his head. The rest of his description is extremely harsh. His face is like the sun. Can you look at the sun without hurting your eyes?

His legs were like pillars of fire. That too is very harsh. It's like the angel comes softly like a lamb but continues like a lion.

Verse: 2

2 and he had a little scroll open in his hand. He placed his right foot on the sea and his left on the land,

The Greek word for 'little scroll' is different from the one in Chapter 5 which is translated 'scroll.' The difference implies that the first one may have been either more important or just contained a lot more information.

The angel was not only powerful but huge since he put one foot on the sea and the other one on the land.

Verse: 3

3 and he cried out with a loud voice like a roaring lion. When he cried out, the seven thunders spoke.

There are several Old Testament passages which mention a voice like this one: Amos 3:8; Hosea 11:10; Psalm 29:3.

Greek Paraphrase of Verses: 1-3

Then I saw another mighty angel coming down from heaven, clothed in a cloud, with a rainbow halo over his head. His face was like the sun, and his legs were like columns of fire, and he had a little book open in his hand. He set his right foot on the sea and his left foot on the land, and he shouted with a loud voice, like the roaring of a lion getting attention and inspiring awe. When he shouted out, the seven peals of thunder spoke with their own voices uttering their message in distinct words.

Verse 4

4 When the seven thunders had spoken, I was about to write, and I heard a voice from heaven saying, "Seal up what the seven thunders have said and do not write them."

4 When the seven thunders had spoken,
    I was about to write,
    and

I heard a voice
from heaven
saying,
"Seal up what the seven thunders have said
and do not write them."

The seven thunders didn't just make noise, they spoke also.

John had been given the command in Revelation 1:19 to write everything down. But when John was getting ready to write down what they said, a voice from heaven told him not to and to seal it up.

Apparently, God wanted John to hear these things but not anyone else. In Daniel 12:4-9 Daniel was told to seal the book until the end times.

Greek Paraphrase of Verse: 4
When the seven peals of thunder had spoken, I was about to write, but I heard a voice from heaven saying, "Seal up the things which the seven peals of thunder have spoken and do not write them down."

Verses 5-7
5 Then the angel I saw standing on the sea and on the land raised his right hand to heaven, 6 and swore by the One who lives forever and ever, who created heaven and what is in it, the earth and what is in it, and the sea and what is in it, that there will no longer be delay, 7 but in the days of the voice of the seventh angel, when he will blow his trumpet, then the mystery of God is finished, as He announced to His servants the prophets.

5 Then
the angel I saw
standing on the sea
and on the land
raised his right hand
to heaven,
6 and
swore by the One
who lives forever and ever,
who created heaven
and what is in it,
the earth
and what is in it,
and
the sea
and what is in it,
that there will no longer be delay,
7 but in the days
of the voice
of the seventh angel,
when he will blow his trumpet,

> then the mystery of God is finished,
> as He announced to His servants
> the prophets.

Verse: 5

⁵ Then the angel I saw standing on the sea and on the land raised his right hand to heaven,

This scene is like one in court. The angel must have the little scroll in his left hand as he raises his right hand toward heaven.

Deuteronomy 32:40, I raise My hand to heaven and declare: As surely as I live forever,

Verse: 6

⁶ and swore by the One who lives forever and ever, who created heaven and what is in it, the earth and what is in it, and the sea and what is in it, that there will no longer be delay,

The angel swore his oath in the name of God. All the rest of that is simply descriptions of God. He is also saying that there will no longer be a delay in the judgments to come.

Verse: 7

⁷ but in the days of the voice of the seventh angel, when he will blow his trumpet, then the mystery of God is finished, as He announced to His servants the prophets.

This 'but' is making a strong contrast. Instead of no further delays like he first said, there will be many more before the mystery of God is finished.

Greek Paraphrase of Verses: 5-7

Then the angel I had seen standing on the sea and the land raised his right hand to swear an oath to heaven, and swore an oath by the name of the One who lives forever and ever, who created heaven and the things in it, the earth and the things in it, and the sea and the things in it, that there will no longer be delay, but when it is time for the trumpet call of the seventh angel, when he is about to sound his trumpet, then the mystery of God that is, His hidden purpose and plan is finished, as He announced the good news to His servants the prophets.

Verse 8

⁸ Then the voice that I heard from heaven spoke to me again saying, "Go, take the scroll that lies open in the hand of the angel standing on the sea and on the land."

[8] Then
  the voice
    that I heard from heaven
    spoke
      to me
      again
      saying,
        "Go,
        take the scroll
          that lies open
          in the hand of the angel
            standing on the sea and on the land."

This is the third time John heard a great voice from heaven (Revelation 4:1; 10:4).

There is much speculation as to what was in this little scroll. Some think it's the same as the book with the seven seals, though I doubt it. Some think it is a message of woe to unbelievers. Others believe it is a message to the church. Still others think it is a further revelation of the events in Chapters 11-19.

I tend to believe it's just the revelation given in Chapter 11.

Greek Paraphrase of Verse: 8
Then the voice that I heard from heaven, *spoke* to me again saying, "Go, take the book which is open in the hand of the angel who is standing on the sea and on the land."

Verse 9
[9] So, I went to the angel, telling him to give me the little scroll. He said to me, "Take and eat it. It will be bitter in your stomach, but sweet as honey in your mouth."

[9] So
  I went to the angel,
    telling him to give me the little scroll.
      He said
        to me,
        "Take and eat it.
          It will be bitter
            in your stomach,
            but sweet
              as honey
              in your mouth."

So, John obeyed the voice from heaven, but the great angel told him to eat the scroll and that it would be sweet in his mouth but bitten in his stomach.

This is very similar to Ezekiel 2:8 – 3:3 where Ezekiel was commanded to eat a book full of lamentation and mourning, yet it would be sweet in his mouth.

I think God wanted John to digest the message. In other words, know it by heart before writing it down or going out to tell others what it said.

Greek Paraphrase of Verse: 9
So, I went up to the angel and told him to give me the little book. He said to me, "Take it and eat it. It will make your stomach bitter, but in your mouth, it will be as sweet as honey."

Verse 10
¹⁰ I took the little scroll out of the angel's hand and ate it. It was sweet as honey in my mouth, but when I ate it, my stomach became bitter.

¹⁰ I took the little scroll
　　out of the angel's hand
　　and ate it.
　　　It was sweet
　　　　as honey
　　　　in my mouth,
　　　　but when I ate it,
　　　　　my stomach became bitter.

When John obeyed, he found it to be just as the angel had said. The judgment day will be sweet for the redeemed but bitter for those unrepentant ones.

Greek Paraphrase of Verse: 10
So, I took the little book from the angel's hand and ate it. It was as sweet as honey in my mouth, but once I swallowed it, my stomach became bitter.

Verse 11
¹¹ And I was told, "You must prophesy again about many peoples, nations, tongues, and kings."

¹¹ And
　　I was told,
　　　"You must prophesy
　　　　again
　　　　about many peoples,
　　　　　nations,
　　　　　tongues,
　　　　　and kings."

The Greek word translated 'about' could also mean 'against.' This difference would only change the understanding right here but not later on. I think John is being told to prophesy about what all will happen to those people. So, the meaning is still the same.

Greek Paraphrase of Verse: 11
Then they said to me, "You must prophesy again concerning many peoples and nations and languages and kings."

Chapter Eleven

Chapter 11 continues the break between the sixth and seventh trumpets. It deals basically with the two witnesses whose identity has caused a great deal of controversy among Bible scholars.

Verse 1
The Two Witnesses
¹ Then I was given a measuring reed like a staff and was told, "Go and measure the temple of God and the altar, and those who worship there.

¹ Then
　I was given a measuring reed
　　like a staff
　　and was told,
　　　"Go and measure
　　　　the temple of God
　　　　and the altar,
　　　　　and those who worship there.

measuring reed – a reed; a staff made of a reed, a reed staff; a measuring reed or rod; a writer's reed, a pen

staff – a staff, a walking stick, a twig, rod, branch; a rod with which one is beaten; a staff as used on a journey, or to lean upon, or by shepherds; with a rod of iron, indicates the severest, most rigorous rule; a royal scepter

measure – to measure, to measure out or off; any space or distance with a measurer's reed or rule; metaphorically to judge according to any rule or standard, to estimate

worship – to kiss the hand to (towards) one, in token of reverence; among the Orientals, especially the Persians, to fall upon the knees and touch the ground with the forehead as an expression of profound reverence; in the NT by kneeling or prostration to do homage (to one) or make obeisance, whether in order to express respect or to make supplication

This command seems to have come from the angel since they were together in the last verse of Chapter 10.

First, John is given a long measuring reed similar to a shepherd's staff to measure the temple, the altar and all who worship there. This can't be Herod's temple since it was destroyed twenty years before John wrote Revelation.

Greek Paraphrase of Verse: 1
Then I was given a measuring rod like a staff and someone said, "Rise, go and measure the temple of God and the altar of incense, and count those who worship in it.

Verse 2
² But exclude the outer court of the temple and do not measure it, for it has been given to the nations, and they will trample the holy city for forty-two months.

² But
  exclude the outer court
    of the temple
    and do not measure it,
      for it has been given to the nations,
        and they will trample the holy city
          for forty-two months.

measure – to measure, to measure out or off; any space or distance with a measurer's reed or rule; metaphorically to judge according to any rule or standard, to estimate
trample – to tread; to trample, crush with the feet; to advance by setting foot upon, tread upon; to tread under foot, trample on, i.e. to treat with insult and contempt: to desecrate the holy city by devastation and outrage

Nations here is the same word often translated gentiles. So, John is being told not to include them because a special judgment has been reserved for them.

Greek Paraphrase of Verse: 2
But leave out the court of the Gentiles which is outside the temple and do not measure it, because it has been given to the Gentiles and they will trample the holy city for three and one-half years.

Verse 3
³ And I will empower my two witnesses, and they will prophesy for 1,260 days, clothed in sackcloth."

³ And
  I will empower my two witnesses,
    and they will prophesy
      for 1,260 days,
      clothed in sackcloth."

empower – give, give out, hand over, entrust, give back, give up; to give; to bestow a gift; to grant, give to one asking, let have; to supply, furnish, necessary things; to grant or permit one; to commission
sackcloth – a sack; a receptacle for holding or carrying various things, as money, food, etc.; a course cloth, a dark course stuff made especially from the hair of animals

The two witnesses appear for 42 months. They ae God's witnesses and they prophesy in sackcloth. Sackcloth usually indicated mourning. These witnesses are telling what will happen, but they are doing so with heavy hearts.

Greek Paraphrase of Verse: 3
And I will grant *authority* to My two witnesses, and they will prophesy for three and one-half years, dressed in sackcloth."

Verse 4
4 These are the two olive trees and the two lampstands that stand before the Lord of the earth.

4 These are the two olive trees
    and the two lampstands
    that stand before the Lord of the earth.

These two olive trees are Zerubbabel, the prince of David's line and Joshua the high priest. They minister, *'Not by strength or by might, but by My Spirit,' says the LORD of Hosts. Zechariah 4:6*

Greek Paraphrase of Verse: 4
These witnesses are the two olive trees and the two lampstands that stand before the Lord of the earth.

Verse 5
5 If anyone wants to harm them, fire comes out of their mouths and devours their enemies, so if anyone wants to harm them, he must be killed in this way.

5 If anyone wants to harm them,
    fire comes out of their mouths
      and devours their enemies,
        so if anyone wants to harm them,
          he must be killed in this way.

harm – to act unjustly or wickedly, to sin; to be a criminal, to have violated the laws in some way; to do wrong; to do hurt; to do some wrong or sin in some respect; to wrong someone, act wickedly towards him; to hurt, damage, harm
devours – to consume by eating, to eat up, devour; to devour, i.e. squander, waste: substance; to strip one of his goods; to ruin (by the infliction of injuries); by fire, to devour, i.e. to utterly consume, destroy; of the consumption of the strength of body and mind by strong emotions

enemies – hated, odious, hateful; hostile, hating, and opposing another; used of men as at enmity with God by their sin; opposing (God) in the mind; a certain enemy; the hostile one; the devil who is the most bitter enemy of the divine government

If anyone wanted to harm them, they would devour them with fire coming from their mouths. This was the accepted way God dealt with those who dissented.

This is similar to when Elijah called down fire from heaven on the soldiers who were coming after him, twice.

Greek Paraphrase of Verse: 5
If anyone tries to harm them, fire comes out of their mouths and consumes their enemies, so if anyone tries to harm them, he must be killed in this way.

Verse 6
⁶ These have the power to shut up the sky, so that rain will not fall during the days of their prophesying, and they have power over the waters to turn them into blood, and to strike the earth with every plague, as often as they want.

⁶ These have the power
    to shut up the sky,
        so that rain will not fall
           during the days of their prophesying
      and they have power
        over the waters
           to turn them into blood,
      and to strike the earth
        with every plague,
        as often as they want.

power – physical and mental power; the power of authority (influence) and of right (privilege); the power of rule or government (the power of him whose will and commands must be submitted to by others and obeyed); the power of judicial decisions; one who possesses authority; a ruler, a human magistrate

42 months without rain would be devastating to the economy. Blood in the waters would be even worse. Then, to top it all off, here come the plagues again.

This is reminiscent of Moses calling down all the plagues on Egypt.

Greek Paraphrase of Verse: 6
These two witnesses have the power from God to shut up the sky, so that no rain will fall during the days of their prophesying regarding judgment and salvation, and they have power over the seas and rivers to turn them

into blood, and to strike the earth with every kind of plague, as often as they wish.

Verse 7
The Witnesses Martyred
⁷ When they have finished their testimony, the beast that comes up out of the bottomless pit will make war with them and overcome and kill them.

⁷ When they have finished their testimony,
>   the beast
>   that comes up out of the bottomless pit
>   will make war with them
>   and overcome and kill them.

beast – a wild animal
bottomless pit – Bottomless; unbounded; the abyss; the pit; the immeasurable depth; of Orcus, a very deep gulf or chasm in the lowest parts of the earth used as the common receptacle of the dead and especially as the abode of demons
overcome – to conquer; to carry off the victory, come off victorious; when one is arraigned or goes to law, to win the case, maintain one's cause

This seems contradictory at first since God had already given the two witnesses the power to breathe fire on their enemies to devour them.
But the key here is their time of power is only 42 months. At the end of that time their power will be gone, and the beast will be able to kill them.

Greek Paraphrase of Verse: 7
When they have finished their testimony *and* given their evidence, the beast that comes up out of the bottomless pit will wage war with them, conquer them and kill them.

Verse 8
⁸ Their dead bodies will lie in the street of the great city, which is spiritually called Sodom and Egypt, where also their Lord was crucified.

⁸ Their dead bodies will lie in the street
>   of the great city,
>   which is spiritually called Sodom and Egypt,
>   where also their Lord was crucified.

Sodom – "burning" - a city destroyed by the Lord raining fire and brimstone on it
Egypt – "double straits" - a country occupying the northeast angle of Africa

It was an extreme sign of disrespect to leave the bodies of enemies in the streets to rot.

It is thought that the 'great city' mentioned here is Jerusalem which has fallen into moral and spiritual degradation.

Greek Paraphrase of Verse: 8
Their dead bodies *will lie exposed* in the open street of the great city Jerusalem, which in a spiritual sense is called by the symbolic and allegorical names of Sodom and Egypt, where also their Lord was crucified.

Verse 9
9 Those from the peoples, tribes, languages, and nations will look at their dead bodies for three and a half days and will not permit their bodies to be laid in a tomb.

9 Those
    from the peoples,
    tribes,
    languages,
    and nations
    will look at their dead bodies
      for three and a half days
      and will not permit their bodies to be laid in a tomb.

It is implied that people, at least representatives from all over the world, would come to view with contempt the dead bodies of the two witnesses.

Greek Paraphrase of Verse: 9
Those from the peoples, tribes, languages and nations will look at their dead bodies for three and a half days and will not allow their dead bodies to be laid in a tomb.

Verse 10
10 Those who live on the earth will gloat over them and celebrate and send gifts to one another, because these two prophets tormented those who live on the earth.

10 Those
    who live on the earth
      will gloat over them
      and
      celebrate
      and send gifts
        to one another,

because these two prophets tormented
those who live on the earth.

tormented – to test (metals) by the touchstone, which is a black siliceous stone used to test the purity of gold or silver by the color of the streak produced on it by rubbing it with either metal; to question by applying torture; to torture; to vex with grievous pains (of body or mind), to torment; to be harassed, distressed; of those who at sea are struggling with a head wind

Remember, the two witnesses had made the people of the earth miserable. Now that they are dead, all the people are going to rejoice. Note also that they are giving each other gifts. It's like a giant Christmas celebration but without any mention of Christ. Does that sound a little too familiar for comfort?

Greek Paraphrase of Verse: 10
And those non-believers who live on the earth will rejoice over them and celebrate, and they will send gifts to one another in celebration, because those two prophets tormented and troubled those who live on the earth.

Verse 11
The Witnesses Resurrected
[11] But after the three and a half days, the breath of life from God entered them, and they stood on their feet. Great fear fell upon those who saw them.

[11] But
after the three and a half days,
the breath
of life
from God
entered them,
and they stood on their feet.
Great fear fell upon those who saw them.

Wow! Can you imagine how frightened the people who saw this were? The two witnesses they had killed and reviled over for three and a half days had now come back to life and stood up to confront their enemies.

Greek Paraphrase of Verse: 11
But after three and a half days, the breath of life from God came into them, and they stood on their feet. Great fear *and* panic fell on those who were watching them.

Verse 12

12 And they heard a loud voice from heaven saying to them, "Come up here." They went up to heaven in the cloud, and their enemies watched them.

12 And
   they heard a loud voice
      from heaven
      saying
         to them,
         "Come up here."
            They went up to heaven
               in the cloud,
               and their enemies watched them.

Okay. There are many similarities between the ascension of Jesus and that of these two witnesses. The people who saw it had to be thinking about all Jesus said before He ascended to heaven.

Now, they should definitely be afraid of what is coming next.

Greek Paraphrase of Verse: 12
And the two witnesses heard a loud voice from heaven saying to them, "Come up here." Then they ascended into heaven in the cloud, and their enemies watched them go.

Verse 13

13 And at that hour, there was a great earthquake, and a tenth of the city fell. Seven thousand people were killed in the earthquake. The rest were terrified and gave glory to the God of heaven.

13 And
   at that hour,
      there was a great earthquake,
      and a tenth of the city fell.
      Seven thousand people were killed
         in the earthquake.
      The rest were terrified
         and gave glory to the God of heaven.

Apparently, while the people are watching the empty sky where the two witnesses had disappeared, a great earthquake hit the city destroying ten percent of it and killed seven thousand people.

The rest were terrified and finally gave glory to God. Is that going to be enough to save them?

Greek Paraphrase of Verse: 13
And in that very hour there was a great earthquake, and a tenth of the city fell and was destroyed. Seven thousand people were killed in the earthquake. And the rest who survived were overcome with terror, and they glorified the God of heaven as they recognized His awesome power.

Verse 14
[14] The second woe has passed. Behold, the third woe is coming quickly.

[14] The second woe has passed.
    Behold,
        the third woe is coming quickly.

    Well, again, we realize that our time is not God's time since the third woe is introduced in Chapter 15 but doesn't really come until Chapter 16.

Greek Paraphrase of Verse: 14
The second woe is past and behold, the third woe is coming quickly.

Verse 15
The Seventh Trumpet
[15] Then the seventh angel blew his trumpet, and there were loud voices in heaven, saying, "The kingdom of the world has become the kingdom of our Lord and of His Christ, and He will reign forever and ever."

[15] Then
    the seventh angel blew his trumpet,
      and there were loud voices
        in heaven,
        saying,
          "The kingdom
           of the world
           has become the kingdom
             of our Lord
             and of His Christ,
               and He will reign forever and ever."

    The seventh trumpet includes the seven bowls and the victory that follows. It is not the last trumpet of judgment mentioned in 1 Corinthians 15:52 and 1 Thessalonians 4:16. The trumpet that calls for the Rapture will be the last one to come before the wrath of God.
    The shout John heard is in expectation of the coming victory.

Greek Paraphrase of Verse: 15
Then the seventh angel sounded his trumpet, and there were loud voices in heaven, saying, "The right to rule the world with royal power belongs to our Lord and to His Christ, and He will reign forever and ever."

Verses 16-17
[16] And the twenty-four elders, who sit on their thrones before God, fell on their faces and worshiped God, [17] saying, "We give thanks to You, O Lord God Almighty, who is and who was, because You have taken Your great power and have begun to reign.

[16] And
   the twenty-four elders,
    who sit
      on their thrones
      before God,
    fell on their faces
    and
    worshiped God,
      [17] saying,
        "We give thanks to You,
          O Lord God Almighty,
          who is
          and who was,
          because You have taken Your great power
            and have begun to reign.

Verse 16
[16] And the twenty-four elders, who sit on their thrones before God, fell on their faces and worshiped God,

John was still in heaven and saw for the eighth time the twenty-four elders who sat before God on their thrones. When the great shout of victory is given, they fall on their faces and worship God.

Verse 17
[17] saying, "We give thanks to You, O Lord God Almighty, who is and who was, because You have taken Your great power and have begun to reign.

They worship God by singing praises to His name. They are also celebrating the fact that God is not only in control as He has been since the beginning of time, but now God is going to reign. This means that God will now literally control everything. That's different from before.

Greek Paraphrase of Verses: 16-17
And the twenty-four elders, who sit on their thrones before God, fell face downward and worshiped God, saying, "To You we give thanks, O Lord God Almighty the Omnipotent, the Ruler of all, Who is and Who was, because You have taken Your great power *and* the sovereignty which is rightly Yours and have[now begun to reign.

Verse 18
[18] The nations were angry, and Your wrath has come. The time has come for the dead to be judged, and to reward Your servants the prophets, to the saints, and those who fear Your name, the small and the great, and to destroy those who destroy the earth."

[18] The nations were angry,
    and Your wrath has come.
  The time has come
    for the dead to be judged,
    and
    to reward Your servants
      the prophets,
      to the saints,
      and those who fear Your name,
        the small and the great,
      and to destroy those who destroy the earth."

destroy – to change for the worse, to corrupt; of minds, morals; to destroy, ruin; to consume; to destroy, to kill

The twenty-four elders are still singing the victory song, but complete victory will still be coming in stages and will take some time to complete.

Greek Paraphrase of Verse: 18
The Gentiles became enraged, and Your wrath and indignation came. The time came for the dead to be judged, and the time came to reward Your bond-servants the prophets, God's people, those who fear Your name, the small and the great, and the time came to destroy those who destroy the earth."

Verse 19
[19] And the temple of God in heaven was opened, and the ark of His covenant appeared in His temple. There were flashes of lightning, rumblings, thunders, an earthquake, and a great hailstorm.

[19] And
  the temple
    of God
    in heaven
    was opened,
      and the ark
        of His covenant
        appeared in His temple.
  There were flashes of lightning,
    rumblings,
    thunders,
    an earthquake,
    and a great hailstorm.

ark – a wooden chest or box; in the NT the ark of the covenant, in the temple at Jerusalem; of Noah's vessel built in the form of an ark

The temple in Jerusalem may have been destroyed but the true temple of God was always in heaven. Now, John is in heaven looking on the majesty of God's temple. That wasn't all though. The ark of God's covenant was also visible in His temple

Greek Paraphrase of Verse: 19
And the temple of God which is in heaven was opened, and the ark of His covenant appeared in His temple. And there were flashes of lightning, loud rumblings, peals of thunder, an earthquake and a great hailstorm.

Chapter Twelve

The woman clothed with the sun (Israel) iso about to give birth. Meanwhile, the great red dragon who swept away one-third of the stars, is waiting to devour the child at birth but when she delivers, God takes the child up to Him.

The archangel and his angels fight the devil and the archangel throws the devil and his angels down to the earth.

Verse 1

The Woman, the Child, and the Dragon

¹ A great sign appeared in heaven: a woman clothed with the sun, with the moon under her feet, and a crown of twelve stars on her head.

¹ A great sign appeared
    in heaven:
    a woman clothed with the sun,
    with the moon under her feet,
        and a crown of twelve stars on her head.

sign – a sign, mark, token; that by which a person or a thing is distinguished from others and is known; a sign, prodigy, portent, i.e. an unusual occurrence, transcending the common course of nature; of signs foretelling remarkable events soon to happen; of miracles and wonders by which God authenticates the men sent by him, or by which men prove that the cause they are pleading is God's

A great sign? In the sky? Who is she and what does she represent? Most think she represents Israel.

This resembles Joseph's second dream in Genesis 37 where Jacob was the sun, Leah was the moon and the 12 stars were him and his 11 brothers.

Thus, the woman probably represents Israel (royal mother, Isaiah 54:1; Galatians 4:26) standing on the moon with authority over lesser things with the redeemed of the 12 tribes as stars in her crown.

Greek Paraphrase of Verse: 1

A great sign, a warning of an ominous and frightening future event, appeared in heaven: a woman clothed with the sun, with the moon beneath her feet, and a crown of twelve stars on her head.

Verse 2

² She was pregnant and cried out in labor and in pain to give birth.

² She was pregnant
    and cried out

> in labor
> and
> in pain
> to give birth.

This could represent the long labor and pains Israel went through in the hundreds of years they expected the Messiah.

Isaiah 26:17, As a pregnant woman about to give birth writhes and cries out in her pains, so we were before You, LORD.

Greek Paraphrase of Verse: 2
She was with child, the Messiah, and being in labor, she cried out in pain to give birth.

Verse 3
³ Then another sign appeared in heaven, and behold, a great red dragon having seven heads and ten horns, and on his heads were seven diadems.

³ Then
  another sign appeared
    in heaven,
    and behold,
      a great red dragon having seven heads and ten horns,
        and on his heads were seven diadems.

diadems – a diadem; a blue band marked with white which Persian kings used to bind on the turban or tiara; the kingly ornament for the head, the crown

The red dragon is in the form of a serpent with seven heads, ten horns and a crown or royal diadem on each head.

In verse 9, he is called the devil, Satan. This signifies that the devil is a murderer and has been a murderer from the beginning. Christ described him as such in John 8:44.

The seven heads don't symbolize wisdom but the shrewdness of the devil. The ten horns show his claim of complete power which of course is false. But he was allowed to have power on earth. The seven crowns or royal diadems signify his claimed authority over the kingdoms of the earth.

Greek Paraphrase of Verse: 3
Then another sign of warning was seen in heaven, and behold, a great fiery red dragon, Satan, with seven heads and ten horns, and on his heads were seven royal crowns.

Verse 4
⁴ His tail swept away a third of the stars in heaven and threw them to the earth. And the dragon stood before the woman who was about to give birth, so that when she gave birth, he might devour her child.

⁴ His tail swept away a third of the stars
    in heaven
    and threw them to the earth.
  And
  the dragon stood
    before the woman
      who was about to give birth,
      so that
        when she gave birth
        he might devour her child.

devour – to consume by eating, to eat up, devour; to devour, i.e. squander, waste: substance; to strip one of his goods; to ruin (by the infliction of injuries); by fire, to devour, i.e. to utterly consume, destroy; of the consumption of the strength of body and mind by strong emotions

He swept one-third of the stars down to the earth. Some think this refers to the time when Satan was thrown out of heaven and he took a third of the angels with him. Others think this was just a display of his power.

Greek Paraphrase of Verse: 4
His tail swept across the sky *and* swept away a third of the stars of heaven and flung them to the earth. And the dragon stood in front of the woman who was about to give birth, so that when she gave birth, he might devour her child.

Verse 5
⁵ And she gave birth to a son, a male child, who is going to rule all the nations with an iron staff. And her child was caught up to God to His throne.

⁵ And
  she gave birth
    to a son,
      a male child,
      who is going to rule all the nations
        with an iron staff.
  And
  her child was caught up to God
    to His throne.

caught up – to seize, carry off by force; to seize on, claim for one's self eagerly; to snatch out or away

Apparently, the serpent's power wasn't what he thought it was. He wanted to devour the child, but God wasn't about to let that happen.

Notice the son, a male child, will rule all the nations. Most think this refers to Christ. But there are some who believe he represents the Church.

Remember, John's focus here is not on salvation but on judgement.

Greek Paraphrase of Verse: 5
And she gave birth to a Son, a male *Child,* who is destined to rule all the nations like a shepherd with a rod of iron. And her Child was caught up to God and to His throne.

Verse 6
⁶ Then the woman fled into the wilderness where she had a place prepared by God, so that there she would be nourished for 1,260 days.

⁶ Then
  the woman fled
    into the wilderness
      where she had a place
        prepared by God,
        so that there she would be nourished for 1,260 days.

From verse 5 to verse 6, the narrative goes from that time to the future. Verse 5 says she was caught up to God's throne. But then verse 6 says she fled into the wilderness to a place God prepared for her. This doesn't happen until toward the end of all these things being revealed.

Greek Paraphrase of Verse: 6
Then the woman fled into the wilderness where she had a place prepared for her by God, so that she would be nourished there for three and one-half years.

Verses 7-8
The Dragon Thrown Out of Heaven
⁷ And there was war in heaven. Michael and his angels fought against the dragon. The dragon and his angels also fought, ⁸ but they did not prevail, and there was no longer a place for them in heaven.

⁷ And
  there was war
    in heaven.
    Michael
      and his angels

fought against the dragon.
The dragon
and his angels
also fought,
⁸ but they did not prevail,
and there was no longer a place
for them
in heaven.

Verse: 7

⁷ *And there was war in heaven. Michael and his angels fought against the dragon. The dragon and his angels also fought,*

Michael – "who is like God" – the first of the chief princes or archangels who is supposed to be the guardian angel of the Israelites

This does not refer to the original battle but to a future one where the devil will fight one more battle against God's angels. The Greek word order implies that Michael started this fight to finally get rid of the devil.

Verse: 8

⁸ *but they did not prevail, and there was no longer a place for them in heaven.*

prevail – to be strong; to be strong in body, to be robust, to be in sound health; to have power; to have power as shown by extraordinary deeds; to exert, wield power, to have strength to overcome; to be a force, avail; to be serviceable; to be able, can

Satan isn't near as strong as he though and bragged that he was. After this, there was no more place for Satan and his angels in the heavenlies.

What conclusion do we draw from this today? Simply that Satan will lose and be destroyed.

Greek Paraphrase of Verses: 7-8

And war broke out in heaven. Michael, the archangel, and his angels fought against the dragon. The dragon and his angels fought, but they were not strong enough *and* did not prevail, and there was no longer a place to be found for them in heaven.

Verse 9

⁹ *The great dragon was thrown out, the ancient serpent who is called the devil and Satan, the one who deceives the whole world. He was thrown down to earth, and his angels with him.*

⁹ The great dragon was thrown out,
    the ancient serpent
      who is called the devil and Satan,
      the one who deceives the whole world.
    He was thrown down
      to earth,
      and his angels with him.

The ancient serpent refers to the fact that this is the same serpent (Satan, the devil) that tempted Eve in the Garden of Eden.

The basic meaning of the word 'devil' is slanderer and the meaning of the word Satan is the adversary. He is also described as the deceiver of the whole world.

But once Michael and his angels defeat the devil and his angels, they will be thrown down to the earth. But he isn't bound yet. That comes later.

Greek Paraphrase of Verse: 9
And the great dragon was thrown down, the age-old serpent who is called the devil and Satan, the one who *continually* deceives *and* seduces the entire inhabited world. He was thrown down to the earth, and his angels were thrown down with him.

Verse 10
¹⁰ *Then I heard a loud voice in heaven, saying, "Now the salvation, and the power, and the kingdom of our God and the authority of His Christ have come, because the accuser of our brothers has been thrown out, the one who accuses them before our God day and night.*

¹⁰ Then
  I heard a loud voice
    in heaven,
  saying,
    "Now
    the salvation,
    and the power,
    and the kingdom
      of our God
    and the authority
      of His Christ
      have come,
        because the accuser
        of our brothers
        has been thrown out,
        the one who accuses them
          before our God
          day and night.
power – strength, power, ability (word we get dynamite from)

authority – physical and mental power; the power of authority (influence) and of right (privilege); the power of rule or government (the power of him whose will and commands must be submitted to by others and obeyed); the power of judicial decisions; one who possesses authority; a ruler, a human magistrate

John is still in heaven when he hears the loud voice. This is not the voice of God. Notice that the voice referred to 'our brothers.' Therefore, the voice could be the collective voice of the people of God who are there or maybe even the 24 elders. Whoever they are, they are rejoicing that Satan has been cast out.

Now, salvation has come!

Greek Paraphrase of Verse: 10
Then I heard a loud voice in heaven, saying, "Now the salvation, power, and reign of our God, and the authority of His Christ have come, because the accuser of our believing brothers and sisters has been thrown down at last. The one who accuses them and keeps bringing charges of sinful behavior against them before our God day and night.

Verse 11
11 They overcame him because of the blood of the Lamb and by the word of their testimony, and they did not love their lives even when faced with death.

11 They overcame him
   because of the blood
     of the Lamb
  and
  by the word
    of their testimony,
  and
  they did not love their lives
    even when faced with death.

overcame – to conquer; to carry off the victory, come off victorious; when one is arraigned or goes to law, to win the case, maintain one's cause

This is referring to the believers who won out over Satan in the end. They did so only by the blood of the Lamb and their testimony. They weren't afraid to lose their lives when Satan threatened to kill them.

Greek Paraphrase of Verse: 11
And they overcame and conquered him because of the blood of the Lamb and because of the word of their testimony, for they did not love their lives and renounce their faith even when faced with death.

Verse 12

¹² For this reason, rejoice, O heavens, and you who live in them. Woe to the earth and the sea, because the devil has come down to you with great wrath, knowing that he has only a short time."

¹² For this reason,
   rejoice,
      O heavens,
         and you who live in them.
   Woe to the earth
      and the sea,
      because the devil has come down
         to you
         with great wrath,
         knowing that he has only a short time."

This is still the loud voice of the believers from verse 10. Again, the voice is calling for rejoicing because of Satan being thrown down.

This does not mean that Satan is defeated yet. He will continue to cause trouble for the inhabitants of the earth throughout the rest of the tribulation period.

Greek Paraphrase of Verse: 12

Therefore, rejoice, O heavens and you who live in them in the presence of God. Woe to the earth and the sea, because the devil has come down to you in great wrath, knowing that he has *only* a short time remaining!"

Verse 13

The Woman Persecuted

¹³ When the dragon saw that he had been thrown down to the earth, he persecuted the woman who gave birth to the male child.

¹³ When the dragon saw
      that he had been thrown down
         to the earth,
      he persecuted the woman
         who gave birth to the male child.

The devil found the woman (Israel) and continued to torment her. Throughout its history, Israel faced hard times and much persecution but this last one will be so much worse. Some think this is what Jeremiah was talking about in:

Jeremiah 30:7, How awful that day will be! There will be none like it! It will be a time of trouble for Jacob, but he will be delivered out of it.

Greek Paraphrase of Verse: 13
And when the dragon saw that he had been thrown down to the earth,
he persecuted the woman who had given birth to the male *Child*.

Verse 14

14 The two wings of the great eagle were given to the woman, so that she could
fly from the presence of the serpent into the wilderness to her place, where
she was nourished for a time, times, and half a time.

14 The two wings
    of the great eagle
    were given to the woman,
      so that she could fly
        from the presence of the serpent
        into the wilderness
        to her place,
          where she was nourished
            for a time,
            times,
            and half a time.

This is the time mentioned in verse 6. The woman (Israel) is able to get away from Satan with the eagle wings given to her.

She is able to stay there for three and a half years.

Greek Paraphrase of Verse: 14
But the two wings of the great eagle were given to the woman, so that she
could fly into the wilderness to her place, where she was nourished for
three and one-half years, away from the presence of the serpent, Satan.

Verse 15

15 The serpent spewed water like a river out of his mouth after the woman, so
that he might cause her to be swept away with the flood.

15 The serpent spewed water
    like a river
    out of his mouth
    after the woman,
      so that he might cause her
        to be swept away with the flood.

Some take the water to be a literal flood in an attempt to drown people. Others think it refers to armies sent to destroy the people like in Jeremiah 46:8.

Greek Paraphrase of Verse: 15
And the serpent spewed water like a river out of his mouth after the woman, so that he might cause her to be swept away with the flood.

Verse 16
16 But the earth helped the woman, and the earth opened its mouth and swallowed up the river which the dragon had spewed out of his mouth.

16 But
  the earth helped the woman,
    and the earth opened its mouth
      and swallowed up the river
        which the dragon had spewed out of his mouth.

God caused the earth to open up and swallow the water before it could harm the people.

Greek Paraphrase of Verse: 16
But the earth helped the woman, and the earth opened its mouth and swallowed up the river the dragon had hurled out of his mouth.

Verse 17
17 So, the dragon was enraged at the woman and went off to make war with the rest of her children, who keep the commandments of God and hold to the testimony of Jesus.

17 So, the dragon was enraged
  at the woman,
  and went off to make war with the rest of her children,
    who keep the commandments
      of God
      and hold to the testimony of Jesus.

Now, the devil is really angry. He decides to go off and attack others who are believers.

Greek Paraphrase of Verse: 17
So, the dragon was furious with the woman, and he went off to wage war on the rest of her children, those who keep *and* obey the commandments of God and have the testimony of Jesus holding firmly to it and bearing witness to Him.

Chapter Thirteen

This chapter is highlighted by the beast out of the sea and the beast out of the earth.

First is the beast rising out of the sea with seven heads, ten horns and ten crowns. He is described as blaspheming and having power and cruelty. The beast coming out of the earth has two horns, deceiving the world by its false miracles and causing everyone to receive his mark on their right hand. His number is 666.

Verse 1
The Beast from the Sea
¹ The dragon stood on the sand of the seashore. Then I saw a beast coming up out of the sea, having ten horns and seven heads, and on his horns were ten diadems, and on his heads were blasphemous names.

¹ The dragon stood on the sand of the seashore.
  Then
  I saw a beast
    coming up
      out of the sea,
    having ten horns and seven heads,
      and on his horns were ten diadems,
      and on his heads were blasphemous names.

diadems – a diadem; a blue band marked with white which Persian kings used to bind on the turban or tiara; the kingly ornament for the head, the crown

This is another one of those differences between the Textus Receptus (KJV) and the Nestle Aland (modern translations).

The Textus Receptus (KJV) has "And I stood upon the sand of the sea."

There are other older manuscripts that back up the Nestle Alan text.

Regardless, there is a new beast coming up out of the sea. This begins the reign of the Antichrist. This beast isn't called that here, but later verses will do so.

Some think this means that he came out of the peoples of the world not the actual earth.

Greek Paraphrase of Verse: 1
And the dragon, Satan, stood on the sandy shore of the sea. Then I saw a vicious beast coming up out of the sea with ten horns and seven heads, and on its horns were ten royal crowns, and on his heads were blasphemous names.

Verse 2

² The beast I saw was like a leopard, his feet were like those of a bear, and his mouth was like the mouth of a lion. The dragon gave him his power, his throne, and great authority.

² The beast I saw
    was like a leopard,
    his feet were like those of a bear,
    and
    his mouth was like the mouth of a lion.
    The dragon gave him
        his power,
        his throne,
        and
        great authority.

authority – strength, power, ability (word we get dynamite from)

The animal John saw was a combination of all four beasts in Daniel's dream in Daniel 7.

This beast seems to represent the Antichrist's kingdom but also the Antichrist himself. His purpose will be to gain religious, political and economic power over the entire world later on during the tribulation period.

The dragon (serpent/Satan) gave him his power and his authority. So, he is sent by Satan to do his dirty work.

Greek Paraphrase of Verse: 2

And the beast that I saw resembled a leopard, but his feet were like those of a bear, and his mouth was like that of a lion. And the dragon gave him his power, his throne and great authority.

Verse 3

³ One of his heads appeared to be fatally wounded, and his fatal wound was healed. The whole earth was amazed and followed the beast.

³ One of his heads
    appeared to be fatally wounded,
        and his fatal wound was healed.
  The whole earth was amazed
    and followed the beast.

Satan is trying to imitate the resurrection by healing one of the heads that had been mortally wounded. But because of this, the whole world was amazed and followed the beast.

Greek Paraphrase of Verse: 3
I saw **one of his heads which seemed to have a fatal wound, but his fatal wound was healed. And the entire earth** *followed* **in amazement after the beast.**

Verse 4
⁴ They worshiped the dragon because he gave authority to the beast. And they worshiped the beast, saying, "Who is like the beast, and who is able to wage war against him?"

⁴ They worshiped the dragon
　　because he gave authority to the beast.
　And
　they worshiped the beast,
　　saying,
　　　"Who is like the beast,
　　　　and who is able to wage war against him?"

authority – different from verse 2 – physical and mental power; the power of authority (influence) and of right (privilege); the power of rule or government (the power of him whose will and commands must be submitted to by others and obeyed); the power of judicial decisions; one who possesses authority; a ruler, a human magistrate

　　As the people worshiped the beast, they were actually worshiping the serpent as well. Their words of praise don't actually mention Satan or the serpent but the beast only.
　　These words are similar to the ones the Israelites used in Exodus 15:11 and Micah 7:18.

Greek Paraphrase of Verse: 4
They fell down and worshiped the dragon because he gave his authority to the beast. They also worshiped the beast, saying, "Who is as great as the beast, and who is able to wage war against him?"

Verse 5
⁵ A mouth was given to him to speak arrogant words and blasphemies, and authority was given to him to act for forty-two months.

⁵ A mouth was given to him
　　to speak arrogant words and blasphemies,
　　and authority was given
　　　to him
　　　to act
　　　　for forty-two months.

arrogant – great; used of intensity and its degrees: with great effort, of the affections and emotions of the mind, of natural events powerfully affecting the senses: violent, mighty, strong; persons, eminent for ability, virtue, authority, power; things esteemed highly for their importance: of great moment, of great weight, importance; splendid, prepared on a grand scale, stately

authority – same as verse 4

The mouth given to him was one with which he could speak eloquently and convincingly to the people. Here's that three and a half years again.

Greek Paraphrase of Verse: 5

And the beast was given a mouth to have the power of speech, uttering arrogant and blasphemous words, and he was given the freedom *and* authority to act *and* to do as he pleased for three and a half years.

Verse 6

⁶ He opened his mouth in blasphemies against God, to blaspheme His name and His dwelling, that is, those who live in heaven.

⁶ He opened his mouth
   in blasphemies
      against God,
         to blaspheme His name
          and His dwelling,
            that is,
               those who live in heaven.

He is sitting in the temple as if he was God, he blasphemies God and everything about Him.

Greek Paraphrase of Verse: 6

And he opened his mouth to speak blasphemies against God, to speak evil of His name and His tabernacle, and those who live in heaven.

Verse 7

⁷ He was permitted to wage war against the saints and to overcome them. He was also given authority over every tribe, people, language, and nation.

⁷ He was permitted to wage war
   against the saints
   and
   to overcome them.
  He was also given authority
   over every tribe,
      people,

language,
and nation.

authority – physical and mental power; the power of authority (influence) and of right (privilege); the power of rule or government (the power of him whose will and commands must be submitted to by others and obeyed); the power of judicial decisions; one who possesses authority; a ruler, a human magistrate

The beast gets his permission and authority from Satan, but Satan can only give it as long as God allows him to do so. This will continue through the last three and a half years of the tribulation

Greek Paraphrase of Verse: 7
He was also permitted to wage war against God's people and to overcome them. He was also given authority *and* power over every tribe, people, language and nation.

Verse 8
8 All who live on the earth will worship him, everyone whose name has not been written from the foundation of the world in the book of life of the Lamb who has been slain.

8 All
　　who live on the earth
　　will worship him,
　　　　everyone whose name has not been written
　　　　　　from the foundation of the world
　　　　　in the book
　　　　　　of life
　　　　　　of the Lamb
　　　　　　　who has been slain.

Only those whose names are not in the Lamb's Book of Life will bow down and worship the beast.

Satan craves for people to worship him. Remember, he tried to get Jesus to worship him.

"Before the foundation of the world" has two different interpretations.

The first is that it refers to the names that were written. The other one is that it refers to the sacrificial death of Christ as God's Lamb.

Greek Paraphrase of Verse: 8
All who live on the earth will fall down *and* worship him, *everyone* whose name has not been written since the foundation of the world in the Lamb's Book of Life, who has been slain as a willing sacrifice.

Verse 9
⁹ If anyone has an ear, let him hear.

⁹ If anyone has an ear,
    let him hear.

This sentence is repeated throughout the book of Revelation and it is always used to draw attention to the importance of what follows or even what was just said.

Greek Paraphrase of Verse: 9
If anyone has an ear, let him hear.

Verse 10
¹⁰ If anyone is destined for captivity, into captivity he goes. If anyone kills with the sword, with the sword he will be killed. Here is the endurance and the faith of the saints.

¹⁰ If anyone is destined for captivity,
    into captivity he goes.
  If anyone kills
    with the sword,
      with the sword he will be killed.
  Here is the endurance
    and the faith
    of the saints.

endurance – steadfastness, constancy, endurance; in the NT the characteristic of a man who is not swerved from his deliberate purpose and his loyalty to faith and piety by even the greatest trials and sufferings; patiently, and steadfastly; a patient, steadfast waiting for; a patient enduring, sustaining, perseverance

This sounds like 'an eye for an eye.' Jesus addressed this in:
Matthew 26:52 Then Jesus said to him, "Put your sword back into its place, for all who take up the sword will perish by the sword.
I think there is special emphasis on the word 'Here.' It draws attention to the excessive trials of their faith the believers will have to go through.

Greek Paraphrase of Verse: 10
If anyone *is destined* for captivity, he will go into captivity. If anyone kills with a sword, he must be killed with a sword. Here is the call for the patient endurance and the faithfulness of the saints which is seen in the response of God's people to difficult times.

Verse 11
The Beast from the Earth
[11] Then I saw another beast coming up out of the earth, and he had two horns like a lamb, but he spoke like a dragon.

[11] Then
  I saw another beast
    coming up out of the earth,
    and he had two horns
      like a lamb,
      but he spoke like a dragon.

The first beast came up out of the sea, now this one is coming up out of the earth. Since he came out of the earth, it is clear that he didn't come from heaven. He's a contradiction. He has the two horns of a lamb but speaks like a serpent.

He will become a part of the triad which will be a false imitation of the Trinity.

Greek Paraphrase of Verse: 11
Then I saw another beast rising up out of the earth and he had two horns like a lamb, but he spoke like a dragon.

Verse 12
[12] He exercises all the authority of the first beast on his behalf and makes the earth and those who live in it to worship the first beast, whose fatal wound was healed.

[12] He exercises all the authority
    of the first beast
      on his behalf,
     and makes the earth
       and those who live in it
      to worship the first beast,
        whose fatal wound was healed.

authority – physical and mental power; the power of authority (influence) and of right (privilege); the power of rule or government (the power of him whose will and commands must be submitted to by others and obeyed); the power of judicial decisions; one who possesses authority; a ruler, a human magistrate

This second beast will have all the power and authority that the first beast has. Again, Satan will be the source of his power too.

Greek Paraphrase of Verse: 12
He exercises all the authority of the first beast when the two are together.
And he makes the earth and those who live in it worship the first beast,
whose deadly wound was healed.

Verse 13

[13] *He performs great signs, so that he even makes fire come down out of heaven to the earth in the presence of men.*

[13] He performs great signs,
> so that he even makes fire come down
>> out of heaven
>> to the earth
>> in the presence of men.

Calling fire out of heaven is clearly an imitation of when Elijah did it at God's instruction in 1 Kings 18:22-39. The second beast is considered to be the false prophet.

Greek Paraphrase of Verse: 13
He performs great awe-inspiring acts, even making fire fall from the sky to the earth, right before men's eyes.

Verse 14

[14] *He deceives those who live on the earth because of the signs that he is permitted to perform on behalf of the beast, telling those who live on the earth to make an image of the beast who had the sword wound and yet lived.*

[14] He deceives
> those who live on the earth
> because of the signs
>> that he is permitted to perform
>>> on behalf of the beast,
>> telling those
>>> who live on the earth
>>> to make an image
>>>> of the beast
>>>>> who had the sword wound
>>>>> and yet lived.

By his apparent miracles, the second beast will mislead the inhabitants or non-believers of the earth.

Jesus warned about this very thing in:

Matthew 24:24 For false Christs and false prophets will arise and will do great signs and wonders, so as to mislead, if possible, even the elect.

The Antichrist and the false prophet will be the end of all of that kind of deception. Thus, the image of the beast will become the focus of the false worship of the beast.

Greek Paraphrase of Verse: 14
He deceives the unconverted ones who live on the earth into believing him because of the signs which he was given by Satan to perform in the presence of the first beast, telling those who live on the earth to make an image of the beast who was fatally wounded by the sword and has come back to life.

Verse 15
15 He was permitted to give breath to the image of the beast, so that the image of the beast could speak and cause all who do not worship the image of the beast to be killed.

15 He was permitted to give breath
   to the image of the beast,
     so that the image
      of the beast
     could speak and cause all who do not worship the image
      of the beast
     to be killed.

The second beast will have the power (from Satan?) to give life to the image of the beast. Some think this will not be real but faked somehow.

All of this will fulfill the prophesy of:

2 Thessalonians 2:9-12, The one coming is based on the work of Satan, with all power and signs and false wonders, and with every unrighteous deception among those who are perishing, because they did not accept the love of the truth in order to be saved. For this reason, God, will send them a strong delusion so that they will believe what is false, so that they all will be judged, those who did not believe the truth, but took pleasure in unrighteousness.

Greek Paraphrase of Verse: 15
He is given the power to give breath to the image of the beast, so that the image of the beast will even appear to speak and cause those who do not bow down *and* worship the image of the beast to be put to death.

Verses 16-17
16 And he causes all, the small and the great, the rich and the poor, and the freemen and the slaves, to be given a mark on their right hand or on their

forehead, ¹⁷ *so that no one will be able to buy or to sell unless he has the mark, either the name of the beast or the number of his name.*

¹⁶ And
   he causes all,
      the small and the great,
      the rich and the poor,
      and the freemen and the slaves,
      to be given a mark
         on their right hand
         or on their forehead,
            ¹⁷ so that no one will be able to buy or to sell
               unless he has the mark,
                  either the name of the beast
                  or the number of his name.

¹⁶ And he causes all, the small and the great, the rich and the poor, and the freemen and the slaves, to be given a mark on their right hand or on their forehead,

mark – a stamp or imprinted mark

No one will escape getting the mark on their foreheads. This will be Satan's substitute for the mark put on the foreheads of the 144,000 in Revelation 7:3.

The mark could be engraved, etched, branded, cut or imprinted. Any of those ways, it would be permanent.

It's very much like the branding of cattle.

¹⁷ so that no one will be able to buy or to sell unless he has the mark, either the name of the beast or the number of his name.

The Antichrist can control the economy of the entire world by means of the mark. Remember in Verse 15 anyone who refused to take the mark would be killed.

Greek Paraphrase of Verses: 16-17
He also compels all, the small and the great, the rich and the poor, the freemen and the slaves, to be given a mark on their right hand or on their forehead signifying allegiance to the beast, so that no one will be able to buy or sell, except the one who has the mark, *either* the name of the beast or the number of his name.

Verse 18
¹⁸ *Here is wisdom. The one who has understanding must calculate the number of the beast, for the number is that of a man. His number is 666.*

¹⁸ Here is wisdom.
> The one
>> who has understanding
>> must calculate the number
>>> of the beast,
>>> for the number is that of a man.
>>> His number is 666.

wisdom – wisdom, broad and full of intelligence; used of the knowledge of very diverse matters; the wisdom which belongs to men; the varied knowledge of things human and divine, acquired by acuteness and experience, and summed up in maxims and proverbs; the science and learning; supreme intelligence, such as belongs to God; the wisdom of God as evinced in forming and executing counsels in the formation and government of the world and the scriptures

Remember there are two types of wisdom, the one that man can accomplish and the one that only comes from God. Here, I think it is implied that only God has the wisdom to understand the number.

The best explanation I've heard is that '6' is the number standing for mankind and '3' of course stands for the Trinity. Therefore, the Antichrist believes he is god or is trying to get the people to believe he is a god.

Greek Paraphrase of Verse: 18
Here is wisdom. Let the person who has enough understanding calculate the number of the beast, for it is the imperfect number of a man. His number is six hundred and sixty-six.

Chapter Fourteen

This chapter starts with the Lamb on mount Zion and with Him are the 144,000. The angel flies in the midst of heaven with the everlasting Gospel. Another angel announces the fall of Babylon. A third angel announces God's judgments against those who worship the beast or his image.

The patience of the saints is mentioned, and the blessedness of those who die in the Lord. Next comes the man on the white cloud with a sickle, reaping the earth.

Then the angel with the sickle is commanded by another angel who had power over fire, to gather the vines of the earth. They gather them and throw them in the great winepress of God's wrath and the blood comes out for a long distance.

Verse 1
The Lamb and the 144,000
¹ Then I looked, and behold, the Lamb was standing on Mount Zion, and with Him 144,000 having His name and the name of His Father written on their foreheads.

¹ Then
  I looked,
    and behold,
      the Lamb was standing
        on Mount Zion,
        and with Him 144,000 having His name
          and the name of His Father
          written on their foreheads.

Don't get confused. This is a glimpse of the future beyond where we've been so far. It's a glimpse of the final victory. Jesus will stand on Mount Zion in Jerusalem, the capital of Christ's millennial kingdom.

The 144,000 is looked at in several different ways. One is that they are the elders mentioned in Chapter 7. Another view is that they are faithful believers of all history. Still another view is that the number 144,000 represents fullness here. Therefore, it includes all believers of all ages.

Greek Paraphrase of Verse: 1
Then I looked, and behold, I saw the Lamb standing firmly established on Mount Zion, and with Him a hundred and forty-four thousand who had His name and His Father's name written on their foreheads signifying God's own possession.

Verse 2
² I heard a voice from heaven, like the sound of many waters and like the sound of loud thunder. The voice I heard was like the sound of harpists playing on their harps.

² I heard a voice
   from heaven,
   like the sound of many waters
   and like the sound of loud thunder.
  The voice
  I heard
  was like the sound
    of harpists playing on their harps.

John is on earth looking up this time. The sound is described much the same way the voice of Jesus was in Revelation 1:15.

Greek Paraphrase of Verse: 2
And I heard a voice from heaven, like the sound of great waters and like the rumbling of mighty thunder. The voice I heard seemed like music and was like *the sound* of harpists playing on their harps.

Verse 3
³ They sang a new song before the throne and before the four living creatures and the elders, but no one could learn the song except the 144,000 who had been redeemed from the earth.

³ They sang a new song
   before the throne
   and
   before the four living creatures
   and
   the elders,
   but no one could learn the song
    except the 144,000
     who had been redeemed from the earth.

This is a new song to the Lord much like those in various Psalms like:
Psalm 33:3, Sing a new song to Him; play skillfully on the strings, with a joyful shout.
It is significant that these singers and harpists are not only in heaven but at the foot of the throne.
The same discussion is here with the 144,000 as in Verse 1.

Greek Paraphrase of Verse: 3
And they sang a new song before the throne of God and before the four living creatures and the elders, but no one could learn the song except the hundred and forty-four thousand who had been ransomed from the earth.

Verses 4-5

⁴ These are the ones not defiled with women, for they have kept themselves pure. These are the ones who follow the Lamb wherever He goes. They have been redeemed from among men as first fruits to God and the Lamb. ⁵ No lie was found in their mouths. They are blameless.

⁴ These are the ones
    not defiled with women,
        for they have kept themselves pure.
  These are the ones
    who follow the Lamb
      wherever He goes.
  They have been redeemed
    from among men
    as first fruits to God
    and the Lamb.
⁵ No lie was found
  in their mouths.
    They are blameless.

Verse: 4

⁴ These are the ones not defiled with women, for they have kept themselves pure. These are the ones who follow the Lamb wherever He goes. They have been redeemed from among men as first fruits to God and the Lamb.

defiled – to pollute, stain, contaminate, defile; used in NT of those who have not kept themselves pure from the defilements of sin, who have soiled themselves by fornication and adultery
redeemed – to be in the marketplace, to attend it; to do business there, buy or sell

There is again, much controversy over the first phrase of Verse 4. Some think it means that these men are virgins. Some think they just haven't been adulterous. Still others think they are simply men who have separated themselves from the world and the apostate church as in:
2 Corinthians 6:17, Therefore, come out from their midst and be separate," says the Lord. "and do not touch what is unclean, and I will welcome you.
I agree with this one. They have left everything to follow God's Lamb. They are completely dedicated. First fruits usually meant the very best.

Verse: 5

⁵ No lie was found in their mouths. They are blameless.

blameless – without blemish; as a sacrifice without spot or blemish; morally: without blemish, faultless, blameless

I think this verse further proves the last theory above. They are true believers whose sins have been cleansed.

Greek Paraphrase of Verses: 4-5
These are the ones who have not been defiled by relations with women, for they have remained celibate. These are the ones who follow the Lamb wherever He goes. These have been purchased *and* redeemed from among the men of Israel as the first fruits sanctified and set apart for special service to God and the Lamb. No lie was found in their mouths, for they are beyond reproach.

Verse 6
Proclamation of Three Angels
⁶ Then I saw another angel flying in mid-heaven, having the eternal good news to proclaim to those who live on the earth, and to every nation, tribe, language, and people.

⁶ Then
  I saw another angel
    flying in mid-heaven,
    having the eternal good news
      to proclaim
        to those
          who live on the earth,
        and
        to every nation,
          tribe,
          language,
          and people.

Remember, John in on earth looking up into heaven. This angel is a good angel from heaven and his mission is to preach the good news about Christ to all the people of the earth so that at the time of judgment, no one would be able to say they never heard.

Greek Paraphrase of Verse: 6
Then I saw another angel flying in midheaven, with the eternal good news to preach to the inhabitants of the earth, to every nation, tribe, language and people.

Verse 7
⁷ He said with a loud voice, "Fear God, and give Him glory, because the hour of His judgment has come. Worship the One who made the heaven and the earth, and sea and springs of waters."

[7] He said
    with a loud voice,
    "Fear God,
      and give Him glory,
      because the hour
        of His judgment
        has come.
   Worship the One
    who made the heaven
      and the earth,
      and sea
      and springs of waters."

The first thing this angel tries to make clear is that all the others, the Antichrist, the false prophet and all the beasts were not the true ones to worship. He makes it clear that God is the One they should give glory to especially since the time of His judgment is coming soon.

Greek Paraphrase of Verse: 7
He said with a loud voice, "Fear God with awe and reverence, and give Him glory, honor and praise in worship, because the hour of His judgment has come. With all your heart, worship the One who created the heaven and the earth, the sea and the springs of water."

Verse 8
[8] Another angel, a second one, followed, saying, "Fallen! Fallen is Babylon the great, she who has made all the nations drink of the wine of the passion of her immorality."

[8] Another angel,
    a second one,
    followed,
    saying,
      "Fallen!
      Fallen is Babylon
        the great,
        she who has made all the nations drink
          of the wine
            of the passion
              of her immorality."

passion – passion, angry, heat, anger forthwith boiling up and soon subsiding again; glow, the wine of passion, inflaming wine (which either drives the drinker mad or kills him with its strength)

This is still the same vision. This angel is saying much the same thing that was in:

Isaiah 21:9-10, Look, riders come— horsemen in pairs." And he answered, saying, "Babylon has fallen, has fallen. All the images of her gods have been shattered on the ground." My people who have been crushed on the threshing floor, I have declared to you what I have heard from the LORD of Hosts, the God of Israel.

The reason for Babylon's fall is that they led so many others astray.

Greek Paraphrase of Verse: 8
Then another angel, a second one, followed, saying, "Fallen, fallen is Babylon the great, she who has made all nations drink the wine of the passion of her immorality corrupting them with idolatry."

Verses 9-11

[9] *Then a third angel followed them, saying with a loud voice, "If anyone worships the beast and his image and receives a mark on his forehead or on his hand, [10] he will also drink of the wine of God's wrath, which is mixed in full strength in the cup of His anger. He will be tormented with fire and brimstone in the presence of the holy angels and the Lamb, [11] and the smoke of their torment goes up forever and ever. There is no rest day and night for those who worship the beast and his image, and whoever receives the mark of his name."*

[9] Then
  a third angel followed them,
    saying
    with a loud voice,
      "If anyone worships the beast
        and his image
        and receives a mark
          on his forehead
          or on his hand,
      [10] he will also drink
        of the wine
        of God's wrath,
          which is mixed
            in full strength
            in the cup of His anger.
He will be tormented
  with fire and brimstone
  in the presence of the holy angels
    and the Lamb,
    [11] and the smoke
    of their torment
    goes up forever and ever.
There is no rest

> day and night
>> for those who worship the beast and his image,
>> and whoever receives the mark of his name."

Verse: 9
⁹ Then a third angel followed them, saying with a loud voice, "If anyone worships the beast and his image and receives a mark on his forehead or on his hand,

This third angel continues the description of what will happen to those who don't repent.

Verse: 10
¹⁰ he will also drink of the wine of God's wrath, which is mixed in full strength in the cup of His anger. He will be tormented with fire and brimstone in the presence of the holy angels and the Lamb,

tormented – to test (metals) by the touchstone, which is a black siliceous stone used to test the purity of gold or silver by the color of the streak produced on it by rubbing it with either metal; to question by applying torture; to torture; to vex with grievous pains (of body or mind), to torment; to be harassed, distressed; of those who at sea are struggling with a head wind

The third angel's pronouncement is probably the most terrifying message describing the final destiny of the lost anywhere in the Bible. But remember that even then God is offering redemption to those who will repent even though few if any will accept.

Verse: 11
¹¹ and the smoke of their torment goes up forever and ever. There is no rest day and night for those who worship the beast and his image, and whoever receives the mark of his name."

torment – to torture, a testing by the touchstone, which is a black siliceous stone used to test the purity of gold or silver by the color of the streak produced on it by rubbing it with either metal

The description just keeps getting worse. This description also tells us that there is no hope for anyone who gets to that point.

Some people think the lake of fire will cleanse those thrown in it, therefore redeeming them. Wow! Can you believe that people actually think that? That belief would refute most of the New Testament, not to mention what Christ accomplished by His death burial and resurrection and why He did it.

Greek Paraphrase of Verses: 9-11
Then another angel, a third one, followed them, saying with a loud voice, "Whoever worships the beast and his image and receives the mark of the

beast on his forehead or on his hand, he too will have to drink of the wine of God's wrath, mixed undiluted into the cup of His anger. He will be tormented with fire and brimstone in the presence of the holy angels and the Lamb, Christ. And the smoke of their torment ascends forever and ever, and they have no rest day and night, those who worship the beast and his image, and whoever receives the mark of his name."

Verse 12

[12] Here is the endurance of the saints who keep the commandments of God and their faith in Jesus.

[12] Here is the endurance of the saints
   who keep
      the commandments of God
      and their faith in Jesus.

endurance – steadfastness, constancy, endurance; in the NT the characteristic of a man who is not swerved from his deliberate purpose and his loyalty to faith and piety by even the greatest trials and sufferings; patiently, and steadfastly; a patient, steadfast waiting for; a patient enduring, sustaining, perseverance

Christ didn't give this vision of these three angels to John to scare those left behind, so to speak. No. He gave it so that those of John's day would know that they would be rewarded for repenting and living for Jesus. Of course, all of that trickles on down to us today. We need that reassurance too.

Greek Paraphrase of Verse: 12
Here is encouragement for the steadfast endurance of God's people, who habitually keep God's commandments and their faith in Jesus.

Verse 13

[13] Then I heard a voice from heaven, saying, "Write, blessed are the dead who die in the Lord from now on!" "Yes," says the Spirit, "so that they may rest from their labors, for their works follow with them."

[13] Then
  I heard a voice
   from heaven,
   saying,
    "Write,
      blessed are the dead
       who die in the Lord
       from now on!"
      "Yes,"

> says the Spirit,
> "so that they may rest
>   from their labors,
>   for their works follow with them."

This voice from heaven was directed at John telling him to write what he was about to hear. Again, there is controversy as to who this message was directed to. I think that as before it was originally directed at those in John's day, but it is equally directed at each of us today. It gives us encouragement to carry on and continue to live for Christ.

Greek Paraphrase of Verse: 13
Then I heard the distinct words of a voice from heaven, saying, "Write, 'Happy, prosperous and to be admired are the dead who die in the Lord from now on!'" "Yes, blessed indeed," says the Spirit, "so that they may rest and have relief from their labors, for their deeds do follow them."

Verse 14
Reaping the Earth's Harvest
[14] Then I looked, and behold, a white cloud, and sitting on the cloud was One like a Son of Man, having a golden crown on His head and a sharp sickle in His hand.

[14] Then
  I looked,
    and behold,
      a white cloud,
        and sitting
          on the cloud
          was One
            like a Son of Man,
            having a golden crown
              on His head
            and
            a sharp sickle in His hand.

This is the same description Daniel used in:
Daniel 7:13, I continued watching in the night visions, and I saw One like a son of man coming with the clouds of heaven. He approached the Ancient of Days and was escorted before Him.
The golden crown on His head proves His royal power and glory. In Zechariah 6:9-13, crowns were put on the head of the high priest. This signifies that Christ would do his priestly work first then later be crowned as King and Judge.

Greek Paraphrase of Verse: 14
Again, I looked, and this is what I saw: a white cloud and sitting on the cloud was One like the Son of Man, with a crown of gold on His head and a sharp sickle of swift judgment in His hand.

Verse 15
15 Another angel came out of the temple, crying out with a loud voice to Him sitting on the cloud, "Take your sickle and reap, for the hour to reap has come, because the harvest of the earth is ripe."

15 Another angel came
    out of the temple,
    crying out
      with a loud voice
      to Him sitting on the cloud,
      "Take your sickle and reap,
        for the hour to reap has come,
        because the harvest of the earth is ripe."

reap – to cut crops down with a sickle

Another angel but this one is talking to the One sitting on the cloud. He is saying that it is time to cut down those who are spiritually dead. It's like a modern farmer going into a field after the good (the crop) has been harvested and cuts down the stalks that were left behind.

Greek Paraphrase of Verse: 15
And another angel came out of the temple, calling with a loud voice to Him who was sitting upon the cloud, "Take your sickle and reap at once, for the hour to reap in judgment has come, because the earth's harvest is fully ripened."

Verse 16
16 So, the One sitting on the cloud swung His sickle over the earth, and the earth was harvested.

16 So,
    the One sitting
      on the cloud
      swung His sickle over the earth,
        and the earth was harvested.

The judgement has begun. One of the things I've heard many times about Jesus is that He is so meek and mild that He could never do what Revelation says He will. Please do not confuse meek with weak. Jesus displayed his anger several times while He was here on earth. He will definitely show that anger again at the end times.

Greek Paraphrase of Verse: 16
So, the One who was sitting on the cloud cast His sickle over the earth, and the earth was judged.

Verse 17
17 Another angel came out of the temple which is in heaven, and he also had a sharp sickle.

17 Another angel came out of the temple
    which is in heaven,
    and he also had a sharp sickle.

    This draws attention to the fact that angels will have a part in the final judgments of the Tribulation.

Greek Paraphrase of Verse: 17
Then another angel came out of the sanctuary in heaven, and he also had a sharp sickle.

Verse 18
18 Then another angel, the one who has authority over fire, came out from the altar, and he called with a loud voice to him who had the sharp sickle, saying, "Take your sharp sickle and gather the clusters from the vine of the earth, because her grapes are ripe."

18 Then
  another angel,
    the one who has authority over fire,
  came out
    from the altar,
  and he called
    with a loud voice
    to him who had the sharp sickle,
    saying,
      "Take your sharp sickle
        and gather the clusters
          from the vine
          of the earth,
          because her grapes are ripe."

authority – physical and mental power; the power of authority (influence) and of right (privilege); the power of rule or government (the power of him whose will and commands must be submitted to by others and obeyed); the power of judicial decisions; one who possesses authority; a ruler, a human magistrate

This angel has the power of fire. The altar is not the one where God sits. It is thought that it might be the incense altar.

Even though the fruit is ripe that does not mean they are good. I once had a lime tree covered with ripe fruit but every single one of them was full of seeds and therefore unfit to eat. That is what I think is referred to here.

Greek Paraphrase of Verse: 18
And another angel, the one who has power over fire, came from the altar, and he shouted with a loud voice to the one who had the sharp sickle, saying, "Put in your sharp sickle and reap the clusters of grapes from the vine of the earth, because her grapes are ripe for judgment."

Verse 19
[19] So, the angel swung his sickle toward the earth and gathered the clusters from the vine of the earth and threw them into the great winepress of the wrath of God.

[19] So,
   the angel swung his sickle
     toward the earth
     and gathered the clusters
      from the vine of the earth,
      and threw them into the great winepress
       of the wrath
       of God.

This vision, like some of those before it, is looking ahead to the time of the final judgment. The great winepress would be where all the bad fruit go to be crushed by the wrath of God.

Greek Paraphrase of Verse: 19
So, the angel swung his sickle to the earth and harvested the grapevine of the earth and threw the grapes into the great wine press of the wrath and indignation of God as judgment of the rebellious world.

Verse 20
[20] Then the wine press was trampled outside the city, and blood flowed out from the winepress, up to the horses' bridles, for a distance.

Trennis E. Killian

20 Then
   the wine press was trampled
     outside the city,
     and blood flowed out
       from the winepress,
       up to the horses' bridles,
       for a distance.

The fact that blood would be coming out of the winepress shows that it is indeed bad fruit being pressed, the unredeemed.

Greek Paraphrase of Verse: 20
Then *the grapes in* the wine press were trampled *and* crushed outside the city, and blood poured from the wine press, *reaching* up to the horses' bridles, for a distance of six hundred feet.

Chapter Fifteen

In this chapter, first we see seven angels with the last seven plagues. Then the sea of glass and those who won out over the beast. Next is the son of Moses and the Lamb.

The temple in heaven is opened and seven angels come out and receive seven golden vials full of the wrath of God from one of the four living creatures.

Verse 1
Preparation for the Bowl Judgments
¹ Then I saw another great and marvelous sign in heaven: seven angels with seven plagues, the last, because with them the wrath of God is finished.

¹ Then
  I saw another great and marvelous sign
    in heaven:
    seven angels
      with seven plagues,
     the last,
       because
        with them
        the wrath of God is finished.

wrath – passion, angry, heat, anger forthwith boiling up and soon subsiding again; glow, the wine of passion, inflaming wine (which either drives the drinker mad or kills him with its strength)

John is seeing into heaven again but he's not there this time.

These seven plagues are called the last plagues because with them, God's wrath and fury will be filled up and completed.

Greek Paraphrase of Verse: 1
Then I saw another sign in heaven, great and wonderful, a warning of terrifying and horrible events: seven angels who had seven plagues, *which are* the last, because with them the wrath of God is completely expressed and reaches its zenith.

Verse 2
² I saw something like a sea of glass mixed with fire, and those who had overcome the beast, his image, and the number of his name, were standing on the sea of glass, holding harps of God.

² I saw something like a sea of glass
  mixed with fire,

and those who had overcome the beast,
   his image,
   and the number of his name,
   were standing on the sea of glass,
     holding harps of God.

overcome – to conquer; to carry off the victory, come off victorious; when one is arraigned or goes to law, to win the case, maintain one's cause

This setting was described in Chapter 4. John sees them as they stand on the sea of glass in front of the throne.

They have persevered even through all that the beast threw at them.

Greek Paraphrase of Verse: 2
Then I saw something like a large expanse of glass like a sea mixed with fire, and those who had been victorious over the beast, his image and the number corresponding to his name were standing on the sea of glass, holding harps of God worshiping Him.

Verse 3
³ They sang the song of Moses, the servant of God, and the song of the Lamb, saying, "Great and marvelous are Your works, O Lord God Almighty. Righteous and true are Your ways, King of the nations!

³ They sang the song of Moses,
   the servant of God,
   and the song of the Lamb,
    saying,
     "Great and marvelous are Your works,
      O Lord God Almighty.
  Righteous and true are Your ways,
  King of the nations!

After God sent the plagues on Egypt and destroyed the Egyptian army, Moses let the people in a great song of praise (Exodus 15:1-18). The main emphasis of the song was the Lord's triumph and the fact that He had become their salvation.

This song sung in heaven anticipates God's final victory over the beast and the joy of believers in heaven.

Greek Paraphrase of Verse: 3
And they sang the song of Moses, the bond servant of God, and the song of the Lamb, saying, "Great, wonderful and awe-inspiring are Your works in judgment, O Lord God, the Almighty, the Omnipotent, Ruler of all. Righteous and true are Your ways, O King of the nations!

Verse 4

⁴ "Who will not fear, O Lord, and glorify Your name? You alone are holy, for all the nations will come and worship before You, for Your righteous acts have been revealed."

⁴ "Who will not fear,
   O Lord,
   and glorify Your name?
You
  alone
  are holy,
    for all the nations will come
     and worship before You,
      for Your righteous acts have been revealed."

fear – to put to flight by terrifying (to scare away); to put to flight, to flee; to fear, be afraid; to be struck with fear, to be seized with alarm; those struck with amazement; to fear, be afraid of one; to reverence, venerate, to treat with deference or reverential obedience

Remember the Greek word translated fear in this context means to revere or to obey reverentially.

Also, 'all the nations' means all the saved from all the nations will come and worship Him. Why? Because He has shown them His righteous acts.

Greek Paraphrase of Verse: 4
"Who will not fear reverently and glorify Your name, O Lord giving You honor and praise in worship? For You alone are holy, for all the nations shall come and worship before You, for your righteous acts have been revealed *and* displayed."

Verses 5-6

⁵ After these things, I looked, and the temple of the tabernacle of testimony in heaven was opened, ⁶ and the seven angels who had the seven plagues came out of the temple, clothed in linen, clean and bright, and girded around their chests with golden sashes.

⁵ After these things,
  I looked,
   and the temple
    of the tabernacle of testimony
    in heaven
    was opened,
     ⁶ and the seven angels
      who had the seven plagues

came out of the temple,
    clothed in linen,
        clean and bright,
        and girded around their chests with golden sashes.

Verse: 5
5 After these things, I looked, and the temple of the tabernacle of testimony in heaven was opened,

Here comes another vision and John is looking into heaven again. The tabernacle of testimony probably refers to the tabernacle in the wilderness which held the Holy of Holies (holiest place of all).

Verse: 6
6 and the seven angels who had the seven plagues came out of the temple, clothed in linen, clean and bright, and girded around their chests with golden sashes.

girded – to fasten garments with a girdle or belt; to gird one's self metaphorically with truth as a girdle; to equip one's self with knowledge of the truth

This vision is of the same seven angels from before who had the seven plagues. They came out of the sanctuary, literally from the presence and glory of God.
The white robes signify their sinlessness while combined with the golden belts was the dress of priests and kings.
These angels are being sent from heaven to earth to exact more of God's righteous judgment on the earth.

Greek Paraphrase of Verses: 5-6
After these things, I looked, and the sanctuary of the tabernacle of the testimony in heaven was opened, and the seven angels who had the seven plagues came out of the temple, arrayed in linen, pure and gleaming, with golden sashes wrapped around their chests.

Verse 7
7 Then one of the four living creatures gave the seven angels seven golden bowls full of the wrath of God, who lives forever and ever.

7 Then
    one
        of the four living creatures
        gave the seven angels
            seven golden bowls full of the wrath of God,
                who lives forever and ever.

wrath – passion, angry, heat, anger forthwith boiling up and soon subsiding again; glow, the wine of passion, inflaming wine (which either drives the drinker mad or kills him with its strength)

This is one of the living creatures that John first met in Chapter 4. He is a guardian of God's throne and a representative of God's creation. As such, it is appropriate that he take part in the events that prepare the way for the coming Kingdom.

When he gives the bowls full of God's wrath to the seven angels, they will then become the ones to bring the last series of judgments on the remaining sinners of the world before Jesus comes back to earth.

Greek Paraphrase of Verse: 7
Then one of the four living creatures gave to the seven angels seven golden bowls full of the wrath *and* indignation of God, who lives forever and ever.

Verse 8
⁸ Then the temple was filled with smoke from the glory of God and from His power, and no one was able to enter the temple until the seven plagues of the seven angels were completed.

⁸ Then
   the temple was filled
     with smoke
       from the glory of God
       and from His power,
       and no one was able to enter the temple
         until the seven plagues
           of the seven angels
           were completed.

Remember, John is still on earth looking into heaven where he sees the smoke that was an indication of God's glory.

The smoke made it impossible for anyone to enter the sanctuary until after the seven angels finished the job of pouring out the seven bowls of the seven plagues. Therefore, nothing could stop the judgment now.

Greek Paraphrase of Verse: 8
Then the temple was filled with smoke from the glory, radiance *and* splendor of God and from His power, and no one was able to enter the temple until the seven plagues of the seven angels were finished.

Chapter Sixteen

This chapter describes what happens when the seven angels pour out the last seven plagues that John saw in his vision.

The first angel pours out his vial on the earth causing bad sores.

The second angel pours out his vial on the sea and it turns into blood.

The third angel pours out his vial on the rivers and fountains and they turn to blood too.

The fourth angel pours out his vial on the sun and men are scorched with fire.

The fifth angel pours out his vial on the throne of the beast.

The sixth angel pours out his vial on the river Euphrates.

Three unclean spirits come out of the mouth of the beast, dragon and false prophet. They go out to gather all the kings of the world to battle in Armageddon.

The seventh angel pours out his vial on the air causing thunder, lightning, earthquakes and huge hail stones.

Verse 1
The First Bowl

[1] *Then I heard a loud voice from the temple, saying to the seven angels, "Go and pour out the seven bowls of the wrath of God on the earth."*

[1] Then
   I heard a loud voice
      from the temple,
      saying
         to the seven angels,
         "Go and pour out the seven bowls
           of the wrath of God
           on the earth."

wrath – passion, angry, heat, anger forthwith boiling up and soon subsiding again; glow, the wine of passion, inflaming wine (which either drives the drinker mad or kills him with its strength)

The voice John heard seems to be the voice of God or Christ since no one else could enter the sanctuary until afterward.

These judgments will be much more harsh and complete with no limits placed on the trumpet judgments.

Greek Paraphrase of Verse: 1
Then I heard a loud voice from the temple, saying to the seven angels, "Go and pour out on the earth the seven bowls of the wrath *and* indignation of God."

Verse 2
² The first angel went and poured out his bowl on the earth, and ugly and painful sores broke out on the people who had the mark of the beast and who worshiped his image.

² The first angel went and poured out his bowl
  on the earth,
  and ugly and painful sores broke out
    on the people
      who had the mark of the beast
      and
      who worshiped his image.

ugly – of a bad nature; not such as it ought to be; of a mode of thinking, feeling, acting; base, wrong, wicked; troublesome, injurious, pernicious, destructive, baneful
painful – full of labors, annoyances, hardships; pressed and harassed by labors; bringing toils, annoyances, perils; of a time, full of peril to Christian faith and steadfastness; causing pain and trouble; bad, of a bad nature or condition; in a physical sense: diseased or blind; in an ethical sense: evil wicked, bad
sores – a wound, especially a wound producing a discharge pus; a sore, an ulcer

All those with the mark of the beast on them will get new marks all over their bodies, ugly painful sores.
This plague is similar to one of the plagues on Egypt in Exodus 9:8-11 but it is much worse.

Greek Paraphrase of Verse: 2
The first *angel* went and poured out his bowl on the earth, and loathsome and malignant sores came on the people who had the mark of the beast and who worshiped his image.

Verse 3
The Second Bowl
³ The second poured out his bowl into the sea. It became blood like that of a dead man, and every living thing in the sea died.

³ The second poured out his bowl
  into the sea.
    It became blood
      like that of a dead man,
      and every living thing
        in the sea
        died.

185

The second plague will change the sea into blood killing every living thing in it. It's not clear if the sea mentioned here is a specific one or all seas and or oceans.

This plague is similar to the first one God sent onto Egypt when the Nile became blood (Exodus 7:20-25).

Greek Paraphrase of Verse: 3
The second *angel* poured out his bowl into the sea, and it turned into blood like that of a corpse, and every living thing in the sea died.

Verse 4
The Third Bowl
⁴ The third poured out his bowl into the rivers and the springs of waters, and they became blood.

⁴ The third poured out his bowl
    into the rivers
        and the springs of waters,
        and they became blood.

The next plague is the same except the blood is poured into the rivers, streams and springs. Therefore, all sources of drinking water will be contaminated. This will cause great suffering of a different kind.

Greek Paraphrase of Verse: 4
Then the third *angel* poured out his bowl into the rivers and the springs of water, and they turned into blood.

Verse 5
⁵ I heard the angel of the waters saying, "You are righteous, who is and who was, the Holy One, because You judged these things.

⁵ I heard the angel
    of the waters
    saying,
      "You are righteous,
        who is
        and who was,
        the Holy One
         because You judged these things.

John now hears the angel of the waters speaking. Who is this angel? The most common answer is that he is an angel that God gave control of all the waters of the earth. If so, this is the only time he is mentioned.

Regardless, this angel is praising God because He is holy and because of His fair judgment.

Greek Paraphrase of Verse: 5
I heard the angel of the waters saying, "Righteous *and* just are You, Who is and Who was, O Holy One, because You judged these things.

Verse 6
⁶ Because they poured out the blood of saints and prophets, You gave them blood to drink. They deserve it."

⁶ Because
   they poured out the blood
      of saints and prophets,
      You gave them blood to drink.
         They deserve it."

deserve – weighing, having weight, having the weight of another thing of like value, worth as much

This is a case of the punishment fitting the crime. Because they shed the blood of saints and prophets, they will be forced to drink blood. I like the little opinion added at the end, "They deserve it."

Greek Paraphrase of Verse: 6
Because they have poured out the blood of God's people and the prophets, and You in turn have given them blood to drink. They deserve Your judgment."

Verse 7
⁷ And I heard the altar saying, "Yes, Lord God Almighty, true and righteous are Your judgments."

⁷ And
   I heard the altar saying,
      "Yes,
         Lord God Almighty,
         true and righteous are Your judgments."

The voice came from the altar and was probably one of the angels there. He is basically saying that no one can question God's judgments for they are true and righteous.

This is similar to *Psalm 19:9, The fear of the LORD is pure, enduring forever; the ordinances of the LORD are reliable and altogether righteous.*

Greek Paraphrase of Verse: 7
And I heard another from the altar saying, "Yes, O Lord God, the Almighty Omnipotent, Ruler of all, Your judgments are true, fair *and* righteous."

Verse 8
The Fourth Bowl
⁸ The fourth poured out his bowl on the sun, and it was given the power to scorch men with fire.

⁸ The fourth poured out his bowl
    on the sun,
    and it was given the power to scorch men with fire.

    The first three plagues will affect the earth, air and water. The fourth plague will affect the sun and indirectly the earth.
    Throughout the Bible, judgment is carried out by fire. This fire will aggravate the suffering the people already have with the sores on their skin.

Greek Paraphrase of Verse: 8
Then the fourth *angel* poured out his bowl on the sun, and it was given the power to scorch men with raging fire.

Verse 9
⁹ The men were scorched with fierce heat, and they blasphemed the name of God who has the power over these plagues, and they did not repent and give Him glory.

⁹ The men were scorched
    with fierce heat,
    and they blasphemed the name
      of God
      who has the power over these plagues,
    and they did not repent
      and give Him glory.

power – physical and mental power; the power of authority (influence) and of right (privilege); the power of rule or government (the power of him whose will and commands must be submitted to by others and obeyed); the power of judicial decisions; one who possesses authority; a ruler, a human magistrate
plagues – a blow, stripe, a wound; a public calamity, heavy affliction, plague

    The men are burned so much that they blaspheme God's name. They now realize that God is in control of all that is happening to them. Up until this time, they thought the Antichrist of his false prophet had control over these plagues.

They still won't give God any glory and stubbornly refuse to recognize their sins against Him and still won't repent.

Greek Paraphrase of Verse: 9
The men were severely burned by the great heat, and they spoke evil of the name of God who has power over these plagues, but they did not repent of their sins and glorify Him.

Verses 10-11
The Fifth Bowl
¹⁰ Then the fifth poured out his bowl on the throne of the beast, and his kingdom was plunged into darkness. They gnawed their tongues because of pain, ¹¹ and they blasphemed the God of heaven because of their pains and their sores, but they did not repent of their actions.

¹⁰ Then
  the fifth poured out his bowl
    on the throne of the beast,
      and his kingdom was plunged into darkness.
  They gnawed their tongues
    because of pain,
    ¹¹ and they blasphemed
      the God of heaven
      because of their pains and their sores,
      but they did not repent of their actions.

Verse 10
¹⁰ Then the fifth poured out his bowl on the throne of the beast, and his kingdom was plunged into darkness. They gnawed their tongues because of pain,

We don't know where the throne of the beast is. Some think it will be Babylon, others think it will be Jerusalem or even Rome. Wherever it is, the whole kingdom will be in darkness. It will be like the plague of darkness on Egypt (Exodus 10:21-23). The pain will be so intense that they will gnaw their tongues.

Verse 11
¹¹ and they blasphemed the God of heaven because of their pains and their sores, but they did not repent of their actions.

pains – great trouble, intense desire; pain

sores – a wound, especially a wound producing a discharge pus; a sore, an ulcer

repent – to change one's mind for better, heartily to amend with abhorrence of one's past sins

actions – business, employment, that which any one is occupied; that which one undertakes to do, enterprise, undertaking; any product whatever, anything accomplished by hand, art, industry, or mind

They also blaspheme God. Notice that all of those who are lost in their sins will automatically blame God and curse him.

It is still implied that repentance will stop the judgment, but no one will repent.

Greek Paraphrase of Verses: 10-11
Then the fifth *angel* poured out his bowl on the throne of the beast, and his kingdom was plunged into darkness. The people gnawed their tongues because of their excruciating anguish and severe torment, and they blasphemed the God of heaven because of their anguish and their sores, but they did not repent of what they had done *nor* hate their wickedness.

Verse 12
The Sixth Bowl
¹² The sixth poured out his bowl on the great river Euphrates, and its water was dried up to prepare for the kings from the east.

¹² The sixth poured out his bowl
   on the great river Euphrates,
      and its water was dried up
         to prepare for the kings from the east.

Euphrates – "the good and abounding river" a large, famous river which rises in the mountains of Armenia Major, flows through Assyria, Syria, Mesopotamia and the city of Babylon, and empties into the Gulf of Persia

prepare – to make ready, prepare; to make the necessary preparations, get everything ready; metaphorically, drawn from the oriental custom of sending on before kings on their journeys persons to level the roads and make them passable; to prepare the minds of men to give the Messiah a fit reception and secure his blessings

The Euphrates was considered to be the major river of the Middle East throughout Biblical times. It formed the northeastern border of the land promised to Abraham and his descendants (Genesis 15:18).

The sixth angel will pour out his bowl and the great river will dry up.

The Euphrates was always a barrier that the kings of the east couldn't cross to invade but now that it is dry, it won't stop future invasions.

Thus, the sixth bowl is part of the preparation for the Battle of Armageddon described in Chapter 19 which will result in victory for the Lamb.

Greek Paraphrase of Verse: 12
Then the sixth *angel* poured out his bowl on the great river Euphrates, and its water was dried up, so that the way would be prepared for the coming of the kings from the east.

Verse 13
¹³ Then I saw three unclean spirits like frogs coming from the dragon's mouth, from the beast's mouth, and from the false prophet's mouth.

¹³ Then
   I saw three unclean spirits
      like frogs
      coming from the dragon's mouth,
         from the beast's mouth,
         and from the false prophet's mouth.

Frogs? Wow!

The dragon is the serpent described in Chapter 12 and identified with the devil and Satan in Chapter12:9. The beast is the Antichrist. This is the first time the second beast, the beast out of the earth or land is named as the false prophet.

Each one of the three had an unclean spirit come out of its mouth.

Greek Paraphrase of Verse: 13
Then I saw three loathsome spirits like frogs, *leaping* from the mouth of Satan, the dragon, and from the mouth of the beast, the Antichrist, and from the mouth of the false prophet.

Verse 14
¹⁴ For they are spirits of demons, performing signs, who travel to the kings of the whole world to assemble them for the battle of the great day of God Almighty.

¹⁴ For
   they are spirits
     of demons,
     performing signs,
     who travel
       to the kings of the whole world
         to assemble them

for the battle of the great day of God Almighty.

These frogs are far worse than the plague of frogs that God sent on Egypt (Exodus 8:2-11). Under the law, frogs were unclean animals therefore in this situation, they are unclean spirits.

The miracles they perform will be the climax of what Jesus warned against in:

Mathew 24:24, For false Christs and false prophets will arise and will do great signs and wonders, so as to mislead, if possible, even the elect.

They will convince the kings of the earth to join the Antichrist in the final battle.

Greek Paraphrase of Verse: 14

For they are actually the spirits of demons, performing miraculous signs. And they go out to the kings of the entire inhabited earth, to gather them together for the war of the great day of God, the Almighty.

Verse 15

[15] *"Behold, I am coming like a thief. Blessed is the one who stays awake and remains clothed, so that he will not go naked and they see his shame."*

[15] "Behold,
    I am coming
      like a thief.
   Blessed is the one
    who stays awake
    and remains clothed,
      so that he will not go naked
        and they see his shame."

There are two parts to this verse. In the first part, Jesus is saying he will come at a time when no one expects him like a thief who comes when everyone is either away or asleep.

The second part is a blessing on those who stay alert and do not allow sins into their lives. The clothing symbolizes keeping sin off and not being naked means, they won't be showing sin that isn't there. Therefore, there will be no shame.

Greek Paraphrase of Verse: 15

"Behold, I am coming like a thief in the night. Blessed is the one who stays awake and stays spiritually ready for the Lord's return, so that he will not be spiritually unprepared, and men will not see his shame."

Verse 16

[16] *And they assembled them at the place called Armageddon in Hebrew.*

¹⁶ And
    they assembled them
      at the place called Armageddon in Hebrew.

Armageddon – the hill or city of Megiddo – the scene of a the struggle of good and evil is suggested by that battle plain of Esdraelon, which was famous for two great victories, of Barak over the Canaanites, and of Gideon over the Midianites; and for two great disasters, the deaths of Saul and Josiah. Hence in Revelation a place of great slaughter, the scene of a terrible retribution upon the wicked. The RSV translates the name as Har-Magedon, i.e. the hill (as Ar is the city) of Megiddo.

This verse goes back to Verse 14 and says that the kings will be assembled at Armageddon which will become the center for the great battle at the end of the Tribulation.

That final battle will fulfill many Old Testament prophesies (Deuteronomy 32:43; Jeremiah 25:31; Joel 3:2, 7-17; Zephaniah 3:8; Zechariah 12:11; 14:2-5).

This battle will end when Jesus returns in all His power and glory and with a word defeats the Antichrist and all his armies.

Greek Paraphrase of Verse: 16
And the demons gathered the kings and armies of the world together at the place which in Hebrew is called Armageddon.

Verse 17
The Seventh Bowl
¹⁷ Then the seventh poured out his bowl into the air, and a loud voice came out of the temple from the throne, saying, "It is done."

¹⁷ Then the seventh poured out his bowl
    into the air,
    and a loud voice
      came out of the temple
        from the throne,
      saying,
        "It is done."

done – to become, i.e. to come into existence, begin to be, receive being; to come to pass, happen; to arise, appear in history, come upon the stage; of men appearing in public; to be made, finished; of miracles, to be performed, wrought

The seventh and final bowl is finally poured out into the air which will fill the air with God's judgment. Then the loud voice will call out that it is done, all over. All of God's judgments (punishments) on the earth and its inhabitants will be finished.

Greek Paraphrase of Verse: 17
Then the seventh *angel* poured out his bowl into the air, and a loud voice came out of the temple from the throne of God, saying, "It is all accomplished.

Verse 18
18 And there was lightning, rumbling, and thunder. And there was a great earthquake, such as there had not been since man has been on the earth, so great was the earthquake.

18 And
   there was lightning,
     rumbling,
     and thunder.
   And
   there was a great earthquake,
     such as there had not been
       since man has been on the earth,
         so great was the earthquake.

This verse begins the description of what happens to the earth with this plague.

The sixth seal in Chapter 6 had an earthquake that seems to have set the stage for this one of much greater magnitude.

Greek Paraphrase of Verse: 18
And there were flashes of lightning, loud rumblings and peals of thunder, and there was a massive earthquake. Nothing like it has ever occurred since mankind originated on the earth, so severe and far-reaching was that earthquake.

Verse 19
19 The great city was split into three parts, and the cities of the nations fell. God remembered Babylon the great and gave her the cup of the wine of His fierce anger.

19 The great city was split
   into three parts,
   and the cities of the nations fell.
  God remembered Babylon the great
   and gave her the cup
     of the wine
     of His fierce anger.

Babylon – confusion – a very large and famous city, the residence of the Babylonian kings, situated on both banks of the Euphrates. Cyrus had formerly captured it, but Darius Hystaspis threw down its gates and walls, and Xerxes destroyed the temple of Belis. At length the city was reduced to almost solitude, the population having been drawn off by the neighboring Seleucia, built on the Tigris by Seleucus Nicanor.

Which city is the 'great city?' Some think that since Babylon is mentioned here that it will be a rebuilt Babylon. Others think it is Rome which was the center of the known world of John's time. Still others think that it is Jerusalem which has often been called 'the great city.'

Whichever city it refers to is split into three parts and the other cities will fall.

Greek Paraphrase of Verse: 19
The great city was split into three parts, and the cities of the nations fell. And God remembered Babylon the great, to give her the cup of the wine of His fierce *and* furious anger.

Verse 20
²⁰ Every island fled, and the mountains were not found.

²⁰ Every island fled,
   and the mountains were not found.

There are two different theories as to the meaning of all islands and mountains being removed.

One theory is that they will be removed to make things ready for the coming kingdom.

Greek Paraphrase of Verse: 20
Then every island fled away, and no mountains could be found.

Verse 21
²¹ Huge hailstones, about one hundred pounds each, fell from heaven on men, and the men blasphemed God because of the plague of the hail, because the plague was extremely severe.

²¹ Huge hailstones,
   about one hundred pounds each,
   fell
      from heaven
      on men,
         and the men blasphemed God

> because of the plague of the hail,
>> because the plague was extremely severe.

The earthquake wasn't bad enough, but can you imagine hailstones weighing one hundred pounds each? Still, men blasphemed God, blaming Him for their being there to suffer this plague.

Greek Paraphrase of Verse: 21
And giant hailstones, about one hundred pounds each, fell from the sky on men; and the men reviled *and* spoke abusively of God for the plague of the hail, because the plague was so very great.

Chapter Seventeen

Chapters 17 and 18 give all the details of the fall of Babylon the great which was already announced in Revelation 14:8 and 16:19.

Verses 1-5 make up the first section of this chapter. One of the seven angels that poured out the seven bowls of God's wrath now speak to John telling him that he would show him the coming judgment.

Verses 1-2
The Woman and the Scarlet Beast
[1] Then one of the seven angels who had the seven bowls came and spoke with me, saying, "Come here, I will show you the judgment of the great prostitute who sits on many waters, [2] with whom the kings of the earth committed acts of immorality, and those who live on the earth were drunk with the wine of her immorality."

[1] Then
  one of the seven angels
    who had the seven bowls
    came and spoke with me,
      saying,
        "Come here,
       I will show you the judgment
        of the great prostitute
          who sits on many waters,
         [2] with whom the kings
          of the earth
          committed acts of immorality,
        and those
          who live on the earth
          were drunk with the wine of her immorality."

Verse 1
[1] Then one of the seven angels who had the seven bowls came and spoke with me, saying, "Come here, I will show you the judgment of the great prostitute who sits on many waters,

There are many places in both the Old Testament and the New Testament where adultery and prostitution are used figuratively to represent false worship, worship of heathen gods or other types of unfaithfulness to God. Sometimes it simply represents rebellion against God.

The waters represent Assyria:

Isaiah 8:7-8, the Lord will certainly bring against them the mighty rushing waters of the Euphrates River— the king of Assyria and all his glory. It will overflow its channels and spill over all its banks. It will pour into Judah, flood over it, and sweep through, reaching up to the neck; and its spreading

streams will fill your entire land, Immanuel!
Verse 2
[2] with whom the kings of the earth committed acts of immorality, and those who live on the earth were drunk with the wine of her immorality."

committed acts of immorality – to prostitute one's body to the lust of another; to commit fornication; metaphorically to be given to idolatry, to worship idols; to permit one's self to be drawn away by another into idolatry
immorality – illicit sexual intercourse; adultery, fornication, homosexuality, lesbianism, intercourse with animals etc.; metaphorically the worship of idols; of the defilement of idolatry, as incurred by eating the sacrifices offered to idols

This great prostitute leads the inhabitants of the earth astray. False prophets encourage the people to follow her false doctrines.

Greek Paraphrase of Verses: 1-2
Then one of the seven angels who had the seven bowls came and spoke with me, saying, "Come here, I will show you the judgment *and* doom of the great prostitute who is seated on many waters influencing nations, with whom the kings of the earth have committed *acts of* immorality, and the inhabitants of the earth have become intoxicated with the wine of her immorality."

Verse 3
[3] And he carried me away in the Spirit to a desert. I saw a woman sitting on a scarlet beast, covered with blasphemous names, having seven heads and ten horns.

[3] And
  he carried me away
    in the Spirit
    to a desert.
  I saw a woman
    sitting on a scarlet beast,
    covered with blasphemous names,
    having seven heads and ten horns.

John was 'in the spirit' two other times, in Revelation 1:10 and 4:2. This one is similar to the one in Ezekiel 8:3 because he was aware of being carried away. There, he saw a beast that is probably the same one described in Revelation 13:1.
Since the woman he sees is carried by the beast, it means that she will allow all the unrighteousness of the ungodly world.

Greek Paraphrase of Verse: 3
And the angel carried me away in the Spirit into a wilderness, and I saw a woman sitting on a scarlet beast that was entirely covered with blasphemous names, having seven heads and ten horns.

Verse 4
4 The woman was dressed in purple and scarlet, adorned with gold, precious stones, and pearls. She had a gold cup in her hand filled with abominations and unclean things of her immorality.

4 The woman was dressed in purple and scarlet,
    adorned with gold,
      precious stones,
      and pearls.
  She had a gold cup
    in her hand
    filled with abominations
      and unclean things
      of her immorality.

abominations – a foul thing, a detestable thing; of idols and things pertaining to idolatry
immorality – illicit sexual intercourse; adultery, fornication, homosexuality, lesbianism, intercourse with animals etc.; metaphorically the worship of idols; of the defilement of idolatry, as incurred by eating the sacrifices offered to idols

This woman is a lot different from the woman in Chapter 12 who was clothed in the sun. This one is dressed in the colors of royalty, purple and scarlet. All the gold, precious stones and pearls added to her status of wealth. But just as it often is, this type of exterior is only covering up the filth inside. Even the beautiful gold cup is filled with filth.

Greek Paraphrase of Verse: 4
The woman was dressed in purple and scarlet, and adorned with gold, precious stones and pearls, and she was holding in her hand a gold cup full of the abominations and the filth of her sexual immorality.

Verse 5
5 On her forehead, a name was written, a mystery, "Babylon the great, the mother of prostitutes and of the abominations of the earth."

5 On her forehead,
  a name was written,
    a mystery,

"Babylon the great,
the mother
  of prostitutes
  and
  of the abominations of the earth."

Babylon – "confusion" – a very large and famous city, the residence of the Babylonian kings, situated on both banks of the Euphrates. Cyrus had formerly captured it, but Darius Hystaspis threw down its gates and walls, and Xerxes destroyed the temple of Belis. At length the city was reduced to almost solitude, the population having been drawn off by the neighboring Seleucia, built on the Tigris by Seleucus Nicanor.
abominations – a foul thing, a detestable thing; of idols and things pertaining to idolatry

Here, the KJV implies that the name written is 'Mystery.' But all modern translations call it a mystery and the title in quotes is considered to be the mystery or a mystery.

Not only is her cup full of filth but she is the mother of prostitutes and abominations of the earth.

Greek Paraphrase of Verse: 5
And on her forehead a name was written, a mystery: "Babylon the great, the mother of prostitutes, false religions, heresies and of the abominations of the earth."

Verse 6
⁶ I saw that the woman was drunk with the blood of the saints, and the blood of the witnesses to Jesus. When I saw her, I was greatly astonished.

⁶ I saw
  that the woman was drunk
    with the blood of the saints,
    and
    the blood of the witnesses
      to Jesus.
  When I saw her,
    I was greatly astonished.

greatly – a wonderful thing, a marvel; wonder; to wonder [with great wonder i.e.] exceedingly
astonished – to wonder, admire, be astonished, be amazed, wonder at, marvel; to be wondered at, to be had in admiration

Her being drunk on the blood of the saints and witnesses to Jesus shows that she represents the entire anti-God world of the time.
John was amazed and probably wondering about the meaning of it all.

Greek Paraphrase of Verse: 6
I saw that the woman was drunk with the blood of God's people, and
with the blood of the witnesses of Jesus who were martyred. When I saw
her, I wondered in amazement.

Verse 7
The Woman and the Beast Explained
7 And the angel said to me, "Why are you astonished? I will tell you the
mystery of the woman and of the beast, with the seven heads and the ten horns
that carries her.

7 And
   the angel said
     to me,
      "Why are you astonished?
       I will tell you the mystery
         of the woman
         and
         of the beast,
            with the seven heads
            and the ten horns that carries her.

astonished – to wonder, admire, be astonished, be amazed, wonder at,
marvel; to be wondered at, to be had in admiration

   It may have been a mystery to John but not to the angel who said he
would explain the mystery to him not only of the woman but also of the beast
she was riding on.

Greek Paraphrase of Verse: 7
But the angel said to me, "Why do you wonder? I will explain to you the
mystery of the woman and of the beast that carries her, which has the
seven heads and ten horns.

Verse 8
8 The beast that you saw was, and is not, and is about to come up out of the
abyss and go to destruction. Those who live on the earth, whose name has
not been written in the Book of Life from the foundation of the world, will be
astonished when they see the beast that was, and is not, and will come.

8 The beast
    that you saw
    was
    and is not,

and is about to come up
  out of the abyss
  and go to destruction.
Those
 who live on the earth,
 whose name has not been written
  in the Book
   of Life
   from the foundation of the world,
   will be astonished
    when they see the beast
     that was,
     and is not,
     and will come.

abyss – Bottomless; unbounded; the abyss; the pit; the immeasurable depth; of Orcus, a very deep gulf or chasm in the lowest parts of the earth used as the common receptacle of the dead and especially as the abode of demons
destruction – destroying, utter destruction; of vessels; a perishing, ruin, destruction; the destruction which consists of eternal misery in hell
astonished – to wonder, admire, be astonished, be amazed, wonder at, marvel; to be wondered at, to be had in admiration

This passage is one of the most difficult to interpret in the entire book of Revelation. Who or what is the beast mentioned here?
There are at least five theories as to who the beast is:
1. The Antichrist. Chapter 13 speaks of him as a beast.
2. A kingdom
3. Both a kingdom and a man.
4. The Antichrist's kingdom
5. Some think the beast 'that was, and is not, and will come' refers to a revived Roman Empire which will be ruled by the Antichrist in the end times.

Greek Paraphrase of Verse: 8
"The beast that you saw was once, but now is not, and it is about to come up out of the bottomless pit, the dwelling place of demons and go to eternal misery in hell. And the inhabitants of the earth, whose names have not been written in the Book of Life from the foundation of the world, will be amazed when they see the beast, because he was and is not and is yet to come to earth.

Verse 9
⁹ Here is the mind with wisdom. The seven heads are seven mountains on which the woman sits.
⁹ Here is the mind
  with wisdom.
 The seven heads are seven mountains

on which the woman sits.

wisdom – wisdom, broad and full of intelligence; used of the knowledge of very diverse matters; the wisdom which belongs to men; the varied knowledge of things human and divine, acquired by acuteness and experience, and summed up in maxims and proverbs; the science and learning; supreme intelligence, such as belongs to God; the wisdom of God as evinced in forming and executing counsels in the formation and government of the world and the scriptures

The mind of wisdom means there is something or someone here to help John to interpret his vision.

The seven heads may represent seven mountains or hills (the Greek isn't specific). Some have tried to find seven hills in Jerusalem but there just aren't seven hills there.

But during that time, Rome was known as the city of seven hills. I'm sure all of John's readers would have immediately thought of Rome.

Greek Paraphrase of Verse: 9
Here is the mind which has wisdom, and this is what it knows about the vision. The seven heads are seven mountains on which the woman sits.

Verse 10
[10] *They are seven kings: five have fallen, one is, the other has not yet come, and when he comes, he must remain a little while.*

[10] They are seven kings:
>   five have fallen,
>   one is,
>   the other has not yet come,
>   and when he comes,
>   he must remain a little while.

The seven heads are also seven kings each with his own kingdom in the empire that Rome maintained.

There are many different guesses (yes, that's what I call them) as to who the seven kings actually are. But since we're not told, I'm not going to guess.

Greek Paraphrase of Verse: 10
And they are seven kings: five of whom have fallen, one exists *and* is reigning; the other, the seventh, has not yet come, and when he does come, he must remain a little while.

Verse 11
¹¹ The beast that was and is not, is himself also an eighth and is one of the seven, and he goes to destruction.

¹¹ The beast
    that was
    and is not,
    is himself
      also
      an eighth
    and is one of the seven,
      and he goes to destruction.

destruction – destroying, utter destruction; of vessels; a perishing, ruin, destruction; the destruction which consists of eternal misery in hell

The beast not only has seven heads but he himself is the eighth one. Here is a little hint of the destruction that is coming for the Antichrist.

Greek Paraphrase of Verse: 11
And the beast that once was but is not, is himself also an eighth king and is one of the seven, and he goes to eternal misery in hell.

Verse 12
¹² The ten horns you saw are ten kings who have not yet received a kingdom, but they receive authority as kings with the beast for one hour.

¹² The ten horns
    you saw
    are ten kings
      who have not yet received a kingdom,
        but they receive authority
          as kings
          with the beast
          for one hour.

received – one's self; to take what is one's own, to take to one's self, to make one's own; to claim, procure, for one's self; to receive what is offered; not to refuse or reject; to receive a person, give him access to one's self
authority – physical and mental power; the power of authority (influence) and of right (privilege); the power of rule or government (the power of him whose will and commands must be submitted to by others and obeyed); the power of judicial decisions; one who possesses authority; a ruler, a human magistrate

Notice that these ten kings have not received a kingdom yet. So, they can't be any who have ever lived before that time.

There are many different thoughts as to who these ten kings are:
They will make up a world confederacy or possibly just Europe.
They are a revived Roman Empire with Italy again being the leader.
They are an empire with a rebuilt city of Babylon as their capital.
Again, I will make no guesses. As I say many times. Sometimes we just can't read too much into what Revelation says, especially when it's as vague as this passage is.

Greek Paraphrase of Verse: 12
The ten horns that you saw are ten kings who have not yet received a kingdom, but together they receive authority as kings for a single hour for a common purpose along with the beast.

Verse 13
¹³ These have one purpose, and they give their power and authority to the beast.

¹³ These have one purpose,
    and they give their power
      and authority
        to the beast.

purpose – the faculty of knowledge, mind, reason; that which is thought or known, one's mind; view, judgment, opinion; mind concerning what ought to be done; by one's self: resolve purpose, intention
power – strength, power, ability (word we get dynamite from)
authority – physical and mental power; the power of authority (influence) and of right (privilege); the power of rule or government (the power of him whose will and commands must be submitted to by others and obeyed); the power of judicial decisions; one who possesses authority; a ruler, a human magistrate

These ten kings and kingdoms will be united in one cause, that of giving the Antichrist more power and authority. That will be their only reason for existing.

Greek Paraphrase of Verse: 13
These kings have one purpose, one mind, one common goal, and they give their power and authority to the beast.

Verse 14
¹⁴ These will wage war against the Lamb, but the Lamb will overcome them, because He is Lord of lords and King of kings, and those who are with Him are the called, chosen and faithful."

¹⁴ These will wage war
    against the Lamb,
      but the Lamb will overcome them,
        because He is Lord of lords
          and King of kings,
          and those who are with Him are the called,
            chosen
            and faithful."

This verse is a prelude of the events in Chapter 19.

These ten kingdoms will join the Antichrist in the fight against the Lamb who will defeat them.

Notice those who will be with the Lamb are "the called, chosen and faithful."

Greek Paraphrase of Verse: 14
They will wage war against Christ the Lamb, and the Lamb will triumph *and* conquer them, because He is Lord of lords and King of kings, and those who are with Him *and* on His side are the called and chosen, elect and faithful."

Verse 15
¹⁵ He said to me, "The waters you saw, where the prostitute sits, are peoples, multitudes, nations, and languages.

¹⁵ He said
    to me,
    "The waters you saw,
      where the prostitute sits,
    are peoples,
      multitudes,
      nations,
      and languages.

The angel from the first verse of this chapter is explaining things to John. Basically, they are all the peoples of the world.

Greek Paraphrase of Verse: 15
Then the angel said to me, "The waters you saw, where the prostitute is seated, are peoples, multitudes, nations and languages.
Verse 16
¹⁶ The ten horns you saw, and the beast, will hate the prostitute and will make her desolate and naked, devour her flesh, and burn her up with fire.

¹⁶ The ten horns
    you saw,
    and the beast,

will hate the prostitute
and
will make her desolate
  and naked,
  devour her flesh,
  and burn her up with fire.

desolate – to make desolate, lay waste; to ruin, bring to desolation; to despoil one, strip her of her treasures

Somewhere along the way, the ten kingdoms will grow to hate the prostitute and turn against her, destroying her. The description here is similar to Ezekiel 23:11-25.

When will all of this happen? Good question! All we know is that it will happen after the Antichrist has declared himself to be god and the kings have given him all their authority and power.

Greek Paraphrase of Verse: 16
And the ten horns you saw, and the beast, these will hate the prostitute and will make her desolate and stripped of her power and influence and will eat her flesh and completely consume her with fire.

Verse 17
[17] For God has put it into their hearts to accomplish His purpose by agreeing to give their kingdom to the beast until the words of God are fulfilled.

[17] For
  God has put it into their hearts
    to accomplish His purpose
      by agreeing to give their kingdom
        to the beast
        until the words
          of God
          are fulfilled.

accomplish – to make; to make ready, to prepare; to produce, bear, shoot forth; to carry out, to execute
purpose – the faculty of knowledge, mind, reason; that which is thought or known, one's mind; view, judgment, opinion; mind concerning what ought to be done; by one's self: resolve purpose, intention

Even though they don't know it, these kings will be fulfilling God's plans of judgment on the prostitute and helping the Antichrist.

Ironically, they are setting up their own judgment.

Greek Paraphrase of Verse: 17
For God has put it in their hearts to carry out His purpose by agreeing together to surrender their kingdoms to the beast until the prophetic words of God will be fulfilled.

Verse 18
¹⁸ The woman you saw is the great city that reigns over the kings of the earth. "

¹⁸ The woman
    you saw
    is the great city
        that reigns over the kings of the earth."

Now the prostitute is identified with the great city that has dominion over the kings of the earth. In Daniel's time, this was Babylon. In John's time, this was Rome

Even though it is called a city, the prostitute is actually the entire anti-God system that will be in place at that time which began at the tower of Babel and has dominated the world since.

Greek Paraphrase of Verse: 18
The woman you saw is the great city, which reigns over, dominates *and* controls the kings *and* the political leaders of the earth."

Chapter Eighteen

The emphasis in Chapter 18 is on the commercial and political aspects of the great Babylon.

This could be a literal city or nation. It could also be that it is the Babylon of the Old Testament times rebuilt.

Ancient Babylon was the economic, political and religious center of the large Mesopotamian area.

Verse 1
The Fall of Babylon the Great
¹ After this, I saw another angel with great authority coming down from heaven, and the earth was illuminated by his splendor.

¹ After this,
    I saw another angel
        with great authority
        coming down
            from heaven,
            and the earth was illuminated
                by his splendor.

authority – physical and mental power; the power of authority (influence) and of right (privilege); the power of rule or government (the power of him whose will and commands must be submitted to by others and obeyed); the power of judicial decisions; one who possesses authority; a ruler, a human magistrate

illuminated – to give light, to shine; to enlighten, light up, illumine; to bring to light, render evident; to cause something to exist and thus come to light and become clear to all; to enlighten, spiritually, imbue with saving knowledge; to instruct, to inform, teach; to give understanding to

splendor – splendor, brightness; of the moon, sun, stars; magnificence, excellence, preeminence, dignity, grace; majesty; a thing belonging to God

There seems to have been a passage of time before the final vision of God's judgment on the Babylon world system was given to John by still another angel who doesn't seem to have taken any part in the proceedings so far. John is on the earth looking up at heaven.

This angel is different in the sense that he has 'great authority' and is so bright, he lights up the earth.

Greek Paraphrase of Verse: 1
After these things I saw another angel coming down from heaven, possessing great power to rule, and the earth was lit up with his magnificence *and* radiance.

Verse 2
² He cried out with a mighty voice, saying, "Fallen, fallen is Babylon the great! She has become a dwelling place of demons, a haunt for every unclean spirit, a prison of every unclean and hateful bird.

² He cried out
>   with a mighty voice,
>   saying,
>   "Fallen,
>   fallen is Babylon the great!
>   She has become
>   a dwelling place of demons,
>   a haunt for every unclean spirit,
>   a prison of every unclean and hateful bird.

mighty – strong, mighty; strong either in body or in mind; strong, violent, forcibly uttered, firm, sure
fallen – to descend from a higher place to a lower; to fall (either from or upon); to be thrust down; metaphorically to fall under judgment, came under condemnation; to descend from an erect to a prostrate position; of those overcome by terror or astonishment or grief or under the attack of an evil spirit or of falling dead suddenly; the dismemberment of a corpse by decay; used of suppliants and persons rendering homage or worship to one; to be cast down from a state of prosperity; to perish, i.e come to an end, disappear, cease
demons – the divine power, deity, divinity; a spirit, a being inferior to God, superior to men; evil spirits or the messengers and ministers of the devil
haunt – guard, watch; a watching, keeping watch; persons keeping watch, a guard, sentinels; of the place where captives are kept, a prison
hateful – to hate, pursue with hatred, detest; to be hated, detested

Regardless of which Babylon this is, it will fall because it has become the home of demons, unclean spirits and every unclean and hateful bird.

When it is destroyed, its inhabitants will be preyed upon by all the unclean and hateful birds.

Greek Paraphrase of Verse: 2
And he shouted with a mighty voice, saying, "Fallen, fallen certainly to be destroyed is Babylon the great! She has become a dwelling place for demons, a dungeon haunted by every unclean spirit, and a prison for every unclean and loathsome bird.

Verse 3
³ For all the nations have drunk the wine of her immorality. The kings of the earth have committed acts of immorality with her, and the merchants of the earth have become rich from her excessive luxuries."

³ For
  all the nations have drunk the wine
    of her immorality.
  The kings
    of the earth
    have committed acts
      of immorality
      with her,
  and
  the merchants
    of the earth
    have become rich from her excessive luxuries."

committed acts of immorality – illicit sexual intercourse; adultery, fornication, homosexuality, lesbianism, intercourse with animals etc.; metaphorically the worship of idols; of the defilement of idolatry, as incurred by eating the sacrifices offered to idols
excessive – strength, power, ability (word we get dynamite from)
luxuries – excessive strength which longs to break forth, over strength; luxury; eager desire

All the nations joined with her in her idolatrous worship and practices. They even encouraged and then forced their subjects to do the same.

This is a case of the more riches the people received the more they wanted, no matter where they came from and no matter what they had to do to get them.

Greek Paraphrase of Verse: 3
For all the nations have drunk from the wine of the passion of her sexual immorality, and the kings and political leaders of the earth have committed acts of immorality with her, and the merchants of the earth have become rich by the wealth *and* economic power of her sensuous luxury."

Verse 4
⁴ *I heard another voice from heaven, saying, "Come out of her, My people, so that you will not share in her sins and receive any of her plagues.*

⁴ I heard another voice
  from heaven,
  saying,
    "Come out of her,
      My people,
      so that you will not share in her sins
        and receive any of her plagues.

share – to become a partaker together with others, or to have fellowship with a thing; to participate, to share with
receive – to take; to take up a thing to be carried; to take upon one's self; to take what is one's own, to take to one's self, to make one's own; to claim, procure, for one's self; to receive what is offered; not to refuse or reject; to receive a person, give him access to one's self
plagues – a blow, stripe, a wound; a public calamity, heavy affliction, plague

John is still on earth and he hears another voice from heaven but this one is not an angel. It is either God or someone speaking for Him.

This voice isn't speaking to John only but to all the people. It is another call for true believers to come out of Babylon so they will not suffer any of the plagues that are coming.

This follows with what God has always wanted, for His people to be separate from the world of the lost.

Greek Paraphrase of Verse: 4
And I heard another voice from heaven, saying, "Come out of her, My people, so that you will not be a partner in her sins and receive her plagues.

Verse 5
5 For her sins have piled up as high as heaven, and God has remembered her crimes.

5 For
    her sins have piled up
        as high as heaven,
        and God has remembered her crimes.

piled – to glue, to glue together, cement, fasten together; to join or fasten firmly together; to join one's self to, cleave to
remembered – to be mindful of, to remember, to call to mind; to think of and feel for a person or thing; to hold in memory, keep in mind; to make mention of
crimes – a misdeed, evil doing, iniquity

The sins of the world have piled up as high as heaven (Greek could also be 'sky'). But the key to this verse is that God never forgets their crimes.

Greek Paraphrase of Verse: 5
Because her sins, crimes and transgressions have piled up as high as heaven, and God has remembered her wickedness *and* crimes for judgment.

Verses 6-7
⁶ Pay her back even as she has paid and give back to her double for her deeds. In the cup, which she has mixed, mix twice as much for her. ⁷ To the degree that she glorified herself and lived luxuriously, give her that much torment and grief. Because she says in her heart, 'I sit as a queen. I am not a widow and will never see grief.'

⁶ Pay her back
    even as she has paid,
    and give back
      to her
      double for her deeds.
  In the cup,
    which she has mixed,
      mix twice as much for her.
        ⁷ To the degree
          that she glorified herself
          and lived luxuriously,
          give her that much torment and grief.
            Because she says
              in her heart,
              'I sit as a queen.
              I am not a widow,
                and will never see grief.'

Verse 6
⁶ Pay her back even as she has paid and give back to her double for her deeds. In the cup, which she has mixed, mix twice as much for her.

The call changes now for those assigned to do God's work to begin doing so.

Verse 7
⁷ To the degree that she glorified herself and lived luxuriously, give her that much torment and grief. Because she says in her heart, 'I sit as a queen. I am not a widow and will never see grief.'

degree – as great as, as far as, how much, how many, whoever
glorified – to praise, extol, magnify, celebrate; to honor, do honor to, hold in honor; to make glorious, adorn with luster, clothe with splendor
luxuriously – to be wanton, to live luxuriously
torment – to torture, a testing by the touchstone, which is a black siliceous stone used to test the purity of gold or silver by the color of the streak produced on it by rubbing it with either metal
grief – mourning, grief

The degree of punishment will be based on two things. First, on how she glorified herself, living luxuriously. Second, on how she bragged that she was above all grief and would never see any grief.

Greek Paraphrase of Verses: 6-7
Repay to her even as she has repaid *others and* pay back to her double her torment in accordance with what she has done. In the cup of sin and suffering which she mixed, mix a double portion of perfect justice for her. To the degree that she glorified herself and reveled *and* gloated in her sensuality, living deliciously and luxuriously, to that same degree impose on her torment, anguish, mourning *and* grief. Because in her heart she boasts, 'I sit as a queen on a throne and I am not a widow, and will never, ever see mourning *or* experience grief.

Verse 8
⁸ For this reason, her plagues will come in one day, death, mourning, and famine. She will be burned up with fire, for the Lord God who judges her is mighty.

⁸ For this reason,
    her plagues will come
        in one day,
        death,
        mourning
         and famine.
    She will be burned up
     with fire,
     for the Lord God
        who judges her
        is mighty.

plagues – a blow, stripe, a wound; a public calamity, heavy affliction, plague

Because Babylon tried to place herself in the place of God in all ways, her punishment will be severe and quick in one day. Burned with fire like the devil will be. He gives the reason for this that the Lord God judges and that He is mighty.

Greek Paraphrase of Verse: 8
For this reason, in a single day her plagues, afflictions and calamities will come, pestilence, mourning and famine. And she will be burned up with fire and completely consumed for the Lord God who judges her is strong and powerful.

Verse 9
The World Mourns Babylon's Fall
⁹ *The kings of the earth, who committed acts of immorality and lived luxuriously with her, will weep and mourn over her when they see the smoke of her burning.*

⁹ The kings
   of the earth,
   who committed acts of immorality
     and lived luxuriously with her,
     will weep and mourn over her
       when they see the smoke of her burning.

The mourning or lamentation that begins here will be the first of three. The rulers of the earth will start to fear that the same thing will happen to them. These are not the ten kings mentioned in Revelation 17:12. They are the rest of the rulers of the world.

Greek Paraphrase of Verse: 9
"And the kings *and* political leaders of the earth, who committed immorality and lived luxuriously with her, will weep and beat their chests in mourning over her when they see the smoke of her burning.

Verse 10
¹⁰ *They will stand at a distance in fear of her torment, saying, 'Woe, woe, the great city, Babylon, the strong city! For in one hour, your judgment has come.'*

¹⁰ They will stand
   at a distance
   in fear of her torment,
   saying,
     'Woe,
     woe,
     the great city,
       Babylon,
       the strong city!
         For in one hour,
           your judgment has come.'

torment – to torture, a testing by the touchstone, which is a black siliceous stone used to test the purity of gold or silver by the color of the streak produced on it by rubbing it with either metal
Babylon – "confusion" – a very large and famous city, the residence of the Babylonian kings, situated on both banks of the Euphrates. Cyrus had formerly captured it, but Darius Hystaspis threw down its gates and walls,

and Xerxes destroyed the temple of Belis. At length the city was reduced to almost solitude, the population having been drawn off by the neighboring Seleucia, built on the Tigris by Seleucus Nicanor.

These kings will not try to help Babylon. Instead, they will stand off at a distance and watch. They are too much afraid that they will be destroyed too if they help.

Calling it 'the great city' and 'the strong city' implies that they as well as the observers thought that it was invincible. But that wasn't the case. This is the judgment that comes on anyone who continues to deny God.

Greek Paraphrase of Verse: 10
They will be standing a long way off in fear of her torment, saying, 'Woe, woe, the great city, the strong city, Babylon! For in a single hour your judgment has come.'

Verses 11-13
[11] "The merchants of the earth will weep and mourn over her, because no one buys their merchandise anymore—[12] merchandise of gold, silver, precious stones, pearls, fine linen, purple, silk, scarlet, every kind of fragrant wood, every article of ivory, every article made from very costly wood, bronze, iron, marble, [13] cinnamon, spice, incense, perfume, frankincense, wine, olive oil, fine flour, wheat, cattle, sheep, horses, chariots and slaves, and human lives.

[11] "The merchants
   of the earth
  will weep and mourn
    over her,
    because no one buys their merchandise anymore—
      [12] merchandise of gold,
        silver,
        precious stones,
        pearls,
        fine linen,
        purple,
        silk,
        scarlet,
        every kind of fragrant wood,
        every article of ivory,
        every article made from very costly wood,
        bronze,
        iron,
        marble,
        [13] cinnamon,
        spice,
        incense,
        perfume,

frankincense,
wine,
olive oil,
fine flour,
wheat,
cattle,
sheep,
horses,
chariots,
slaves,
and human lives.

Verse 11
[11] *"The merchants of the earth will weep and mourn over her, because no one buys their merchandise anymore—*

The fall of Babylon seems to be accompanied by a worldwide economic collapse. The merchants don't seem to be weeping and mourning about Babylon, just that they no longer have a market for their merchandise.

Verse 12
[12] *merchandise of gold, silver, precious stones, pearls, fine linen, purple, silk, scarlet, every kind of fragrant wood, every article of ivory, every article made from very costly wood, bronze, iron, marble,*

merchandise – a lading or freight of a ship, cargo, merchandise conveyed in a ship; any merchandise

Prior to this time, Babylon and the areas nearby seems to have had a time of great prosperity, economic activity and excessive luxury. Just look at all the merchandise that is mentioned in this verse. All of them are luxury items.

Verse 13
[13] *cinnamon, spice, incense, perfume, frankincense, wine, olive oil, fine flour, wheat, cattle, sheep, horses, chariots and slaves, and human lives.*

More proof that it will be a time of excessive luxury. The slave trade was one of the most profitable trades of the time. Often, the only expense the merchant had was transporting them from where they were captured to where they were sold.

Greek Paraphrase of Verses: 11-13
"And the merchants of the earth will weep and grieve over her, because no one buys their cargo anymore—cargoes of gold, silver, precious stones, pearls, fine linen, purple, silk and scarlet, all *kinds of* fragrant scented wood and every article of ivory and every article of very costly

and lavish wood, bronze, iron and marble, and cinnamon, spices, incense, perfume, frankincense, wine, olive oil, fine flour, wheat, cattle, sheep, and *cargoes* **of horses, chariots, carriages, slaves and human lives.**

Verse 14
[14] The fruit you long for is gone from you. All your splendid and glamorous things are gone, and men will never find them.

[14] The fruit you long for is gone from you.
   All your splendid and glamorous things are gone
      and men will never find them.

This is a general statement that sums up what the situation will be like for the people who have grown accustomed to all the luxuries that were mentioned in Verses 12 and 13. They will sorely miss all of those things.

But what they don't know and probably won't benefit from is that the future, beyond this point when Christ rules, things will be so many times better than before the fall of Babylon.

Greek Paraphrase of Verse: 14
The ripe fruits *and* **delicacies of your soul's desire have gone from you, and all things that were luxurious and extravagant are lost to you, never again to be found.**

Verses 15-18
[15] The merchants of these things, who became rich from her, will stand far off in fear of her torment, weeping and mourning, [16] saying, 'Woe, woe, the great city, clothed in fine linen, purple, and scarlet, adorned with gold, precious stones, and pearls; [17] for in one hour such great wealth has been destroyed!' Every shipmaster, passenger, sailor, and all who make their living by the sea, stood far off [18] and were crying out as they saw the smoke of her burning, saying, 'What city is like the great city?'

[15] The merchants
   of these things,
   who became rich from her,
      will stand far off
         in fear of her torment,
         weeping and mourning,
         [16] saying,
            'Woe,
            woe,
            the great city,
               clothed in fine linen,
               purple,
               and scarlet,

adorned with gold,
precious stones,
and pearls;
   ¹⁷ for in one hour such great wealth
    has been destroyed!'
Every shipmaster,
  passenger,
  sailor,
  and all who make their living by the sea,
    stood far off
      ¹⁸ and were crying out
      as they saw the smoke of her burning,
      saying,
        'What city is like the great city?'

Verse 15

¹⁵ The merchants of these things, who became rich from her, will stand far off in fear of her torment, weeping and mourning,

This verse is basically a repetition of Verse 11. But actually, Verses 12-14 are stuck in to explain Verse 11 and the description continues with Verse 15.

This verse indicates that the merchants were not concerned about all the people in Babylon, but they were only concerned about their own loss of income. They were friends with the people of Babylon only as long as they made a profit off them. Once that was gone, so was their friendship. (Sound familiar?)

Verse 16

¹⁶ saying, 'Woe, woe, the great city, clothed in fine linen, purple, and scarlet, adorned with gold, precious stones, and pearls;

Here are the woes again. The word conveys a mixture of judgment, warning and sorrow.

Verse 17

¹⁷ for in one hour such great wealth has been destroyed!' Every shipmaster, passenger, sailor, and all who make their living by the sea, stood far off

Look at how quickly years of trading and hording just disappeared, in one hour. Again, it is those who made a huge profit off the trade that are lamenting the loss of it.

Verse 18

¹⁸ and were crying out as they saw the smoke of her burning, saying, 'What city is like the great city?'

They are not only upset over what they have lost but they can't believe that such a great city could be destroyed the way it will be.

Greek Paraphrase of Verses: 15-18
The merchants who handled these things, who grew wealthy from their business with her, will stand far away in fear of her torment, weeping and mourning aloud, saying, 'Woe, woe, for the great city that was clothed in fine linen, purple and scarlet, gilded *and* adorned with gold, precious stones, and pearls; because in one hour all the vast wealth has been laid waste.' And every ship captain *or* navigator, and every passenger and sailor, and all who make their living by the sea, stood a long way off, and cried out as they watched the smoke of her burning, saying, 'What could be compared to the great city?'

Verse 19
19 They threw dust on their heads and were crying out, weeping, and mourning, saying, 'Woe, woe, the great city, where all who had ships at sea became rich from her wealth, for in one hour she was destroyed!'

19 They threw dust on their heads
    and were crying out,
    weeping,
    and mourning,
    saying,
     'Woe,
     woe,
     the great city,
      where all
       who had ships at sea
       became rich from her wealth,
        for in one hour she was destroyed!'

More of the same! Again, the merchants are more concerned for their loss than that of the city of Babylon.

Greek Paraphrase of Verse: 19
And they threw dust on their heads and were crying out, weeping and mourning, saying, 'Woe, woe, for the great city, where all who had ships at sea grew rich from her great wealth, because in one hour she has been laid waste!'

Verse 20
20 Rejoice over her, O heaven, and you saints, apostles, and prophets, because God has pronounced judgment for you against her."

^{20} Rejoice over her,
    O heaven,
    and you saints,
    apostles,
    and prophets,
    because God has pronounced judgment
      for you
        against her."

Instead of mourning, heaven and especially those Christians who were persecuted should rejoice over Babylon being destroyed. It is their judgment against those who had persecuted them.

The Lord has taken vengeance as only He can do, and the outcome will be great for all believers.

Greek Paraphrase of Verse: 20
Rejoice over her, O heaven, and you God's people, apostles and prophets who were martyred, because God has executed vengeance for you through righteous judgment upon her."

Verse 21
The Finality of Babylon's Fall
^{21} *Then a mighty angel picked up a stone like a large millstone and threw it into the sea, saying, "Thus will Babylon, the great city, be thrown down violently and will never be found again.*

^{21} Then
    a mighty angel picked up a stone
      like a large millstone
      and threw it into the sea,
        saying,
          "Thus will Babylon,
            the great city,
            be thrown down
              violently
              and will never be found again.

This is a symbolic gesture saying that the same thing will happen to Babylon and it will never rise again.

Greek Paraphrase of Verse: 21
Then a single powerful angel picked up a stone like a great millstone and flung it into the sea, saying, "Thus will Babylon the great city be hurled down with violence by the sudden, spectacular judgment of God, and will never again be found.

Verse 22
²² The sound of harpists, musicians, flute-players, and trumpeters will never be heard in you again, and no craftsman of any craft will ever be found in you again, and the sound of a mill will never be heard in you again.

²² The sound
    of harpists,
    musicians,
    flute-players,
    and trumpeters
    will never be heard
      in you
      again,
and
no craftsman
    of any craft
    will ever be found
      in you
      again,
    and the sound of a mill
      will never be heard
        in you
        again.

This is further proof of what will be missing. There will be no joy, or celebrations of any kind. There will be no work of any kind performed. In fact, no sounds will be heard at all.

Greek Paraphrase of Verse: 22
The sound of harpists, musicians, flutists and trumpeters will never again be heard in you, and no skilled craftsman of any craft will ever again be found in you, and the sound of the millstone grinding grain will never again be heard in you for business will no longer flourish, and normal life will cease.

Verse 23
²³ The light of a lamp will never shine in you again, and the voice of the bridegroom and bride will never be heard in you again, for your merchants were the great men of the earth, because all the nations were deceived by your sorcery.

²³ The light
    of a lamp
    will never shine
      in you
      again
and

the voice
   of the bridegroom and bride
   will never be heard
      in you
      again,
      for your merchants were the great men
         of the earth,
            because all the nations were deceived by your sorcery.

deceived – to cause to stray, to lead astray, lead aside from the right way; to go astray, wander, roam about; metaphorically to lead away from the truth, to lead into error, to deceive; to be led into error; to be led aside from the path of virtue, to go astray, sin; to sever or fall away from the truth; to be led away into error and sin
sorcery – the use or the administering of drugs; poisoning; sorcery, magical arts, often found in connection with idolatry and fostered by it; metaphorically the deceptions and seductions of idolatry

Not only no sounds but no lights of any kind will ever be seen in the city of Babylon. Not only that but no more marriages. All of that is just to emphasize that there will be nothing and no one left after the destruction of Babylon. Such is the great judgment of God.

Greek Paraphrase of Verse: 23
And the light of a lamp will never again shine in you, and the voice of the bridegroom and bride will never again be heard in you, because your merchants were the great and prominent men of the earth, since all the nations were deceived *and* misled by your magic spells and poisonous charm.

Verse 24
²⁴ And the blood of prophets and of saints and all who have been slain on the earth was found in her."

²⁴ And
   the blood
      of prophets
      and
      of saints
      and
      all who have been slain
         on the earth
         was found in her."

After the city was destroyed, they found proof of all the prophets and saints who were killed there. This further proves that the city needed to be destroyed.

Greek Paraphrase of Verse: 24
And the blood of prophets, God's people and of all those who have been slaughtered on the earth was found in Babylon."

Chapter Nineteen

This chapter tells about what is taking place in heaven while the Tribulation rages. The halleluiahs, marriage of the Lamb, second coming in glory, Armageddon, doom of the beast, False Prophet, and kings.

During those days when the wrath of God is poured out upon the earth, the Bride of Christ will celebrate the long looked for marriage celebrations. Dressed in her cleansed clothes, she will be eternally united with the King of Kings and Lord of Lords. When He comes to end all evil, His Bride will come with Him, linked in judgment, and later to rule with Him.

Verses 1-2
Heaven Exults over Babylon
¹ After this, I heard something like the loud voice of a great multitude in heaven, saying, "Hallelujah! Salvation, glory, and power belong to our God, ² because His judgments are true and righteous. He has judged the great prostitute who corrupted the earth with her immorality, and He has avenged the blood of His servants on her."

¹ After this,
    I heard something like the loud voice
      of a great multitude
      in heaven,
      saying,
        "Hallelujah!
        Salvation,
        glory
         and
        power
          belong to our God,
            ² because His judgments are true and righteous.
He has judged the great prostitute
    who corrupted the earth
      with her immorality,
and
He has avenged the blood
    of His servants
    on her."

Verse 1
¹ After this, I heard something like the loud voice of a great multitude in heaven, saying, "Hallelujah! Salvation, glory, and power belong to our God,

Another vision is coming. Chapters 17 and 18 mostly dealt with the fall of the world system that Babylon had accumulated. Chapter 19 deals with the final defeat of the Antichrist at the end of the Tribulation when Christ makes his triumphant return.

Angels don't introduce this vision but loud voices of a combined heavenly choir singing a Hallelujah chorus.

Verse 2
² because His judgments are true and righteous. He has judged the great prostitute who corrupted the earth with her immorality, and He has avenged the blood of His servants on her."

corrupted – to corrupt, to destroy; to be destroyed, to perish; in an ethical sense, to corrupt, deprave; to lead away a Christian church from that state of knowledge and holiness in which it ought to abide
immorality – illicit sexual intercourse; adultery, fornication, homosexuality, lesbianism, intercourse with animals etc.; metaphorically the worship of idols; of the defilement of idolatry, as incurred by eating the sacrifices offered to idols
avenged – to vindicate one's right, do one justice; to protect, defend, one person from another; to avenge a thing; to punish a person for a thing

The chorus is praising God that His judgments are true and righteous. They also seem to be celebrating His judgment on Babylon for avenging the believers who were persecuted there.

Greek Paraphrase of Verses: 1-2
After these things I heard something like the great *and* mighty shout of a great multitude in heaven, shouting, "Hallelujah! Salvation, splendor, majesty dominion and might belong to our God, because His judgments are true and righteous. He has convicted and pronounced sentence on the great idolatress who was corrupting, ruining and poisoning the earth with her sexual immorality, and He has imposed the penalty for the blood of his servants on her."

Verse 3
³ A second time they said, "Hallelujah! Her smoke rises up forever and ever."

³ A second time they said,
"Hallelujah!
Her smoke rises up forever and ever."

The smoke rising forever is looked at in two different ways. One is that it is reminiscent of the destruction of Edom in Isaiah 34:9-10. The other one is that the smoke will continue on through the atmosphere into distant galaxies forever.

Greek Paraphrase of Verse: 3
And a second time they said, "Hallelujah! Her smoke will ascend forever and ever."

Verse 4
⁴ And the twenty-four elders and the four living creatures fell down and worshiped God who is sitting on the throne saying, "Amen. Hallelujah!"

⁴ And
  the twenty-four elders
  and
  the four living creatures
    fell down and worshiped God
      who is sitting on the throne
      saying,
        "Amen.
        Hallelujah!"

The twenty-four elders and the four living creatures respond to the Hallelujah chorus by saying amen and Hallelujah. They are giving their full approval of what God has done to Babylon.

Greek Paraphrase of Verse: 4
Then the twenty-four elders and the four living creatures also fell down and worshiped God who sits on the throne, saying, "Amen. praise the Lord!"

Verse 5
⁵ A voice came from the throne, saying, "Praise our God, all you His servants, you who fear Him, both small and the great."

⁵ A voice came
  from the throne,
  saying,
    "Praise our God,
      all you His servants,
      you who fear Him,
      both small and the great."

Some think that the voice is one of the four living creatures. Others think it is another angel out of sight.

The servants are all those who revere, worship and serve God. They are devoted to Him.

Greek Paraphrase of Verse: 5
Then a voice came from the throne, saying, "Praise our God, all you His servants, you who fear Him, both the small and the great."

Verse 6
Marriage of the Lamb Announced
⁶ Then I heard something like the voice of a great multitude, like the sound of rushing waters and like the sound of loud thunder, saying, "Hallelujah! For the Lord God Almighty reigns.

⁶ Then
    I heard something like the voice
      of a great multitude,
      like the sound of rushing waters
      and like the sound of loud thunder,
      saying,
        "Hallelujah!
        For the Lord God Almighty reigns.

The praise here is louder and more joyful than the previous praise.

Greek Paraphrase of Verse: 6
Then I heard *something* like the shout of a great multitude, and like the sound of many pounding waves, and like the roar of mighty peals of thunder, saying, "Hallelujah! For the Lord our God, the Almighty, the Omnipotent, the Ruler of all reigns.

Verse 7
⁷ Let us rejoice, be glad, and give Him the glory, for the marriage of the Lamb has come, and His bride has made herself ready."

⁷ Let us rejoice,
    be glad,
    and
    give Him the glory,
    for the marriage
      of the Lamb
      has come,
        and
      His bride has made herself ready."

glory – splendor, brightness; of the moon, sun, stars; magnificence, excellence, preeminence, dignity, grace; majesty; a thing belonging to God

The Marriage Supper of the Lamb is coming. This will fulfill the parables and prophecies of the relationship of the Church to Christ.

Note that the time is after the judgment on the prostitute which is contrasted with the true Church

Greek Paraphrase of Verse: 7
"Let us rejoice, be glad and shout for joy! Let us give Him glory and honor, for the marriage of the Lamb has come at last and His bride has prepared herself."

Verse 8
⁸ Fine linen, bright and clean was given her to wear. The fine linen represents the righteous acts of the saints.

⁸ Fine linen,
   bright and clean
   was given her to wear.
  The fine linen represents the righteous acts of the saints.

The fine linen being bright and clean signifies that she is free from all impurity. The fine linen itself represents the righteousness of the saints.

The Greek word for 'righteous' is plural therefore it includes all believers.

Greek Paraphrase of Verse: 8
She was permitted to wear fine linen, dazzling white and clean--for the fine linen represents the righteous acts, ethical conduct, personal integrity, moral courage, and godly character of God's people.

Verse 9
⁹ Then he said to me, "Write, 'Blessed are those who are invited to the marriage supper of the Lamb.'" And he said to me, "These are the true words of God."

⁹ Then
  he said
   to me,
   "Write,
    'Blessed are those
     who are invited
      to the marriage supper
       of the Lamb.'"
  And
  he said
   to me,
   "These are the true words of God."

Trennis E. Killian

invited – to call or invite

The same angelic voice is now commanding John to write. Some think that John was to give a special word to the seven churches. But more than likely, it is to all churches.

Some translate this as being called instead of being invited. Even though the Greek word can mean to be called, I don't think the context supports that translation. We don't want to confuse a calling to salvation or ministry with a simple invitation to a wedding supper.

There have been many words spoken throughout all the visions but this one wants us to know that these words are the true words of God.

Greek Paraphrase of Verse: 9
Then the angel said to me, "Write, 'Blessed are those who are invited to the marriage supper of the Lamb.'" And he said to me, "These are the true *and* exact words of God."

Verse 10
[10] Then I fell at his feet to worship him. But he said to me, "Do not do that. I am a fellow servant of yours and your brothers who have the testimony of Jesus. Worship God, for the testimony of Jesus is the spirit of prophecy."

[10] Then
  I fell at his feet
    to worship him.
      But he said
        to me,
        "Do not do that.
        I am a fellow servant
          of yours
          and
          your brothers
            who have the testimony of Jesus.
        Worship God,
          for the testimony
          of Jesus
          is the spirit of prophecy."

All the wonder, glory and hope overwhelmed John and he wanted to worship the voice, but the angel told him that he was a fellow servant and to only worship God. Kind of the reverse of killing the messenger.

Greek Paraphrase of Verse: 10
Then I fell down at his feet to worship him, but he stopped me and said to me, "Do not do that, I am a fellow servant with you and your brothers and sisters who have and have the testimony of Jesus. Worship God

alone, because the testimony of Jesus is His life and teaching are the heart of prophecy."

Verse 11
The Rider on a White Horse
[11] I saw heaven opened, and behold, a white horse. The One sitting on it is called Faithful and True, and in righteousness He judges and makes war.

[11] I saw heaven opened,
   and behold,
     a white horse.
       The One sitting on it
         is called Faithful and True,
         and
         in righteousness He judges and makes war.

The Marriage Supper of the Lamb is not described here but goes on to another vision. In that vision, John sees heaven opened and Jesus returning on a white horse which means He is returning a mighty conqueror and triumphant King of kings and Lord of lords.

Greek Paraphrase of Verse: 11
I saw heaven opened, and behold, a white horse, and the One who was riding it is called Faithful and True, and He judges in righteousness and wages war on the rebellious nations.

Verse 12
[12] His eyes are a flame of fire, and on His head are many crowns. He has a name written on Him that no one knows except Himself.

[12] His eyes are a flame
   of fire,
   and on His head are many crowns.
  He has a name
   written on Him
   that no one knows except Himself.

His eyes being a flame mean that nothing will escape Christ's righteous judgment. No one can hide from Him.

The many royal crowns (diadems) show that He comes as King of kings to make David's throne eternal and to fulfill the many prophecies that He will reign on earth.

The name (or names) speaks of the divine nature and inner glory he shares with God the Father (Luke 10:22).

Greek Paraphrase of Verse: 12
His eyes are a flame of fire, and many royal crowns are on His head. He has a name inscribed on Him which no one knows *or* understands except Himself.

Verse 13
[13] He is dressed in a robe dipped in blood, and His name is called The Word of God.

[13] He is dressed
   in a robe dipped in blood,
      and His name is called The Word of God.

His robe dipped in blood proves that this is the same Jesus who shed His blood, rose from the dead and ascended into heaver.
Dipped in blood can also mean spattered by the blood of His enemies after He judged them.

Greek Paraphrase of Verse: 13
He is dressed in a robe dipped in blood, and His name is called The Word of God.

Verse 14
[14] The armies that were in heaven were following Him on white horses, wearing pure white linen.

[14] The armies
   that were in heaven
   were following Him
      on white horses,
      wearing pure white linen.

This is the final battle of Armageddon and all the armies in heaven are following Jesus into battle. Notice that they also ride white horses and wear pure white linen. This identifies them with Christ.

Greek Paraphrase of Verse: 14
And the armies of heaven followed Him on white horses, and they were dressed in dazzling white and clean fine linen.

Verse 15
[15] From His mouth comes a sharp sword, so that with it He may strike down the nations. He will rule them with an iron scepter. He treads the winepress of the fierce anger of God Almighty.

¹⁵ From His mouth comes a sharp sword,
   so that with it He may strike down the nations.
He will rule them
   with an iron scepter.
He treads the winepress
   of the fierce anger
     of God Almighty.

scepter – a staff, a walking stick, a twig, rod, branch; a rod with which one is beaten; a staff as used on a journey, or to lean upon, or by shepherds; with a rod of iron, indicates the severest, most rigorous rule; a royal scepter

There are three pictures of how terrible the judgment that Jesus brings will be.

First, the sharp sword out of the mouth of the rider represents:
Ephesians 6:17, "the sword of the Spirit, which is the word of God."

Second, the sharp sword striking down the nations is parallel to the shattering of the nations with a rod of iron in Psalm 2:9. This means that the shepherd will destroy all the enemies of the sheep.

The third one is that the day of judgment will come like:
2 Peter 3:10, "But the day of the Lord will come like a thief."

Greek Paraphrase of Verse: 15
From His mouth comes His sharp sword with which He may strike down the nations, and He will rule them with a rod of iron. He will tread the wine press of the fierce wrath of God, the Almighty in judgment of the rebellious world.

Verse 16
¹⁶ And on His robe, and on His thigh, He has a name written, "King of kings, and Lord of lords."

¹⁶ And
   on His robe,
   and
   on His thigh,
     He has a name written,
      "King of kings,
      and
      Lord of lords."

Jesus is called "King of kings and Lord of lords" only one place in the New Testament outside of Revelation, 1 Timothy 6:15 and only one other place in Revelation, 17:14.

On His thigh probably means on His robe at His thigh but some think the literal interpretation is best and that it is both on His robe and on His thigh. Either way, it is in plain sight for all to see.

Greek Paraphrase of Verse: 16
And on His robe and on His thigh, He has a name inscribed, "King of kings, and Lord of lords."

Verses 17-18
The Beast and His Armies Defeated
[17] Then I saw an angel standing in the sun, and he cried out in a loud voice, saying to all the birds flying in mid-heaven, "Come, gather together for the great supper of God, [18] so that you may eat the flesh of kings, the flesh of commanders, the flesh of mighty men, the flesh of horses and of their riders, and the flesh of all men, both free and slave, small and great."

[17] Then
  I saw an angel
    standing in the sun,
    and
    he cried out
      in a loud voice,
     saying
       to all the birds flying in mid-heaven,
       "Come,
       gather together
        for the great supper of God,
         [18] so that you may eat
          the flesh of kings,
          the flesh of commanders,
          the flesh of mighty men,
          the flesh of horses and of their riders,
          and the flesh of all men,
            both free and slave,
            small and great."

Verse 17
[17] Then I saw an angel standing in the sun, and he cried out in a loud voice, saying to all the birds flying in mid-heaven, "Come, gather together for the great supper of God,

This next vision is a drastic contrast to the marriage Supper of the Lamb. Some think the angel was actually standing in the sun. Most think he was standing directly in the sunlight.

The big battle will soon be over and he's calling the birds to be ready.

Verse 18
¹⁸ *so that you may eat the flesh of kings, the flesh of commanders, the flesh of mighty men, the flesh of horses and of their riders, and the flesh of all men, both free and slave, small and great."*

Now, the birds will be let loose on all the dead of the war which will include all men, high or low, free or slave and even the horses.

Greek Paraphrase of Verses: 17-18
Then I saw a single angel standing in the sun, and he shouted with a loud voice to all the birds that fly at the highest point in the heavens, saying, "Come, gather together for the great supper of God, so that you may feast on the flesh of kings, the flesh of commanders, the flesh of powerful *and* mighty men, the flesh of horses and of those who sit on them, and the flesh of all mankind, both free and slaves, both small and great in a complete conquest of evil."

Verse 19
¹⁹ *Then I saw the beast, the kings of the earth, and their armies gathered together to make war against the One sitting on the horse and against His army.*

¹⁹ Then
  I saw
    the beast,
    the kings of the earth,
      and their armies
      gathered together
        to make war
        against the One sitting on the horse
        and
        against His army.

It's finally coming, the war to end all wars and Christ is ready, sitting on His horse.

Greek Paraphrase of Verse: 19
Then I saw the beast, the kings *and* political leaders of the earth with their armies gathered together to make war against the One who is mounted on the white horse and against His army.

Verse 20
²⁰ *But the beast was captured, and with him the false prophet who performed the signs in his presence, by which he deceived those who had received the*

mark of the beast and those who worshiped his image. Both of them were thrown alive into the lake of fire that burns with sulfur.

[20] But
  the beast was captured,
    and with him the false prophet
      who performed the signs
        in his presence,
        by which he deceived those
          who had received the mark
            of the beast
        and
        those who worshiped his image.
      Both of them were thrown
        alive
        into the lake of fire
          that burns with sulfur.

The battle won't last long. The wild beast (Antichrist0 and his false prophet will both be captured right away. This false prophet will be the last in the long line of them as in:

Matthew 24:24, For false Christs and false prophets will arise and will do great signs and wonders so as to mislead, if possible, even the elect.

It is ironic that the wild beast and the false prophet will be thrown into the lake of fire that was prepared for the devil and his angels, these two qualify in that sense. They are truly agents of the devil.

Greek Paraphrase of Verse: 20
But the beast, the Antichrist, was seized and overpowered, and with him the false prophet who, in his presence, had performed amazing signs to deceive those who had received the mark of the beast and those who worshiped his image. They were both thrown alive into the lake of fire which burns with sulfur.

Verse 21
[21] The rest were killed with the sword that came from the mouth of the One sitting on the horse, and all the birds were filled with their flesh.

[21] The rest were killed
  with the sword
    that came
      from the mouth
      of the One sitting on the horse,
  and all the birds were filled with their flesh.

None of the other followers of the Antichrist will escape. Christ will kill them with the sword of His mouth. Then the birds will eat them all.

Greek Paraphrase of Verse: 21
The rest were killed with the sword which came from the mouth of the One who sat on the horse, and all the birds fed themselves on their flesh.

Chapter Twenty

This is an eventful chapter. It starts out with an angel binding the devil for a thousand years in the bottomless pit.

All of those beheaded for their testimony of Jesus will have part in the first resurrection and will reign with Christ for a thousand years.

Once the thousand years are over, the devil will be released from his prison and go out doing what he always did and also gather Gog and Magog from the four corners of the earth.

Then they will lay siege to the holy city, but fire will come down from heaven and consume them then they will be cast into the lake of fire.

The dead will be all judged according to their works.

The dead will come up from the sea, death and hades which will be destroyed. Then all whose names aren't written in the book of life will be thrown into the lake of fire.

Verse 1
Satan Bound
¹ Then I saw an angel coming down from heaven with the key to the abyss and a great chain in his hand.

¹ Then
  I saw an angel
    coming down from heaven
    with the key to the abys
    and
    a great chain in his hand.

abyss – Bottomless; unbounded; the abyss; the pit; the immeasurable depth; of Orcus, a very deep gulf or chasm in the lowest parts of the earth used as the common receptacle of the dead and especially as the abode of demons

Here comes the angel who will capture the devil and put him in chains before putting him in the bottomless pit.

Greek Paraphrase of Verse: 1
And then I saw an angel coming down from heaven, holding the key of the bottomless pit and a great chain was in his hand.

Verse 2
² He seized the dragon, that ancient serpent, who is the devil and Satan, and bound him for a thousand years.

² He seized the dragon,
    that ancient serpent,
    who is the devil and Satan,

and bound him for a thousand years.

This is when the long-anticipated event happens. The devil is finally bound and imprisoned for a thousand years.

Greek Paraphrase of Verse: 2
He overpowered and seized the dragon, that old serpent of primeval times, who is the devil and Satan, and bound him securely for a thousand years.

Verse 3
3 He threw him into the abyss, closed and sealed it over him, so that he would not deceive the nations any longer, until the thousand years were completed. After that, he must be released for a short time.

³ He threw him into the abyss,
    closed and sealed it over him,
    so that he would not deceive the nations any longer,
    until the thousand years were completed.
        After that,
            he must be released for a short time.

abyss – Bottomless; unbounded; the abyss; the pit; the immeasurable depth; of Orcus, a very deep gulf or chasm in the lowest parts of the earth used as the common receptacle of the dead and especially as the abode of demons

The angel threw the devil in the bottomless pit and sealed it over him so he could have no more sway over the nations. Also, the pit is sealed to prevent anyone from rescuing him.

Greek Paraphrase of Verse: 3
The angel threw him into the bottomless pit and closed it and sealed it over him preventing his escape or rescue, so that he would no longer deceive and seduce the nations, until the thousand years were at an end. After these things he must be released for a short time.

Verse 4
The Saints Reign with the Messiah
4 Then I saw thrones, and they sat on them, and judgment was given to them. I saw the souls of those who had been beheaded because of their testimony about Jesus and because of the word of God, and those who had not worshiped the beast or his image and had not received the mark on their foreheads and on their hands. They came to life and reigned with Christ for a thousand years.

⁴ Then
>   I saw thrones,
>   and they sat on them,
>   and judgment was given to them.
>   I saw the souls
>   of those who had been beheaded
>   because of their testimony
>   about Jesus
>   and
>   because of the word of God,
>   and
>   those who had not worshiped the beast or his image,
>   and had not received the mark
>   on their foreheads
>   and
>   on their hands.
>   They came to life
>   and reigned
>   with Christ
>   for a thousand years.

Now begins the thousand-year reign of Christ with His saints (the Millennium).

This verse describes two groups of people. First, the souls (people) who sit on thrones to judge (rule).

The second group is all those who were faithful to Christ and were martyred during the Tribulation.

Greek Paraphrase of Verse: 4
Then I saw thrones and sitting on them were those to whom the authority to act as judges was given. *I saw* the souls of those who had been beheaded because of their testimony of Jesus and because of the word of God, and those who had refused to worship the beast or his image and had not received his mark on their foreheads and on their hands. They came to life and reigned with Christ for a thousand years.

Verse 5
⁵ The rest of the dead did not come to life until the thousand years were completed. This is the first resurrection.

⁵ The rest of the dead did not come to life
>   until the thousand years were completed.
>   This is the first resurrection.

The rest of the dead is all those not in the first two groups.

Jesus spoke of two resurrections in John 5:29. The first resurrection is that of the believers and the second resurrection is all the rest.

Greek Paraphrase of Verse: 5
The rest of the dead, the non-believers, did not come to life until the thousand years were completed. This is the first resurrection.

Verse 6
⁶ Blessed and holy is the one who has a part in the first resurrection. The second death has no power over these, but they will be priests of God and of Christ and will reign with Him for a thousand years.

⁶ Blessed and holy is the one
    who has a part
    in the first resurrection.
  The second death has no power over these,
    but they will be priests
      of God
      and
      of Christ
      and
      will reign
        with Him
        for a thousand years.

God's special blessing will be on those of the first resurrection. They won't be affected by the second death, but they will be with Christ and help Him reign for a thousand years.

Greek Paraphrase of Verse: 6
Blessed and holy is the one who takes part in the first resurrection. The second death, which is the lake of fire, eternal separation from God, has no power *or* authority over these, but they will be priests of God and of Christ and they will reign with Him for a thousand years.

Verses 7-8
Satan's Rebellion Defeated
⁷ When the thousand years are completed, Satan will be released from his prison ⁸ and will go out to deceive the nations at the four corners of the earth, Gog and Magog, to gather them together for battle. Their number is like the sand of the seashore.

⁷ When the thousand years are completed,
    Satan will be released from his prison
      ⁸ and will go out
        to deceive the nations
        at the four corners of the earth,

> Gog and Magog,
> to gather them together for battle.
> Their number is like the sand of the seashore.

Verse 7
⁷ When the thousand years are completed, Satan will be released from his prison

There is nothing else mentioned about the Millennium. Now, the next phase will start with the devil being released.

I wonder if the devil will still think he can defeat God. No way!

Verse 8
⁸ and will go out to deceive the nations at the four corners of the earth, Gog and Magog, to gather them together for battle. Their number is like the sand of the seashore.

Gog – "mountain" – the king of the land of Magog who will come from the north and attack the land of Israel

Magog – "overtopping: covering" – a land north of Israel from which the King, Gog will come to attack Israel

But the devil will still be able to deceive all those left behind after the first resurrection. Of course, he already had them to begin with.

The nations are here called Gog and Magog which are terms from Ezekiel Chapters 38 and 39.

Greek Paraphrase of Verses: 7-8
When the thousand years are completed, Satan will be released from his prison the bottomless pit and will come out to deceive *and* mislead the nations at the four corners of the earth, including Gog and Magog, to gather them together for the war. Their number is like the sand of the seashore.

Verse 9
⁹ They came up over the breadth of the earth and surrounded the camp of the saints and the beloved city. Fire came down from heaven and devoured them.

⁹ They came up
> over the breadth of the earth
> and surrounded the camp
> > of the saints
> > and the beloved city.
> Fire came down from heaven and devoured them.

As they tried to surround the saints, fire from heaven destroyed them.

Greek Paraphrase of Verse: 9
And they came up over the broad plain of the earth and surrounded the camp of God's people and the beloved city Jerusalem. But fire came down from heaven and consumed them.

Verse 10

[10] The devil who deceived them was thrown into the lake of fire and sulfur where the beast and the false prophet are also, and they will be tormented day and night forever and ever.

[10] The devil
    who deceived them
    was thrown into the lake
      of fire and sulfur
      where the beast and the false prophet are also,
        and they will be tormented
          day and night
          forever and ever.

tormented – to test (metals) by the touchstone, which is a black siliceous stone used to test the purity of gold or silver by the color of the streak produced on it by rubbing it with either metal; to question by applying torture; to torture; to vex with grievous pains (of body or mind), to torment; to be harassed, distressed; of those who at sea are struggling with a head wind

Not only will the devil lose but he will be thrown into the lake of fire with the beast and the false prophet to be tormented all day long forever.

Greek Paraphrase of Verse: 10
And the devil who had deceived them was thrown into the lake of fire and burning brimstone, where the beast, the Antichrist and false prophet are also, and they will be tormented day and night, forever and ever.

Verse 11
The Great White Throne Judgment

[11] Then I saw a great white throne and the One sitting on it. Earth and heaven fled away from His presence, and no place was found for them.

[11] Then
    I saw a great white throne
      and the One sitting on it.
    Earth and heaven fled away
      from His presence,
      and no place was found for them.

Now that the devil is out of the way forever, those who followed him and never turned to Christ will be found and judged.

Greek Paraphrase of Verse: 11
Then I saw a great white throne and the One who was seated on it. Earth and heaven fled away from His presence, and no place was found for them because this heaven and earth are passing away.

Verse 12
12 I saw the dead, the great and the small, standing before the throne, and books were opened. Another book was opened, which is the Book of Life, and the dead were judged according to their works by what was written in the books.

12 I saw the dead,
    the great
    and the small,
    standing before the throne,
      and books were opened.
  Another book was opened,
    which is the Book of Life,
    and the dead were judged
      according to their works
      by what was written in the books.

Now it is time for the dead to be judged according to what they did while alive. This only includes those who were not resurrected during the first resurrection. This will only be those non-believers throughout time.

Greek Paraphrase of Verse: 12
I saw the dead, the great and the small, standing before the throne, and books were opened. Then another book was opened, which is *the Book* of Life; and the dead were judged according to everything they had done while on earth which was written in the books.

Verse 13
13 The sea gave up the dead that were in it, and death and Hades gave up the dead that were in them, and they were each judged according to their works.

13 The sea gave up the dead
    that were in it,
    and death and Hades gave up the dead
      that were in them,
      and they were each judged according to their works.

To make sure that we know none will escape, all the dead from everywhere were killed and sent after death and will now stand before the judgment seat.

Greek Paraphrase of Verse: 13
The sea gave up the dead who were in it, and death and Hades, the realm of the dead, surrendered the dead who were in them, and they were judged *and* sentenced, each one according to their deeds.

Verse 14
[14] Then death and Hades were thrown into the lake of fire. This is the second death, the lake of fire.

[14] Then
    death and Hades were thrown
        into the lake of fire.
            This is the second death,
                the lake of fire.

Just to prove that everything will be new, death and Hades will be thrown into the lake of fire with the devil and all the rest. Thus, the lake of fire is called the second death.

Greek Paraphrase of Verse: 14
Then death and Hades, the realm of the dead, were thrown into the lake of fire. This is the second death, the lake of fire the eternal separation from God.

Verse 15
[15] If anyone's name was not found written in the Book of Life, he was thrown into the lake of fire.

[15] If anyone's name was not found
        written in the Book of Life,
        he was thrown into the lake of fire.

No more second chances. All who will not be found in the Lamb's Book of Life will be thrown into the lake of fire with the devil and the rest.

Greek Paraphrase of Verse: 15
And if anyone's name was not found written in the Book of Life, he was thrown into the lake of fire.

Chapter Twenty-One

This chapter starts with the new heaven and the new earth appearing. Then the new Jerusalem where God will live with men.

An angel shows John the holy city with its light coming from God and its wall, gates and foundations.

Verse 1
The New Creation
¹ *Then I saw a new heaven and a new earth, for the first heaven and the first earth passed away, and there was no longer any sea.*

¹ Then
  I saw a new heaven and a new earth,
    for the first heaven
    and the first earth
      passed away,
        and there was no longer any sea.

new – recently made, fresh, recent, unused, unworn; of a new kind, unprecedented, novel, uncommon, unheard of

Since the Greek word translated 'new' means something that wasn't there shortly before, then we gather that the new heaven and the new earth were just created.

But there are several other ideas about that. Some think it was there all along but just appeared to the human eye. Others think it appeared at the beginning of the Millennium.

I like to think it was literally new right then.

The new earth will be completely different especially since there won't be any seas. The people of that time thought of the sea as being restless, unstable and full of danger. (Isaiah 57:20; James 1:6).

Because there will be no seas, then the whole economy of the earth will be quite different than before.

Greek Paraphrase of Verse: 1
Then I saw a new heaven and a new earth, because the first heaven and the first earth had vanished, and there was no longer any sea.

Verse 2
² *I saw the holy city, new Jerusalem, coming down out of heaven from God, prepared as a bride adorned for her husband.*

² I saw the holy city,
    new Jerusalem,
    coming down

out of heaven
from God,
prepared as a bride adorned for her husband.

Finally, this new Jerusalem is truly holy and set apart for God in a special sense. Unlike the new earth, the new Jerusalem already exists in heaven.
Galatians 4:26, But the Jerusalem above is free, and she is our mother.
It is a specially prepared place for a people who have been specially prepared.

Greek Paraphrase of Verse: 2
And I saw the holy city, new Jerusalem, coming down out of heaven from God, arrayed like a bride adorned for her husband.

Verse 3
³ Then I heard a loud voice from the throne, saying, "Behold, the dwelling of God is with men, and He will live with them. They will be His people, and God Himself will be with them and be their God.

³ Then
   I heard a loud voice
     from the throne,
     saying,
      "Behold,
      the dwelling of God is with men,
       and He will live with them.
        They will be His people,
         and God Himself will be with them
         and be their God.

The great voice from heaven is God Himself and He is making an announcement of great importance. He will be visibly present with us at all times.
This is fantastic! God will no longer be set apart from His people. He will live among them and they will have full access to Him at all times.
This sounds a little like heaven and earth will merge.

Greek Paraphrase of Verse: 3
And then I heard a loud voice from the throne, saying, "See! The tabernacle of God is among men, and He will live among them. And they will be His people, and God Himself will be with them as their God.

Verse 4
⁴ He will wipe away every tear from their eyes. There will be no more death, or mourning, or crying, or pain, for the former things have passed away."

247

[4] He will wipe away every tear
    from their eyes.
  There will be no more death,
    or mourning,
    or crying,
    or pain,
    for the former things have passed away."

former – first in time or place; first in rank; influence, honor; chief; principal; first, at the first

Those things that came first are now gone forever.
He is giving great comfort and assurance.
No more death! No more mourning! No more crying! No more pain!
Why? Because all the old things will be gone, and everything will be new and with God present all the time.
Do you know what this means? It means there will also be no more evil.

Greek Paraphrase of Verse: 4
And He will wipe away every tear from their eyes. And there will no longer be death, sorrow *and* anguish, or crying, or pain, since the former order of things has passed away."

Verse 5
[5] *The One sitting on the throne said, "Behold, I am making all things new." Then He said, "Write, because these words are faithful and true."*

[5] The One sitting on the throne said,
    "Behold,
      I am making all things new."
  Then He said,
    "Write,
      because these words are faithful and true."

The voice is saying that these words are to be trusted and believed because they are the true word of God.
Some believe the 'One sitting on the throne' is the Lamb but others think it is God the Father. I see no problem with either one. Basically, they are working together then as they have throughout all of history.
Not only are the new heaven and earth new but everything in each one will be as well.
Again, the absence of evil needs to be reemphasized.

Greek Paraphrase of Verse: 5
And the One who sits on the throne said, "Behold, I am making all things new." Also, He said, "Write, because these words are accurate, incorruptible, and trustworthy."

Verse 6
6 Then He said to me, "It is done. I am the Alpha and the Omega, the Beginning and the End. I will give freely to the one who thirsts from the spring of the water of life.

6 Then
  He said
    to me,
    "It is done.
    I am the Alpha and the Omega,
      the beginning and the end.
    I will give freely
      to the one who thirsts
      from the spring of the water of life.

Alpha – the first letter of the Greek alphabet
Omega – the last letter of the Greek alphabet

Jesus said on the cross, "It is finished." Now God is saying the same thing. All the things that were revealed to John throughout this book have now become real and there is no more to be done.

Because He is the "Beginning and the End" He is the source of all that is good.

Greek Paraphrase of Verse: 6
Then He said to me, "It is done. I am the Alpha and the Omega, the Beginning and the End. I will give water from the spring of the water of life freely to the one who thirsts.

Verse 7
7 The one who overcomes will inherit these things, and I will be his God and he will be My son.

7 The one
  who overcomes
  will inherit these things,
    and I will be his God
      and he will be My son.

overcomes – to conquer; to carry off the victory, come off victorious; when one is arraigned or goes to law, to win the case, maintain one's cause
inherit – to receive a part of an inheritance, receive as an inheritance, obtain by right of inheritance; to be an heir, to inherit; to receive the portion assigned to one, receive an allotted portion, receive as one's own or as a possession

Those who win the victory will receive everything that was set up for them to receive. It will be their inheritance.

Greek Paraphrase of Verse: 7
The one who overcomes the world by adhering faithfully to Christ Jesus as Lord and Savior will inherit these things, and I will be his God and he will be My son.

Verse 8
⁸ But the cowardly, unbelieving, vile, murderers, sexually immoral, sorcerers, idolaters, and all liars—their place will be in the lake that burns with fire and sulfur, which is the second death."

⁸ But
   the cowardly,
   unbelieving,
   vile,
   murderers,
   sexually immoral,
   sorcerers,
   idolaters,
   and all liars—
      their place will be
         in the lake
            that burns with fire and sulfur,
               which is the second death."

cowardly – timid, fearful
vile – to render foul, to cause to be abhorred; abominable; to turn one's self away from on account of the stench; metaphorically to abhor, detest
immoral – a man who prostitutes his body to another's lust for hire; a male prostitute; a man who indulges in unlawful sexual intercourse, a fornicator
sorcerers – pertaining to the magical arts
second death – eternal death

We now see what happens to those who did not come to Christ for any of the reasons listed here.
They will go into the lake of fire with the devil and his minions.

Greek Paraphrase of Verse: 8
But the cowards and unbelieving and abominable who are devoid of character and personal integrity and practice or tolerate sexual immorality, and murderers, sorcerers with intoxicating drugs, idolaters, those who practice and teach false religions and all the liars who knowingly deceive and twist truth, their place will be in the lake that blazes with fire and brimstone, which is the second death."

Verse 9
The New Jerusalem
⁹ Then one of the seven angels, who had the seven bowls full of the seven last plagues, came and spoke with me, saying, "Come here, I will show you the bride, the wife of the Lamb."

⁹ Then
   one of the seven angels,
    who had the seven bowls
     full of the seven last plagues,
    came and spoke
     with me,
     saying,
      "Come here,
      I will show you the bride,
       the wife of the Lamb."

plagues – a blow, stripe, a wound; a public calamity, heavy affliction, plague

John's first vision of the new Jerusalem was very short. Now he is being addressed by one of the seven angels. Now the angel who had delivered the last seven plagues is telling John he will show him the bride of the Lamb.

This means that the New Jerusalem will be the home of the church forever.

Greek Paraphrase of Verse: 9
Then one of the seven angels who had the seven bowls filled with the seven final plagues came and spoke with me, saying, "Come here, I will show you the bride, the wife of the Lamb."

Verses 10-11
¹⁰ He carried me away in the Spirit to a great and high mountain, and showed me the holy city, Jerusalem, coming down out of heaven from God, ¹¹ having the glory of God. Her brilliance was like a very precious stone, as a stone of crystal-clear jasper.

¹⁰ He carried me away
   in the Spirit
   to a great and high mountain,
   and showed me the holy city,
    Jerusalem,
    coming down
     out of heaven
     from God,
     ¹¹ having the glory of God.

Her brilliance was like a very precious stone,
as a stone of crystal-clear jasper.

Verse 10
[10] He carried me away in the Spirit to a great and high mountain, and showed me the holy city, Jerusalem, coming down out of heaven from God,

Now, John is being carried away in the Spirit to a place where he can see the whole city which is still coming down out of heaven from God.

This event will mark the beginning of the eternal kingdom of God on earth.

Verse 11
[11] having the glory of God. Her brilliance was like a very precious stone, as a stone of crystal-clear jasper.

Since a jasper has so many beautiful colors, it is the perfect stone to represent what John saw in the new city of God. I'm sure words will not describe is sufficiently.

Greek Paraphrase of Verses:10-11
And he carried me away in the Spirit to a great and high mountain, and showed me the holy city of Jerusalem, coming down out of heaven from God, having God's glory, filled with His radiant light. The brilliance of it resembled a rare and very precious jewel, like jasper, shining *and* clear as crystal.

Verse 12
[12] It had a great, high wall, with twelve gates, and at the gates twelve angels, names were written on them, which are the names of the twelve tribes of the sons of Israel.

[12] It had a great, high wall,
    with twelve gates,
        and at the gates
        twelve angels,
    names were written on them,
        which are the names
        of the twelve tribes
            of the sons of Israel.

The high wall always represented security and it will here as well. Believers will finally be safe and secure. It also means that the city is real, and it will have boundaries. With twelve gates, the believers will be able to come and go freely. That should mean that they will be free to explore the new heaven as well.

Greek Paraphrase of Verse: 12
It had a massive, high wall, with twelve large gates, and at the gates were stationed twelve angels, and on the gates were written the names of the twelve tribes of the sons of Israel.

Verse 13

[13] There were three gates on the east, three gates on the north, three gates on the south, and three gates on the west.

[13] There were three gates
    on the east,
  three gates
    on the north,
  three gates
    on the south,
  and
  three gates
    on the west.

This arrangement of the gates is like that of the camp of the twelve tribes of Israel at Sinai for their journeys through the wilderness (Ezekiel 48:31-35). There were three tribes on each side.

Greek Paraphrase of Verse: 13
On the east side there were three gates, on the north three gates, on the south three gates, and on the west three gates.

Verse 14

[14] The wall of the city had twelve foundations, and on them were the twelve names of the twelve apostles of the Lamb.

[14] The wall
  of the city
  had twelve foundations,
    and on them were the twelve names
      of the twelve apostles
        of the Lamb.

Wow! The very foundations of the city will be the twelve apostles of Christ making it the perfect place for the new church.

The names of the twelve apostles will include Matthias since he was selected to replace Judas and accepted by God.

Greek Paraphrase of Verse: 14
And the wall of the city had twelve foundation stones, and on them the twelve names of the twelve apostles of the Lamb, Christ.

Verse 15
15 The one who spoke with me had a gold measuring rod to measure the city, its gates, and its wall.

15 The one
   who spoke
     with me
     had a gold measuring rod
       to measure the city,
         its gates,
         and its wall.

measuring rod – a reed; a staff made of a reed, a reed staff; a measuring reed or rod; a writer's reed, a pen

The fact that the angel is measuring it shows that it is an actual city, not just a spiritual symbol of the Church.
Everything about the city proves that no human could have built it. It could only be built or created by God Himself.

Greek Paraphrase of Verse: 15
The one who was speaking with me had a gold measuring rod to measure the city, and its gates and wall.

Verse 16
16 The city is laid out as a square, and its length is as great as the width. He measured the city with the rod, 12,000 stadia. Its length, width, and height are equal.

16 The city is laid out
   as a square,
     and its length is as great as the width.
  He measured the city
   with the rod,
   12,000 stadia.
   Its length, width, and height are equal.

stadia – a space or distance of about 600 feet

Some translations convert 12,000 stadia into fifteen hundred miles, but my calculations only make it around 1350 miles. That would be roughly the distance from Phoenix, AZ to St. Louis, MO.

Either way, it is huge as far as cities go. Modern cities are usually only a fraction of that size.

Greek Paraphrase of Verse: 16
The city is laid out as a square, its length is the same as its width. He measured the city with his rod, about 1,400 miles. Its length, width and height are equal.

Verse 17
17 He measured its wall, 144 cubits according to human measurements, which the angel was using.

17 He measured its wall,
   144 cubits
      according to human measurements,
      which the angel was using.

cubits – a measure of length equal to distance from the joint of the elbow to the tip of the middle finger (i.e. about 18 inches, (.5 m) but its precise length varied and is disputed)

That would make the wall at 216 feet high. That's pretty high.
Some think that the city was a cube, therefore the walls would be 1,350 miles high. They say that the wall would be 216 feet thick.
Frankly, I don't see it that way.

Greek Paraphrase of Verse: 17
He also measured its wall, about 200 feet, *according to* man's measurements, which the angel was using.

Verse 18
18 The material of the wall was jasper, and the city was pure gold like clear glass.

18 The material
   of the wall
   was jasper,
      and the city was pure gold
         like clear glass.

John's human vocabulary places a limit on how well he can describe the beauty that he sees before him. It is better and more beautiful than John could accurately describe.

Trennis E. Killian

Greek Paraphrase of Verse: 18
The wall was built with jasper and the city was pure gold, transparent like clear crystal.

Verses 19-20
[19] The foundations of the city wall were adorned with every kind of precious stone. The first foundation was jasper, the second, sapphire, the third, chalcedony, the fourth, emerald, [20] the fifth, sardonyx, the sixth, sardius, the seventh, chrysolite, the eighth, beryl, the ninth, topaz, the tenth, chrysoprase, the eleventh, jacinth, the twelfth, amethyst.

[19] The foundations
    of the city wall
    were adorned with every kind of precious stone.
The first foundation was jasper,
the second, sapphire,
the third, chalcedony,
the fourth, emerald,
[20] the fifth, sardonyx,
the sixth, sardius,
the seventh, chrysolite,
the eighth, beryl,
the ninth, topaz,
the tenth, chrysoprase,
the eleventh, jacinth,
the twelfth, amethyst.

Verse 19
[19] The foundations of the city wall were adorned with every kind of precious stone. The first foundation was jasper, the second, sapphire, the third, chalcedony, the fourth, emerald,

sapphire – this is not the modern sapphire but the ancient lapis lazuli which is a deep blue stone sprinkled with brilliant bits of iron pyrite (fool's gold).

    The twelve foundations which have the names of the twelve apostles written on them are described by using almost every precious stone known to man.

Verse 20
[20] the fifth, sardonyx, the sixth, sardius, the seventh, chrysolite, the eighth, beryl, the ninth, topaz, the tenth, chrysoprase, the eleventh, jacinth, the twelfth, amethyst.

Greek Paraphrase of Verses: 19-20
The foundation stones of the city wall were adorned with every kind of precious stone. The first foundation stone was jasper; the second,

sapphire, the third, chalcedony, the fourth, emerald, the fifth, sardonyx; the sixth, sardius; the seventh, yellow topaz, the eighth, beryl; the ninth, topaz; the tenth, chrysoprase, the eleventh, jacinth, and the twelfth, amethyst.

Verse 21

21 The twelve gates were twelve pearls, each one of the gates was a single pearl. The street of the city was pure gold, like transparent glass.

21 The twelve gates were twelve pearls,
  each one of the gates was a single pearl.
 The street
  of the city
  was pure gold,
   like transparent glass.

The gates were each a huge pearl that could only be created by God. The ancient people looked at the pearl as something that only the richest people could afford. Jesus talked about a pearl of great value in Matthew 13:45-46.

When John mentions the street, it is assumed that he is talking about all the streets in the city being pure gold as well.

Greek Paraphrase of Verse: 21
The twelve gates were twelve pearls, each separate gate was of one single pearl. And the broad street of the city was pure gold, like transparent crystal.

Verse 22

22 I did not see a temple in it, for the Lord God Almighty and the Lamb are its temple.

22 I did not see a temple
  in it,
  for the Lord God Almighty
   and the Lamb
    are its temple.

In ancient times, God manifested His presence in the Holy of Holies, the inner sanctuary of the tabernacle, then in the temple of Solomon. Now there is no need for any of that since God will dwell with and fellowship openly with all believers.

Greek Paraphrase of Verse: 22
I did not see a temple in it, for the Lord God Almighty, the Omnipotent, the Ruler of all, and the Lamb are its temple.

Verse 23

²³ The city does not need the sun or the moon to shine on it, for the glory of God illumines it, and its lamp is the Lamb.

²³ The city does not need the sun
    or the moon
    to shine on it,
    for the glory of God illumines it,
        and its lamp is the Lamb.

Now, all light, heat and energy come from the sun. That won't be necessary when God is with us. He will be our light, our heat and our energy. The Lamb will still light up and show the way to God the father.

Greek Paraphrase of Verse: 23
And the city has no need of the sun nor of the moon to give it light, for the glory, splendor and radiance, of God has illumined it, and the Lamb is its lamp *and* light.

Verse 24

²⁴ The nations will walk by its light, and the kings of the earth will bring their glory into it.

²⁴ The nations will walk
    by its light,
and
the kings of the earth will bring their glory
    into it.

glory – splendor, brightness; of the moon, sun, stars; magnificence, excellence, preeminence, dignity, grace; majesty; a thing belonging to God

This verse indicates that the New Jerusalem will be the capital city, the headquarters of all believers and the dwelling place of God.

Nations is a Greek word that is often translated as Gentiles but sometimes includes the Jews. Here, I think it is John's way of saying all peoples of the new earth.

Greek Paraphrase of Verse: 24
The redeemed people from the earth will walk by its light, and the kings of the earth will bring their glory into it.

Verse 25
25 In the daytime, its gates will never be closed, for there will be no night there.

25 In the daytime,
    its gates will never be closed,
        for there will be no night there.

In ancient times, the city gates were always closed at night to help prevent a surprise attack from their enemies. With the New Jerusalem, there will be no enemies, and there will be no night anyway. They will be safe all day long every day.

Another point to make here is that with God there, there can be no darkness. That's why there will be no night.

Greek Paraphrase of Verse: 25
By day, since there will be no night there, its gates will never be closed in fear of evil.

Verse 26
26 They will bring the glory and the honor of the nations into it.

26 They will bring the glory
    and the honor
    of the nations
    into it.

glory – splendor, brightness; of the moon, sun, stars; magnificence, excellence, preeminence, dignity, grace; majesty; a thing belonging to God

Again, nations probably refers to all the people (the saved) who live in the new earth. Glory and honor will come to them.

Greek Paraphrase of Verse: 26
They will bring the glory, splendor, majesty and the honor of the nations into it.

Verse 27
27 Nothing impure nor anyone who practices abomination and lying, will ever come into it, but only those whose names are written in the Lamb's Book of Life.

²⁷ Nothing impure
    nor anyone who practices abomination and lying,
    will ever come into it,
      but only those
        whose names are written in the Lamb's Book of Life.

impure – common; ordinary, belonging to generality; by the Jews, unhallowed, profane, unclean
abomination – a foul thing, a detestable thing; of idols and things pertaining to idolatry

Here we finally get the indication that only those whose names are written in the Lamb's Book of Life will be able to be there.

Greek Paraphrase of Verse: 27
Nothing that defiles *or* profanes *or* is unwashed will ever enter it, nor anyone who practices detestable, morally repugnant things and lying, but only those will be admitted whose names have been written in the Lamb's Book of Life.

Chapter Twenty-Two

John is shown the river of the water of life. The tree of life grows down the middle of the street. There is no curse nor darkness in the city.

John tries to worship the angel who stops him from doing so.

The theme of this chapter seems to be the coming of Jesus Christ soon.

Verses 1-2
The Source of Life
¹ Then he showed me a river of living water, clear as crystal, flowing from the throne of God and of the Lamb. ² Down the middle of its street, on each side of the river was the tree of life, bearing twelve kinds of fruit, yielding its fruit every month. The leaves of the tree were for healing the nations.

¹ Then
   he showed me a river
     of living water,
     clear as crystal,
     flowing from the throne
      of God
      and of the Lamb.
² Down the middle of its street,
   on each side
     of the river
     was the tree of life,
       bearing twelve kinds of fruit,
       yielding its fruit every month.
     The leaves
       of the tree
       were for healing the nations.

Verse 1
¹ Then he showed me a river of living water, clear as crystal, flowing from the throne of God and of the Lamb.

The angel shows John the river of the water of life that comes from the throne of God and the Lamb.

The throne seems to be in the middle of the city and the river flows out from it.

Verse 2
² Down the middle of its street, on each side of the river was the tree of life, bearing twelve kinds of fruit, yielding its fruit every month. The leaves of the tree were for healing the nations.

healing – service rendered by one to another; spec. medical service: curing, healing; household service; body of attendants, servants, domestics

The river reminds the inhabitants that they are still just as much dependent on God and the Lamb for their very lives as they ever were, possibly even more so now.

The leaves of the tree will heal all the people of the new earth.

Greek Paraphrase of Verses: 1-2
Then the angel showed me a river of the water of life, clear as crystal, flowing from the throne of God and of the Lamb, Christ, in the middle of its street. On each side of the river was the tree of life, bearing twelve *kinds of* fruit, yielding its fruit every month. And the leaves of the tree were for the healing of the nations.

Verse 3
³ There will no longer be any curse, and the throne of God and of the Lamb will be in it, and His servants will serve Him.

³ There will no longer be any curse,
    and the throne
      of God
      and of the Lamb
      will be in it,
        and His servants will serve Him.

The reference to the curse is the curse of sickness and disease. That curse will no longer affect the people of the new earth.

Greek Paraphrase of Verse: 3
There will no longer be anything that is cursed because sin and illness and death are gone and the throne of God and of the Lamb will be in it, and His servants will serve *and* worship Him with great awe, joy and loving devotion.

Verse 4
⁴ They will see His face, and His name will be on their foreheads.

⁴ They will see His face,
    and His name
      will be on their foreheads.

I think seeing His face will refer to seeing the face of Jesus (the Lamb) first, then God Himself.

This will be a new phenomenon. Remember that Moses was told that no one could see God and live (Exodus 33:20).

All will be instantly recognizable because they will all have His name on their foreheads.

Greek Paraphrase of Verse: 4
They will be privileged to see His face, and His name will be on their foreheads.

Verse 5
5 There will no longer be night, and they will not need the light of a lamp nor the light of the sun, because the Lord God will give them light, and they will reign forever and ever.

5 There will no longer be night,
    and they will not need the light
      of a lamp
      nor the light of the sun,
        because the Lord God will give them light,
          and they will reign forever and ever.

Again, the emphasis is on the fact that there will be no night in the presence of God. The fact that this is repeated makes it all the more important.

Greek Paraphrase of Verse: 5
There will no longer be night, they have no need for lamplight or sunlight, because the Lord God will give them light, and they will reign as kings forever and ever.

Verse 6
The Time Is Near
6 And he said to me, "These words are faithful and true." The Lord, the God of the spirits of the prophets, sent His angel to show His servants what must soon take place.

6 And
  he said
    to me,
    "These words are faithful and true."
  The Lord,
    the God
      of the spirits
        of the prophets,
    sent His angel
     to show
      His servants
      what must soon take place.

This verse begins the conclusion to the whole book of Revelation.

There is no longer any doubt about the security of the believers, and it is coming soon.

Once God's time comes, everything will come together, and all prophesies will be fulfilled.

Greek Paraphrase of Verse: 6

Then he said to me, "These words are faithful and true." And the Lord, the God of the spirits of the prophets, has sent His angel as a representative to show His servants the things that must soon take place.

Verse 7

7 "And behold, I am coming quickly. Blessed is the one who keeps the words of the prophecy of this book."

7 "And
  behold,
    I am coming quickly.
    Blessed is the one
      who keeps the words
        of the prophecy
        of this book."

quickly – without delay

Jesus makes this announcement that He is coming without delay.

Some think this means that when He comes, it will be very suddenly. But the word translated quickly means soon and without delay. We also need to remember that to Him a thousand years is like a day.

If you carry that out, then it has only been two days since Jesus came the first time. Interesting?

Nevertheless, the meaning is that all believers should be ready since we don't know when He will come.

Revelation started with a blessing on those who read the book aloud and on those who hear it. Now, the blessing is on those who not only hear it but keep on keeping, observing and obeying the words, teachings and prophecies of this book.

Greek Paraphrase of Verse: 7

"And behold, I am coming quickly. Blessed, happy, prosperous and to be admired is the one who heeds, takes to heart *and* remembers the words of the predictions, consolations, and warnings contained in this book."

Verse 8

8 I, John, am the one who heard and saw these things. When I heard and saw, I fell down to worship at the feet of the angel who showed me these things.

8 I,
    John,
    am the one
      who heard and saw these things.
  When I heard and saw,
    I fell down
      to worship
      at the feet of the angel
        who showed me these things.

John was so overwhelmed with the message and the messenger that he fell down and worshiped the angel who brought the message.

Greek Paraphrase of Verse: 8

I, John, am the one who heard and saw all of these things. And when I heard and saw them, I fell down to worship before the feet of the angel who showed me these things.

Verse 9

9 But he said to me, "Do not do that. I am a fellow servant with you, your brothers the prophets and those who keep the words of this book. Worship God."

9 But
  he said
    to me,
    "Do not do that.
      I am a fellow servant
        with you,
        your brothers the prophets
        and those
          who keep the words
            of this book.
    Worship God."

The angel immediately corrected John and told him not to worship him. He also makes it clear that John should worship only God.

Greek Paraphrase of Verse: 9

But he said to me, "Do not do that. I am a fellow servant with you. Your brothers the prophets and those who heed *and* remember the truths contained in the words of this book. Worship God only."

Verse 10
¹⁰ He said to me, "Do not seal the words of the prophecy of this book, because the time is near.

¹⁰ He said
    to me,
    "Do not seal the words
      of the prophecy
      of this book,
      because the time is near.

    It is important to note that the message of Revelation is not to be sealed since it will be happening soon. It could happen at any moment.

Greek Paraphrase of Verse: 10
And he said to me, "Do not seal up the words of the prophecy of this book, for the time of their fulfillment is near.

Verse 11
¹¹ "Let the one who does wrong, continue to do wrong, and the one who is filthy, continue being filthy, and let the one who is righteous, continue being righteousness, and the one who is holy, continue being holy."

¹¹ "Let the one
    who does wrong,
      continue to do wrong,
  and
  the one
    who is filthy,
      continue being filthy,
  and
  let the one
    who is righteous,
      continue being righteousness,
  and
  the one
    who is holy,
      continue being holy."

    Some believe that the time this statement is talking about is only in the future when Jesus comes again and that the people themselves will be able to come to Him all the way up until He does finally come again.
    I believe that it is not only talking about that future time but also right now, this instant. It's a final appeal to those who need to change for them to change and accept Christ as their savior.

Greek Paraphrase of Verse: 11
Let the one who does wrong, continue to do wrong, and the one who is vile, impure, continue being filthy, and the one who is just and upright, continue being righteous, and the one who is holy, continue being holy."

Verse 12
¹² "Behold, I am coming quickly, and My reward is with Me, to repay each man according to what he has done.

¹² "Behold,
    I am coming
        quickly,
        and My reward is with Me,
            to repay each man
                according to what he has done.

reward – dues paid for work; wages, hire; reward: used of the fruit naturally resulting from toils and endeavors; in both senses, rewards and punishments

This is the fifth time Jesus announces that He is coming quickly (Revelation 2:5,16; 3:11; 22:7).

Again, we need to remember that God doesn't look at time the way we do (1 Peter 3:8).

This is the first time the word reward is used. The word means to be paid what is owed to you.

Greek Paraphrase of Verse: 12
"Behold, I, Jesus, am coming quickly, and My reward is with Me, to give to each one according to his earthly works and faithfulness.

Verse 13
¹³ I am the Alpha and the Omega, the First and the Last, the Beginning and the End.

¹³ I am the Alpha and the Omega,
    the first and the last,
    the beginning and the end.
Alpha – the first letter of the Greek alphabet
Omega – the last letter of the Greek alphabet

This is the second time Jesus has made this statement, but this time it is appropriate to the verse above it. He is stressing that he and only he is capable of doing what He is saying He will do.

Greek Paraphrase of Verse: 13
I am the Alpha and the Omega, the First and the Last, the Beginning and the End the Eternal One."

Verse 14

14 Blessed are those who wash their robes, so that they may have the right to the tree of life and may enter through the gates into the city.

14 Blessed are those
  who wash their robes,
    so that they may have the right
      to the tree of life,
      and may enter
        through the gates
        into the city.

This is another one of those differences between the Textus Receptus (KJV) and the Nestle Aland (modern translations).

The TR has "they that do his commandments" and the NA has "those who wash their robes." The meaning is very much the same, so nothing is really gained or lost with either text.

Jesus is stressing that only those who are 'clean' so to speak, may enter His holy city and enjoy the fruit of the tree of life.

Greek Paraphrase of Verse: 14
Happy, prosperous and to be admired are those who wash their robes in the blood of Christ by believing and trusting in Him, so that they may have the right to the tree of life and may enter through the gates into the city.

Verse 15

15 Outside are the dogs, the sorcerers, the immoral, the murderers, the idolaters, and everyone who loves and practices lying.

15 Outside are the dogs,
    the sorcerers,
    the immoral,
    the murderers,
    the idolaters,
    and everyone
      who loves and practices lying.

sorcerers – pertaining to the magical arts
immoral – a man who prostitutes his body to another's lust for hire; a male prostitute; a man who indulges in unlawful sexual intercourse, a fornicator

It's interesting that lying is the last sin to be condemned here since the devil has always used lying and deceit in an attempt to keep people away from Christ.

Greek Paraphrase of Verse: 15
Outside are the godless, and the sorcerers with their intoxicating drugs, and magic arts, the immoral persons, and the murderers, the idolaters and everyone who loves and practices lying, deception and cheating.

Verse 16
16 I, Jesus, have sent My angel to testify these things to you for the churches. I am the Root and the Offspring of David, the bright Morning Star."

16 I,
    Jesus,
    have sent My angel
      to testify these things
        to you
        for the churches.
  I am the Root
    and the Offspring of David,
    the bright Morning Star."

Jesus is Himself verifying that He sent all the angels to warn the churches and the individuals of all that is written in this book.

He identifies Himself in two different ways which fulfill Old Testament prophecies.

Greek Paraphrase of Verse: 16
"I, Jesus, have sent My angel to testify to you *and* to give you assurance of these things for the churches. I am the Source, the Life and the Offspring of David, the radiant and bright Morning Star."

Verse 17
17 The Spirit and the bride say, "Come." And let the one who hears say, "Come." And let the one who is thirsty come. Let the one who wishes, take the free gift of the water of life.

17 The Spirit and the bride say,
    "Come."
  And

let the one
  who hears
  say,
    "Come."
And
let the one
  who is thirsty
  come.
Let the one
  who wishes take the free gift
    of the water
    of life.

This is the last mention of the Holy Spirit in the Bible. He is joining in with Jesus, the Son, in saying 'Come.'

Those who hear, those who are thirsty, and the ones wo want to drink of the water of life are told to 'Come.'

Greek Paraphrase of Verse: 17
The Holy Spirit and the church, the believers say, "Come." And let the one who hears say, "Come." And let the one who is thirsty come. Let the one who wishes, take and drink the free gift of the water of life.

Verse 18
18 I testify to everyone who hears the words of the prophecy of this book: If anyone adds to them, God will add to him the plagues that are written in this book.

18 I testify
  to everyone
    who hears the words
      of the prophecy
      of this book:
      If anyone adds to them,
        God will add to him the plagues
        that are written in this book.

plagues – a blow, stripe, a wound; a public calamity, heavy affliction, plague
    I have known individuals who think this is talking about commentaries. Well ... I must be honest and say that some commentaries do exactly this. But a true commentary written by a person who is prayed up and seeking God's will does not add to or take anything away from the Bible.

Greek Paraphrase of Verse: 18
I testify *and* warn everyone who hears the words of the prophecy of this book, its predictions, consolations and admonitions: If anyone adds

anything to them, God will add to him the afflictions and calamities which are written in this book.

Verse 19

19 If anyone takes away from the words of this book of prophecy, God will take away his share of the tree of life and from the holy city, which are written in this book.

19 If anyone takes away
    from the words
      of this book
      of prophecy,
      God will take away his share
        of the tree
        of life
        and from the holy city,
          which are written in this book.

This is dangerous territory for many people over the years have tried to do exactly that. Remember all of those people who claim that Revelation told them that Jesus was coming on such and such a date and it never happened. Those people try to become famous off false predictions.

I totally stay away from any and all predictions. As I noted in the introduction, if God wanted us to know exactly when, He would have told us.

The one thing I know is this: we are to be ready for whenever it happens. Period!

Greek Paraphrase of Verse: 19
If anyone takes away from *or* distorts the words of this book of prophecy, God will take away from that one his share of the tree of life and from the holy city, new Jerusalem, which are written in this book.

Verse 20

20 He who testifies to these things says, "Yes, I am coming quickly." Amen. Come, Lord Jesus.

20 He
    who testifies
      to these things
    says,
      "Yes,
        I am coming quickly."
  Amen.
  Come,
    Lord Jesus.

I know I say this about a lot of verses in the Bible, but this one is one of my favorites. I love the fact that John just heard Jesus say He was coming quickly (or without delay) and John stands up and essentially says, "I'm ready, come now Lord Jesus.

Greek Paraphrase of Verse: 20
He who testifies *and* affirms these things says, "Yes, I am coming quickly." Amen. Come, Lord Jesus.

Verse 21
[21] The grace of the Lord Jesus be with all. Amen.

[21] The grace
    of the Lord Jesus
    be with all.
  Amen.

Isn't it truly fitting that the book of Revelation ends on a benediction? It assures all believers that our Lord and Savior Jesus Christ will be with us until He comes again.

Shall we also add our own "Amen!"

Greek Paraphrase of Verse: 21
The grace of the Lord Jesus, the Christ, the Messiah, be with all the believers, who are set apart for God. Amen.

End Matters (Index)

The Beast and the Dragon

Daniel 7:3-7, *³ Four huge beasts came up from the sea, each different from the other. ⁴ "The first was like a lion but had eagle's wings. I continued watching until its wings were torn off. It was lifted up from the ground, set on its feet like a man, and given a human mind. ⁵ "Suddenly, another beast appeared, a second one, that looked like a bear. It was raised up on one side, with three ribs in its mouth between its teeth. It was told, 'Get up! Gorge yourself on flesh.' ⁶ "While I was watching, another beast appeared. It was like a leopard with four wings of a bird on its back. It had four heads and was given authority to rule. ⁷ "While I was watching in the night visions, a fourth beast appeared, frightening and dreadful, and incredibly strong, with large iron teeth. It devoured and crushed, and it trampled with its feet whatever was left. It was different from all the beasts before it, and it had 10 horns.*

Four Great Beasts
    1. Lion with eagle's wings and two man-like feet and is given a man's heart
    2. Bear
    3. Leopard with four bird wings and four heads
       Given dominion
    4. Frightening and dreadful
       Strong
       Large iron teeth
       Different from all before
       Ten horns

In Verse 11, the beast was killed, his body destroyed and thrown into the burning fire

In Verse 23, sounds like Satan or the Antichrist?

Revelation 11:7 (The Beast)

Antichrist?
    Same as Rev. 13:11 and 17:8

In the Book of Revelation, the characteristics of the "beast" are:

    1.   It has its origin from beneath, in the bottomless pit. The sea. The earth. (11:7; 13:1, 11)
    2.   It has great power. (13:4, 13:12; 17:12-13)

    3. It claims and receives worship. (13:3, 13:12, 13:14-15; 14:9, 14:11)

    4. It has a certain "seat" or throne where it gets its power. (16:10)

    5. It is of scarlet color. (17:3)

    6. It receives power given to it by the kings of the earth. (17:13)

    7. It is known by its mark. (13:17; 19:20)

    8. It has a specific number, 666. (13:18)

The origin of the imagery may be traced back to Daniel: 7-7 and that the same beast is being described in Revelation.

Revelation 12:3-17 (The Dragon)

Revelation 13:1-11 (The Beast and the Dragon)
    The Antichrist again.

Revelation 13:11-18 (The Beast)
    The false prophet

Symbols and Definitions

In this table I'm only listing the leading symbols and words that John used, giving their apparent meaning.

Adultery – Idolatry or apostasy; especially the latter. As Christ is represented as a bridegroom and the church as a bride, apostasy, or unfaithfulness to him, would be spiritual adultery, and a false church properly represented as a harlot.

Angel – Any agent or messenger of the divine will. The term may be a symbol of any movement of nations, or in history which carries out the divine purposes.

Ascension to Heaven – Exaltation in power and glory. Prosperity.

Babylon – The city which carried Israel into captivity. Hence, a symbol of any power that renders them captive, whether it be pagan or so-called religious.

Balances – A symbol of justice, but when used to denote the weighing out of food, a symbol of scarcity.

Black – The color of mourning; hence a symbol of calamity and sorrow.

Black Horse – The horse was not used as a beast of burden by the ancients, but for purposes of war. Hence it is a symbol of war, and a black horse is a symbol of catastrophic war.

Blood – A symbol of the slaughter of war.

Beast – As the term is used in the Revelation, it means a savage wild beast. Hence it is a symbol of a cruel, oppressive power.

Binding – This symbol means to restrain, to hold; also, to deprive of power and render helpless.

Book – The record of the divine will. To seal a book is to conceal its meaning, since ancient books were rolls and could not be read when sealed. To open a seal is to disclose the meaning. To devour a book is to become master of its contents. The book with seven seals is the book of human destiny, an outline of the great events which connect themselves with the church until its final triumph. The opening of its seals is the revelation of future history.

Bow – The bow, a warlike weapon, when held in the hand is a symbol of war.

Bride – The Church, the New Jerusalem.

Bridegroom – Jesus Christ.

Lampstand – A symbol of a church, which should be a light in the world. The seven golden lampstands are the seven churches. A symbol of any light-giving agency.

Chain – A symbol of bondage or affliction. To chain is to render powerless. To bind Satan with a chain is to destroy his power.

Cloud – An emblem of power and majesty. To ride upon the clouds is to appear in glory and exaltation.

Crown – The symbol of royal majesty. To enjoy exaltation and honor. To receive the crown of life is to receive the honors of eternal life.

Darkness – The well-known symbol of disaster and suffering.

Death – A symbol of destruction.

Dragon – The old Roman Empire. The dragon was originally a symbol of a monarch. In Revelation it means the persecuting monarchy of Rome.

Earth – The ancient civilized world, which corresponded in John's time with the Roman Empire. Political powers.

Earthquake – Political and moral revolutions and convulsions of society. The shaking of the established order of things. The undermining of states and fortunes.

Eclipse – The darkening of heavenly bodies, means the obscuration of the glory of kings and potentates of which sun, moon and stars are symbols.

Egypt – The place of spiritual bondage. A condition of sinfulness. Opposition to Christ.

Euphrates – The symbol of the Turkish power. To be "bound by the Euphrates" is to be restrained at that river.

Elders – Probably princes of righteousness.

False Prophets – A false spiritual power which falsely claims divine authority for its teaching.

Fire – Fierce destruction. Never the symbol of a blessing, but of a curse.

Fire from Heaven – Divine destruction. But fire brought down from heaven by the two-horned dragon means excommunication and curses of a false spiritual power.

Flood – Symbol of overpowering. Distress from persecution or any cause.

Forehead – A mark on the forehead means a public profession.

Grave – To put in the grave, signifies to consign to oblivion. "Not to suffer dead bodies to be put into the grave," means that they shall be remembered.

Hail – Ravages and destruction.

Hand – A mark on the hand means the manner of life, or practice.

Harlot – An idolatrous community. The great Harlot is the apostate church. See Adultery.

Heavens and the Earth – The world. The political and religious universe. A new heaven and a new earth imply a passing away of the old order of things and the establishment of a new order.

Horse – Used only for warlike purposes by the ancients and hence a symbol of war. The color of the horse indicates the condition of his rider and the status of the war.

Horns – "The great horn of the first king," Daniel. A symbol of kings, kingdoms, or power. Seven horns indicate enormous power.

Incense – The prayers of the saints.

Islands – The European states. In the prophets the "isles of the sea" meant the countries in and beyond the Mediterranean which was Europe.

Jerusalem – The capital of Judea and the seat of the temple becomes a symbol of the church of Christ. The "holy city" is contrasted with the "great city," Jerusalem with Babylon, or the true with the false church.

Jezebel – An unholy woman is a symbol of an unholy influence in the church.

Key – A symbol of power to deliver or imprison, to open heaven or hell, or to shut them. It can also mean power to save or destroy.

King – Supreme power of any kind. A government; a kingdom.

Lamb – The symbol of a sinless, sacrificial offering. The Lamb of God is Christ, slain as a lamb from the foundation of the world.

Lion – A symbol of kingly power.

Locusts – The locusts, a devouring pest bred in the deserts of Arabia, are a symbol of devouring Arabian armies. The Arabians under Mohammed.

Manna – The bread of life. The truth of Christ.

Measuring Rod – The standard by which the church is measured. The Word.

Mountain – Some person or power noticeable among men. Highly elevated. A great prince or government. A burning mountain is a sinister, destructive power.

Moon – A symbol of powers, rulers and great men which are not supreme. A light which shines only by reflecting another light.

Merchants – A symbol of those who make money off godliness and traffic in religious privileges.

Palm – A symbol of joy or victory.

Pale Horse – An image of destructive war, and a reign of death.

Red Horse – An image of cruel, bloody war, distinguished by slaughter.

River of Life – Christ is the fountain of life. The abundant, ever flowing life that Christ bestows, is appropriately symbolized by a river. The river, and tree of life mean essentially the same.

Rod – The symbol of rule. The rod of iron is a symbol of limitless control.

Scarlet – This color, the color of blood, symbolizes bloody cruelty. A scarlet woman is a persecuting church.

Seven – The perfect number. Completeness.

Stars – Shining lights in the world. Prominent men, whether in the church or the state.

Sun – As the great light giver, in one sense a symbol of Christ. Also, a supreme ruler. The moon and stars indicate great lights of society, but inferior to the sun.

Sword – A symbol of slaughter. Also, of conquest. A sword in the hand indicates by carnal weapons. A sword proceeding from the mouth indicates conquests by the word of God.

Temple of God – The church and the tabernacle and temple were types. The temple of God in heaven, open, is the abode of God, heaven itself, the church above.

Throne – A symbol of authority.

Trumpet – The blast of a trumpet signifies the forward march of armies, carnal or spiritual. Also, the declaration of war or peace.

Time – Time, times and half a time is an annual revolution of the earth, a year, two years, a half year, or three and a half years. "Seven times" passed over Nebuchadnezzar, or seven years.

Wine Press – A symbol of an outpouring of blood and of distress.

White – To be clothed in white is to be innocent, pure and to be triumphant.

White Horse – Triumphant and glorious war.

Whore – Apostate church. See Adultery.

Winds – Symbol of commotion, of mighty movements. The "Four Winds" are four invasions of the Roman Empire.

Witness – The two witnesses are the two Testaments, which is the meaning of testament.

Woman – The "woman clothed with the sun" is the pure and faithful church. The Great Harlot is the false, faithless, apostate church. The church is often symbolized by a bride, or a woman bearing children. A pure woman represents a faithful church. An adulterous woman, "a harlot," represents a false, apostate church.

The Letters to the Seven Churches

Summaries of the Letters

Ephesus 2:1-7
For:

> Can't tolerate evil
> Tested false apostles
> Possess endurance
> Tolerated many things because of Him

Against:

> Abandoned your first love

Warning:

> Remember how far you've fallen
> Repent and do the works you did at first
> Otherwise He will remove your lampstand

Yet:

> You hate the Nicolaitans

Smyrna 2:8-11
For:

> Tribulation and poverty
> Jews slander you

Warning:

> Don't be afraid of what you're about to suffer
> The devil will throw some in prison (tribulation for 10 days)

> Be faithful unto death and receive the crown of life

Pergamos 2:12-17
For:

> You live where Satan's throne is
> You are holding onto my name
> You did not deny your faith

Against:

> Some follow the teaching of Balaam
> Some follow the teaching of the Nicolaitans

Warning:

> Repent
> He will come quickly with sword of His mouth

Thyatira 2:18-29
For:

> Love, faithfulness, service and endurance
> Last works greater than the first

Against:
> You tolerate Jezebel the prophetess

Warning:
> I will overthrow her
> Throw her into a sickbed
> Also, those who commit adultery with her (unless they repent)
> I will kill her children with the plague

> Do not hold to this teaching
> Hold on to what you have until I come

Sardis 3:1-6

Against:
> You have a reputation for being alive, but you are dead
> I have not found your works complete before God

Warning:
> Be alert and strengthen what remains which is about to die
> Remember what you have received and heard, keep it and repent
> If you are not alert, I will come, and you won't know when

But a few people are worthy

Philadelphia 3:7-13

For:
> You have limited strength
> You have kept My word

Warning:
> He will make the synagogue of Satan bow down at your feet
> I will keep you because you have kept my command to endure
> I am coming quickly
> Hold on to what you have

Laodicea 3:14-22

Against:
> Neither cold nor hot

Warning:
> Vomit you out of My mouth
> Buy from Me

A Comparison of the Beginnings

All seven of the letters to the churches begin with:
To the angel of the church in _____ write:

2:1 Ephesus
The One who holds the seven stars in His right hand and who walks among the seven gold lampstands

2:8 Smyrna
The First and the Last, the One who was dead and came to life

2:12 Pergamos
The One who has the sharp, two-edged sword

2:18, Thyatira
The Son of God, the One whose eyes are like a fiery flame, and whose feet are like fine bronze

3:1 Sardis
The One who has the seven spirits of God and the seven stars

3:7 Philadelphia
The Holy One, the True One, the One who has the key of David, who opens, and no one will close, and closes and no one opens

3:14 Laodicea
The Amen, the faithful and true Witness, the Originator of God's creation

A Comparison of the Endings

All seven of the letters to the churches end with:
"Anyone who has an ear should listen to what the Spirit says to the churches."
Then they go on to add another sentence or two.
The exception is the last four churches, Thyatira, Sardis, Philadelphia and Laodicea, do not add any more.

2:7 Ephesus
I will give the victor the right to eat from the tree of life, which is in the paradise of God.

2:11 Smyrna
The victor will never be harmed by the second death.

2:17 Pergamos
I will give the victor some of the hidden manna. I will also give him a white stone, and on the stone a new name is inscribed that no one knows except the one who receives it.

2:29 Thyatira
No additional words to this church.

3:6 Sardis
No additional words to this church.

3:13 Philadelphia
No additional words to this church.

3:22 Laodicea
No additional words to this church.

The Plan of Salvation

I include this section for two possible reasons.

The first reason is that if you have never accepted the Lord as your Savior, it can guide you to doing so.

The second reason is that if you are already a Christian, you have my permission to use this section to help others come to the Lord.

* * *

It is my prayer that you have come to a point in your life where you feel that you need to come closer to Christ, He will help you to do just that.

If you are ready right now to accept Him as your personal savior and Lord, would you pray this simple prayer right now?

"Lord Jesus, I know I have fallen away from You, and now I want to come back to You. Please forgive me where I have failed You. I am rededicating my life to You. In Your name I pray. Amen."

If you need to know a little more in order to accept Christ as your personal savior and make Him Lord of your life, please work your way through the following verses and instructions.

The Roman Road to Salvation

The Roman Road is a group of Bible verses from the book of Romans in the New Testament. If you work your way down this road, you will understand how to take advantage of the salvation that Christ offers so freely. You need to understand some other facts first. Read and think about the following verse.

Romans 3:23, *For all have sinned and fall short of the glory of God*

We know what sin is. Many people think sin is whatever we do that hurts others in any way. That is part of it, but God does not look at sin that way. God looks at sin as anything that goes against His commandments. In other words, no matter what we do or who we do it to, we are sinning against God. We must admit our sin against God so He can forgive us. The first step on the Roman Road is to realize that we have sin in our hearts.

Do you recognize that you are a sinner? You need to admit that you are a sinner.

Romans 6:23a, *For the wages of sin is death.*

Sin has a penalty. The penalty for sin is death. This is not physical death. Physical death is a result of sin that entered the world when Adam and Eve disobeyed God in the Garden of Eden. Everyone faces physical death.

The death referred to in Romans 6:23a is not physical death. This death is far worse. It is spiritual death. Spiritual death pushes us away from God. Spiritual death will last for all of eternity. The Bible teaches there is a place called the Lake of Fire where lost people will be in torment forever. Spiritually dead people will go there and never leave.

You need to realize that this means you too.

Romans 6:23b, *but the gift of God is eternal life in Christ Jesus our Lord.*

There is hope! God offers us His salvation. The best part is that this salvation is a gift from God to you. You cannot earn this gift, but you must reach out and receive it. That is all you have to do. He is waiting for you to do just that. Ask God to forgive you of your sins and then ask Him to save you.

Romans 5:8, *God demonstrates His own love for us, in that while we were still sinners, Christ died for us.*

If we had to pay the penalty for our sins, it would be spiritual death. Jesus changed all that when He died on the cross for our sins. He paid the penalty for our sins. He paid it for all sin, and when He did that, we no longer have to be slaves to sin and death! He only asks that we believe in Him and all He has done for us. Because of this, we are one with Him, and He has become our life. He gave Himself for us because He loved us so much that He was willing to die for us!

Turn your life over to God. His love poured out to us in Jesus on the cross. He is your only hope to have forgiveness and change. Because of His love, we are no longer slaves to sin. There is only one way to salvation. It is not religion or church membership. It is turning everything over to God. God loves you, and His love saves you.

Romans 10:13, *For "Whoever calls on the name of the Lord will be saved."*

Verse 13 does not say He will save some. It does not say only those who do certain good deeds. It does not say those who have religion. It does not say those who go to church. You can do all those things and still be lost.

Verse 13 says those who call on the name of the Lord will be saved. Call on His name right now. Call out to God in the name of Jesus!

Romans 10:9-10, *if you confess with your mouth Jesus as Lord, and believe in your heart that God raised Him from the dead, you will be saved. [10] With the heart, you believe, resulting in righteousness, and with the mouth you confess, resulting in salvation.*

This passage is saying that you have to believe that God raised Jesus from the dead, and then you need to confess aloud that you are a sinner and you want Jesus to come into your heart and save you.

If you believe that God raised Jesus from the dead, confess that you are a sinner and ask Him to come into your heart.

Jesus said,

Revelation 3:20, *Behold, I stand at the door and knock. If anyone hears My voice and opens the door, I will come in to him and will dine with him, and he with Me.*

Is Jesus knocking on your heart's door? All He is asking is for you to believe in Him. He wants you to ask Him to come into your heart by faith, so He can reveal Himself to you.

Open the Bible now to the Gospel of John and read what God says in Chapter One about Jesus, about you, and about salvation.

God will help you. He loves you.

Now that you have worked your way through the "Plan of Salvation," You should be ready to accept Jesus Christ as your savior and make Him Lord of your life. Please pray the following prayer.

"Lord Jesus, I come to you now, a sinner. I ask you to forgive me of all my sins, to save me, and make me whole again. Please come into my life and make me yours and be Lord of my life. In your name I prey, Amen."

Epilogue

Now that you have tried the commentary on *Revelation* in the *Easy Study Bible Commentary* series, you will want to look for all the other books in this series as they are published. The ones published to date are listed below.

Please leave an honest review of this book wherever you have access to reviews. Thank you.

If you received a blessing from this title, please tell others so they too may receive a blessing from reading and studying God's word in this new translation and commentary.

If you find any typos or other types of errors, please feel free to contact me through my web page listed below.

I am currently working on the rest of the commentaries in this series and am excited about how God has already used *The Easy Study Bible* and *The Easy Study Bible Diagramed* to help many people around the world to better understand His word.

I am here to help you no matter what your need may be. You may contact me through my web page: http://www.trenniskillian.com

May God bless you in your efforts to learn more about Him and come closer to Him.

* * *

The Easy Study Bible Commentary Series

Ephesians

Philippians

Titus and Philemon

James

Jude

Revelation

About Trennis E. Killian

Dr. Trennis E. Killian was a high school English teacher until God called him into the Gospel Ministry more than thirty-five years ago. He immediately enrolled in seminary.

After seminary, he was a pastor for ten years. Since then, he has been a chaplain to various hospitals and police agencies.

All the time he was doing each of the above, he also served as a pastoral counselor with two different agencies.

He has always been an avid student of the Bible, always spending as much time as possible in the original Greek and Hebrew.

In 2010, wanting to do his own modified diagram of the Bible and not being allowed to do so by any of the publishers of existing translations, he set out to translate the New Testament from the Greek so he could do his modified diagram.

The result was that he published *The Easy Study Bible: New Testament* and *The Easy Study Bible: New Testament Diagramed* in 2011.

He and his wife, Ann, live in Black Canyon City, Arizona, where he continues to study and write full time.

Manufactured by Amazon.ca
Bolton, ON